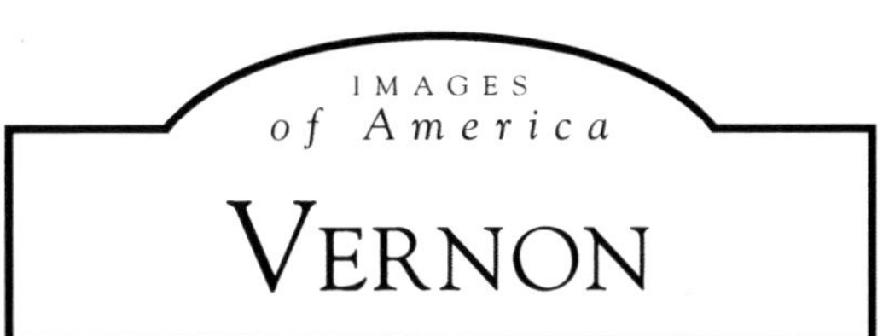
IMAGES
of America
VERNON

On the Cover: Men are standing in front of the new Texas Wagon Yard on Texas Street. The picture also shows the back and side view of Norwood Dry Goods, which faces east on Main Street. This picture was taken around 1905. (Author's collection.)

IMAGES
of America

VERNON

Preston Cary

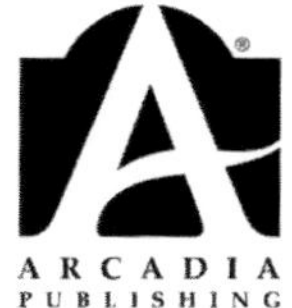

ISBN 978-0-7385-9546-7

Published by Arcadia Publishing
Charleston, South Carolina

Printed in the United States of America

Library of Congress Control Number: 2012952318

For all general information, please contact Arcadia Publishing:
Telephone 843-853-2070
Fax 843-853-0044
E-mail sales@arcadiapublishing.com
For customer service and orders:
Toll-Free 1-888-313-2665

Visit us on the Internet at www.arcadiapublishing.com

In memory of Earnest Bismarck Schmoker

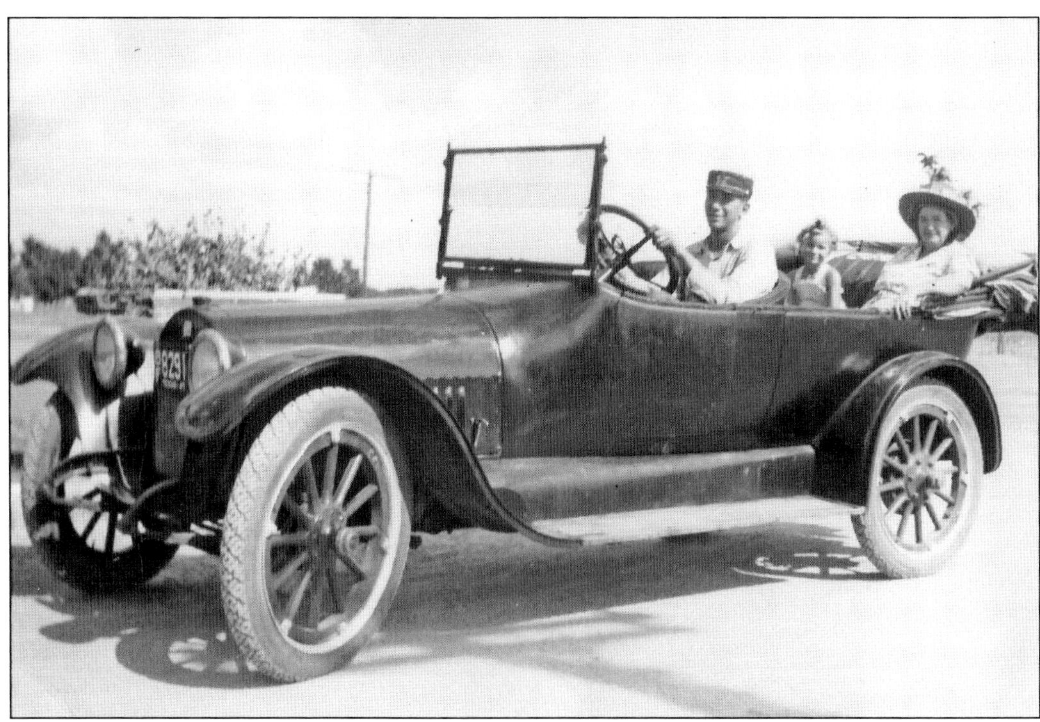

Earnest Schmoker is pictured driving his touring car with his sister Myrtle June and his mother, Clara (Ramsey) Schmoker, in the back seat. (Author's collection.)

Contents

ACKNOWLEDGMENTS

In the preparation of Images of America: *Vernon*, all data, material, and information were gathered from a copy of the "Old Settlers Edition," published in 1927 by the *Vernon Times*, and also from a copy of the newspaper's book, titled *Early-day History of Wilbarger County*, published in 1933 and written mostly by J.E. Collins.

Material was also obtained from a copy of the book written in 1986 by Sylvia "Jo" Jones and published by the Wilbarger County Historical Commission. The majority of the images used in the book are from the archives of the Wilbarger County Historical Society and the private collection of the author.

Special thanks go to my family, especially my wife, Paula, for the encouragement. Thanks go out to my sons, Mark and Nick, for all of their help and support. Also, this book would not be a reality without the support given by Karen Gfeller and her daughter Carrie Hawkins.

INTRODUCTION

Vernon has the distinction of being on the western branch of the Chisholm Trail. This trail has also been known as the Western Trail, the Dodge City Trail, the trail to Kansas, and the Fort Griffin Trail.

On October 10, 1878, C.F. Doan, his wife, and their child became the first settlers in Wilbarger County. The adobe house that they built near the Red River in 1880 is still standing today. Doan also built a trading post and the Cowboy Saloon that same year. At this time, the nearest railroad was in Gainesville, Texas, and the nearest post office was in Henrietta.

In 1879, W.B. Worsham established the R2 Ranch in Wilbarger County, with headquarters at Big Springs, later known as Condon Springs and now as the Hillcrest Country Club. During this year, the mail and stage line was established between Wichita Falls and Mobettie, with a passenger rate of 10¢ per mile.

In the spring of 1880, G.W. Darby and Lon Byars shoveled out a dugout and called the place Eagle Flat because of all the eagles in the area. The name Eagle Flat was adopted on April 23, 1880. In 1881, Eagle Flat was awarded a post office, but the postal department said there were too many towns in Texas with the name eagle in them; therefore, the name Vernon was chosen on March 27, 1881. The people in the area then applied to be county seat on October 5, 1881, organized October 10, and Vernon became county seat on March 4, 1882. In 1881, there were only 56 eligible voters in the county. In that year, saloons were voted out but came back and ran for a few more years.

Wilbarger County was named in 1858 after two pioneers, Texas surveyors Josiah and Mathias Wilbarger. While on a surveying expedition near Austin, Josiah Wilbarger was shot down and scalped by Indians but lived to tell the story. Wilbarger and his companions were attacked by a large band of Indians. The first man killed in the group was a Mr. Christian. Wilbarger tried to help him to safety but was shot by an arrow from behind. The arrow pierced through the back of Wilbarger's neck and out under his chin. Believing Wilbarger was dead, the Indians scalped him. When he regained consciousness, he managed to pull the arrow out of his neck and drag himself about a half mile to Pecan Springs, where he was rescued.

Around 1867, due to the shortage of beef in the northern states and the abundance of free range cattle in South Texas, a new enterprise sprang up—the business of cattle drives. Cattle by the thousands were gathered in South Texas and herded to northern markets. Years before the cattle drives, Jessie Chisholm had used a trail for his trading post business and had left a well-used wagon trail through the Indian territory (Oklahoma) to Kansas. When the cattle drives came out of South Texas, they got on Jesse Chisholm's wagon trail, heading north to Kansas, so they adopted the name Chisholm for the entire trail. This cattle trail was used from 1867 to around 1875, when the Chisholm Trail moved over to the west to avoid the quarantine line that Kansas had placed on Texas cattle for what was called Texas fever. The fever was actually caused from the bite of a tick the southern cattle carried with them. The infection, caused by a tick bite, would sometimes kill the entire northern herds that the southern cattle had come in contact with. While in the womb, southern cattle became immune to the infection caused by the tick bite. A cure was not discovered until after 1890. The western branch of the Chisholm Trail ran from 1876 to around 1884. Trains later moved cattle. Cattle are still being driven through Vernon but in trucks, which truck drivers call "bull wagons."

An early resident, Ella Jones, wife of Robert Franklin Jones, recalls when the cattle, being driven through town to northern markets, not only stirred up the dust but also brought with them large cattle and horse flies. The cattle could be heard before they got to town. Everyone would shut his or her doors and cover windows with mosquito netting to prevent the flies from coming in. Robert Franklin Jones came to Wilbarger County in 1879 and filed on a section of land running south from the Pease River to where the center of town is now located. He later donated half of this section to the townsite that bears his name today (the Jones addition). Ella Jones came to Vernon in 1880. At that time, the area was known as Eagle Flat, and there were only three buildings established, including the store owned by her husband, which was located at the southwest corner of the intersection of Main and Pease Streets; a café run by the Ruppert family, located where the courthouse now stands; and another structure occupied by four men, located across Main Street and west of the café. A Mrs. Ruppert and Ella Jones were the only two ladies. Ella said she thought they had a big town when C.M. Byars arrived three weeks later with his wife, giving them three women. The four old bachelors living nearby were G.W. Darby, T. Windsor Robinson, J.A. Nabers, and Uel Misick. Robert and Ella Jones first made their home in the back of the store. Later, they added a little log house on the back of the store for a kitchen. Ella Jones said that when the Indians came to Vernon, they camped just west of her home. At one time, there were as many as 50 teepees.

In 1887, a streetcar franchise was issued to the Vernon Street Railway Company. A single set of tracks was built down the center of Main Street from the Fort Worth & Denver Railroad to the city square. This horse-drawn trolley lasted a few years but finally played out and was sold at auction for $350 to W.O. Anderson. Jack Thomson used one of the cars for a shoe repair shop. Another was traded for 50 bushels of wheat to John Coffee.

Farming and ranching have always been the main businesses in Vernon, but oil was discovered in 1908, and Vernon made its move to prosperity. In 1923, a thriving oil field was recognized just south of Vernon. Just like all oil booms, the bottomed dropped out, and Vernon went back to its normal growth.

The first paved street was Main Street, which was completed about 1916. Soon after Word War I, in 1922, the first highway was paved through Vernon.

The Wilbarger County Courthouse now standing in Vernon was built in 1928, replacing the old one constructed in 1886. The old one had an outhouse and windmill.

By 1930, Vernon had become, and still is today, recognized as one of the outstanding cities of its kind. Vernon had become the heart of the Greenbelt and the center hub for a vast network of highways

One

1880s–1915

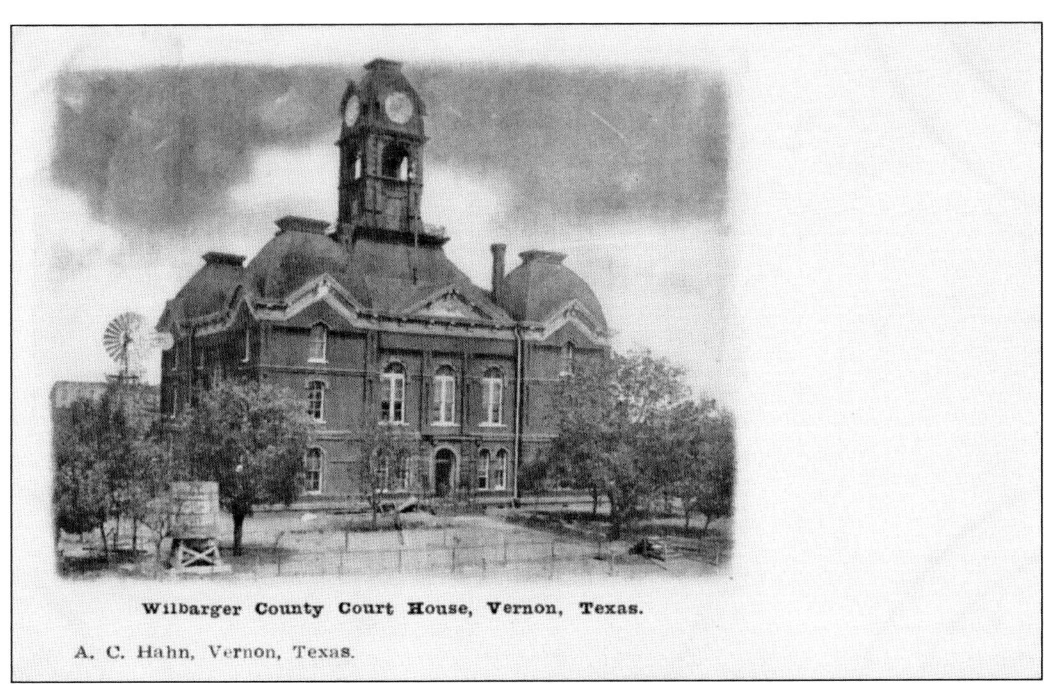

The first contract for a new courthouse was awarded to W.V. Evans on February 16, 1883. This was a wood frame structure. On August 11, 1885, the county commissioners voted to receive plans for a new courthouse to be built of brick. The contract for this courthouse was awarded to architect J.E. Flanders on March 10, 1886. Brick used for the courthouse was made at the Vernon Brick Factory northeast of town. The clock tower was destroyed by a tornado and was replaced with a tower without a clock. This building was demolished in 1928 to make room for the courthouse now standing. (Author's collection.)

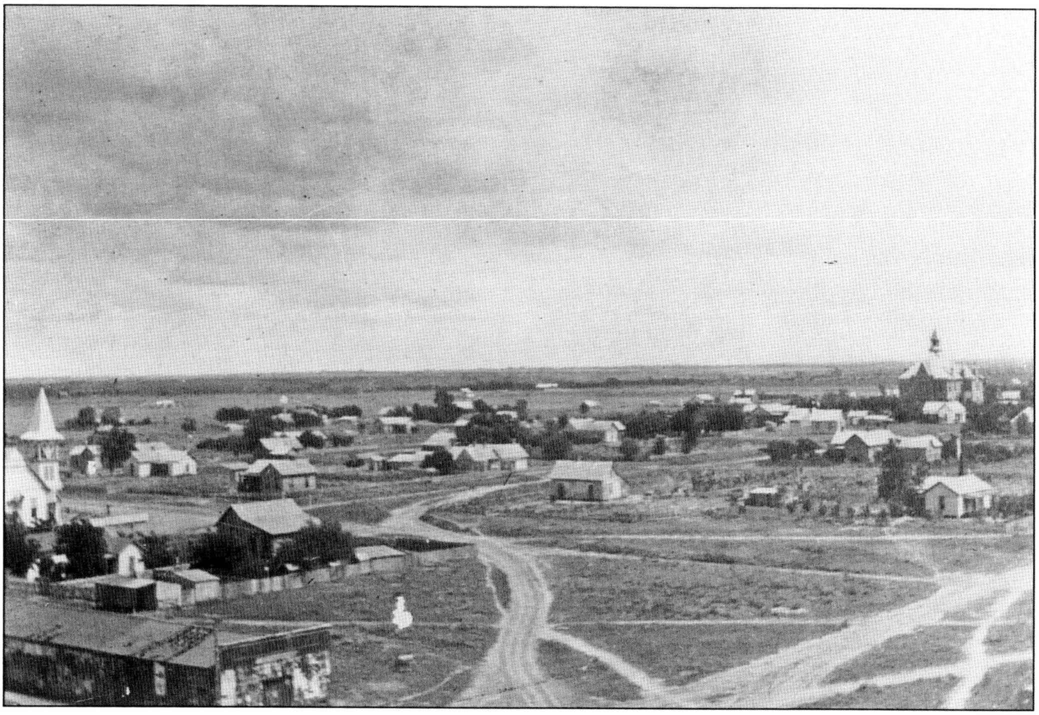

This c. 1895 view is from the 1886 courthouse clock tower. Looking southeast, one can see the First Baptist Church on the left and the old public high school on the right. The county records show that on April 23, 1880, J.W. Chowing, W.C. Chowing, T. Chowing, R.F. Jones, G.W. Darby, and T. Windsor Robinson (the six original townsite owners) did settle on and improve State School Section No. 18 and the northern half of State Section No. 64. The area was originally called Eagle Flat but the name was changed to Vernon on March 27, 1881. (Courtesy of First Baptist Church.)

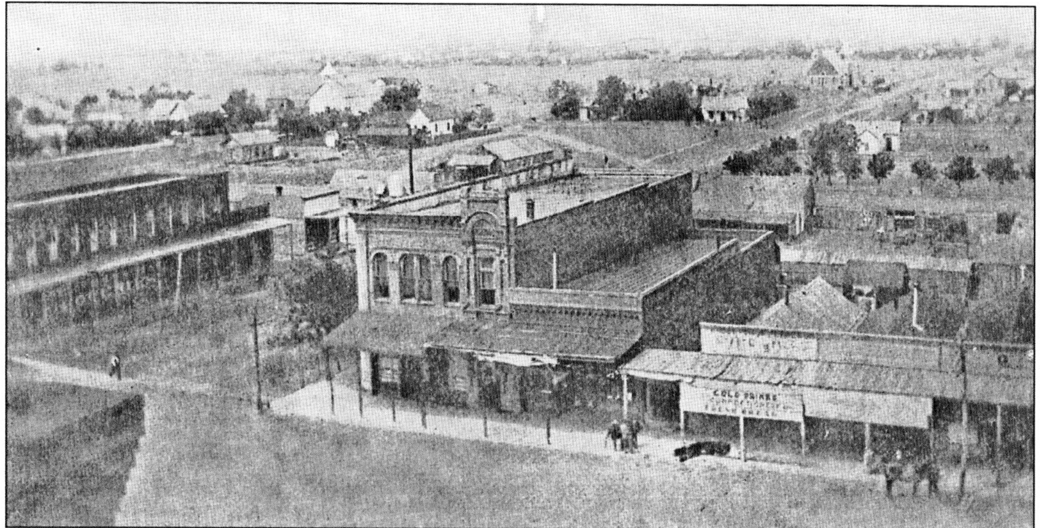

This is a view from the top of the courthouse at the corner of Main and Wilbarger Streets in 1896. The structure to the left is the Panhandle Hotel, and the corner building to the right is Wood & Company Mercantile. (Author's collection.)

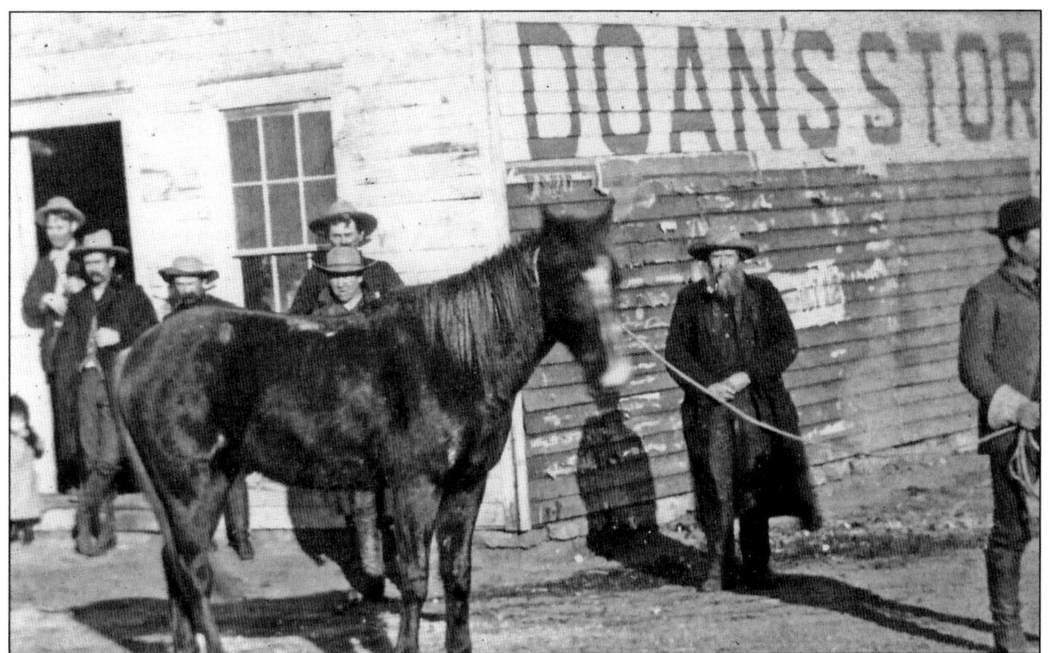

Corwin and Jonathan Doan established Doan's Store in 1878, a few miles north of Vernon on the Red River. They traded with the Kiowa and Comanche Indians and with the cowboys that came through on the cattle drives going north up the western branch of the Chisholm Trail. (Courtesy of Wilbarger County Historical Society.)

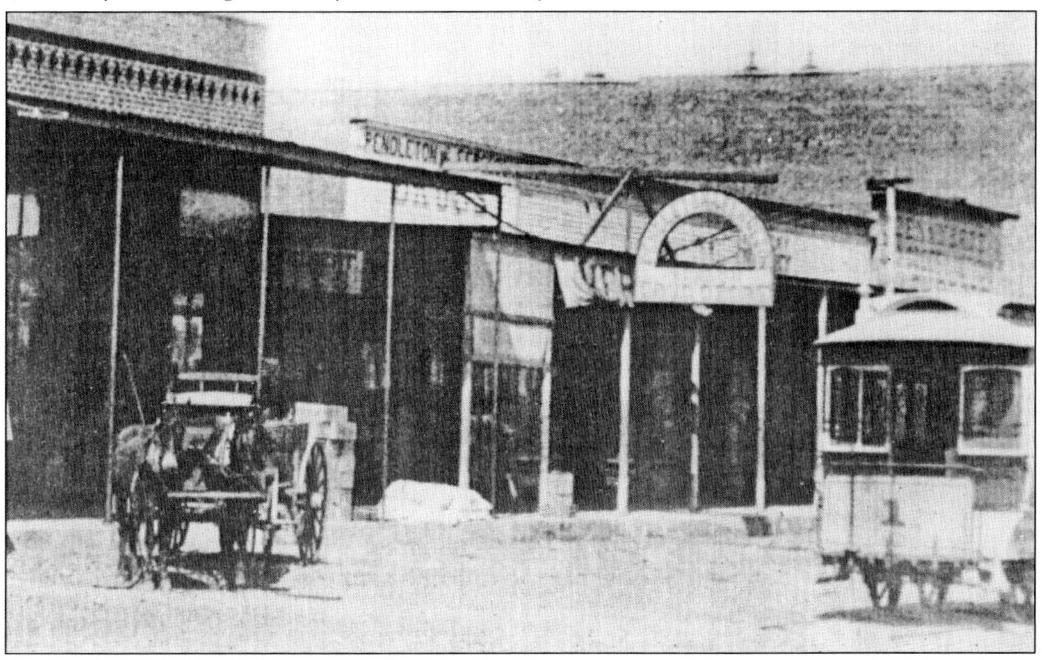

A street railway franchise was issued to the Vernon Street Railway Company in 1887. A single set of tracks was built down the center of Main Street from the Fort Worth & Denver tracks to the city square. It operated with success for a few years but gradually played out. It was sold at auction for $350 to W.O. Anderson. (Courtesy of Wilbarger County Historical Society.)

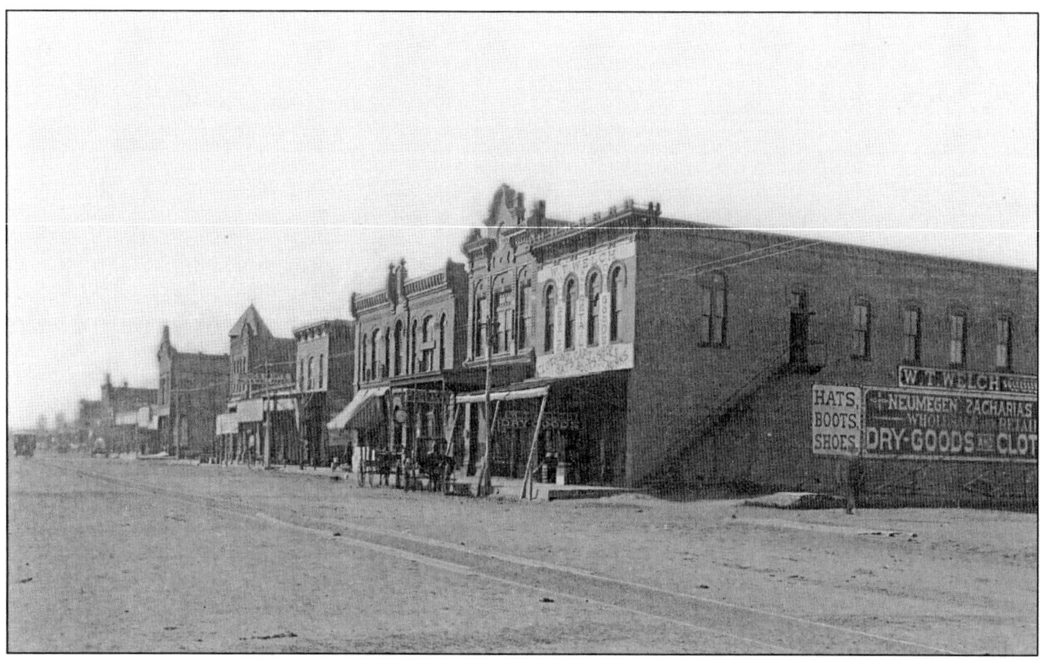

Looking south, this single set of trolley tracks was built down the center of Main Street, from the Fort Worth & Denver station to the city square. The businesses paralleling the trolley line are W.T. Welch Dry Goods, the Red Store (dry goods), and Waggoner National Bank with L.J. Massie Grocery in first floor of the bank's building. (Courtesy of Wilbarger County Historical Society.)

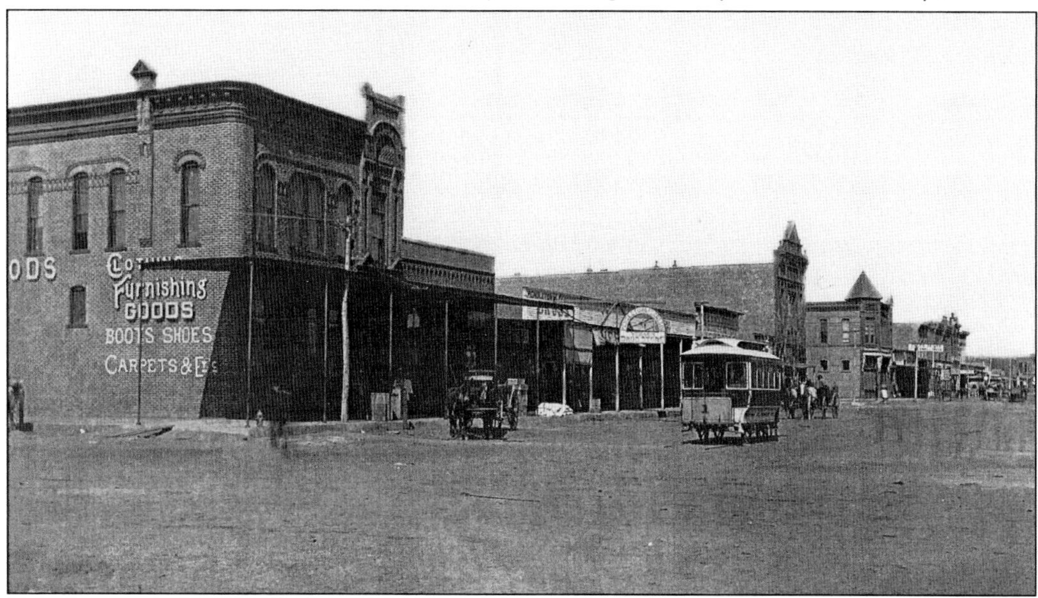

Pictured looking north is the same set of trolley car tracks. The business shown are Woods & Company Dry Goods, Parker & Colbert Grocery, Pendleton & Fergesons, Vernon Drugstore, Denny Brothers Dry Goods, and Perkins Watkins Dry Goods. Johnson, Cooke & Murray Dry Goods was also on Main Street. The street railway franchise was issued to the Vernon Street Railway Company in 1887. It operated with success for a few years but gradually played out. It was sold at auction for $350. (Courtesy of Wilbarger County Historical Society.)

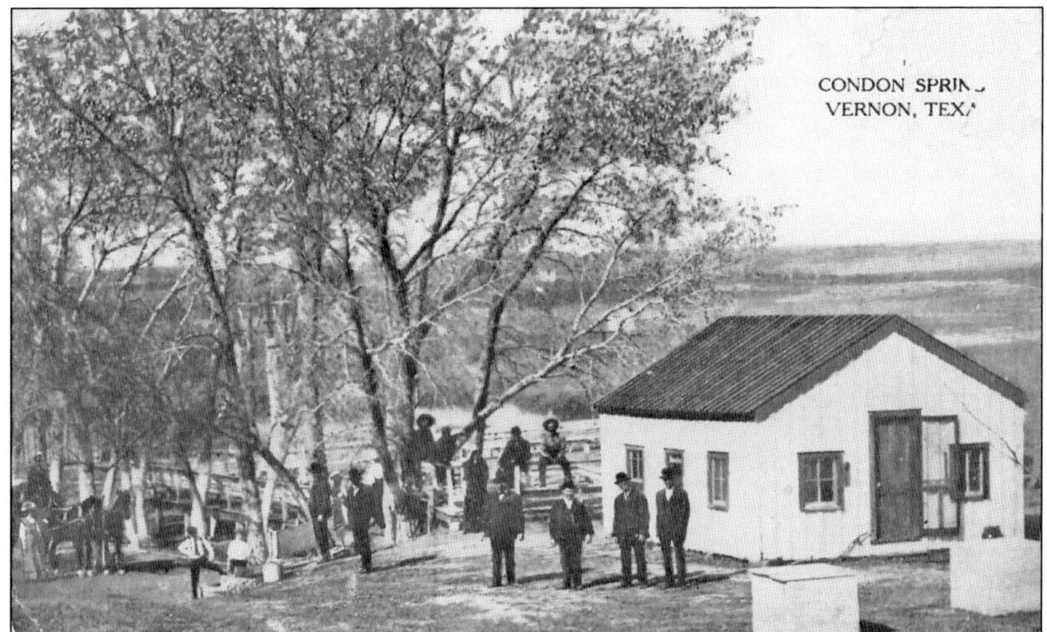

In 1879, W.B. Worsham of Henrietta established the R2 Ranch in Wilbarger County, with headquarters at Big Springs, more commonly called Condon Springs and now Hillcrest Country Club. Robert D. Rector, who worked for Worsham, became postmaster of the post office established there in 1880. That office was later discontinued, and the mail service went to Vernon. (Author's collection.)

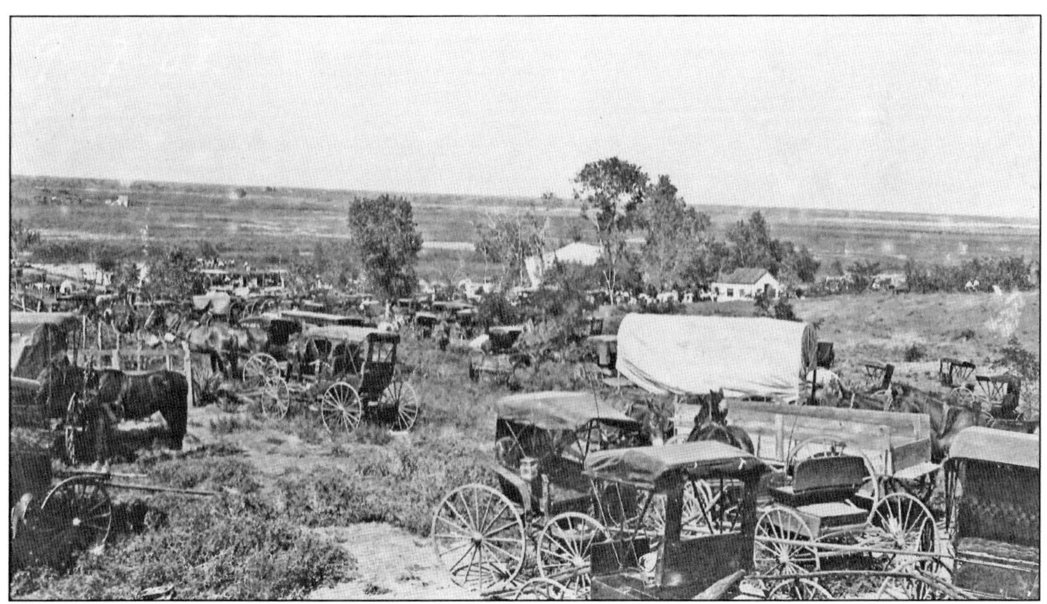

Here, wagons and buggies are at the Fourth of July picnic in 1908 at Condon Springs. The small, white building in the background is the location of the springs, where spring water was sold in the early 1890s. (Author's collection.)

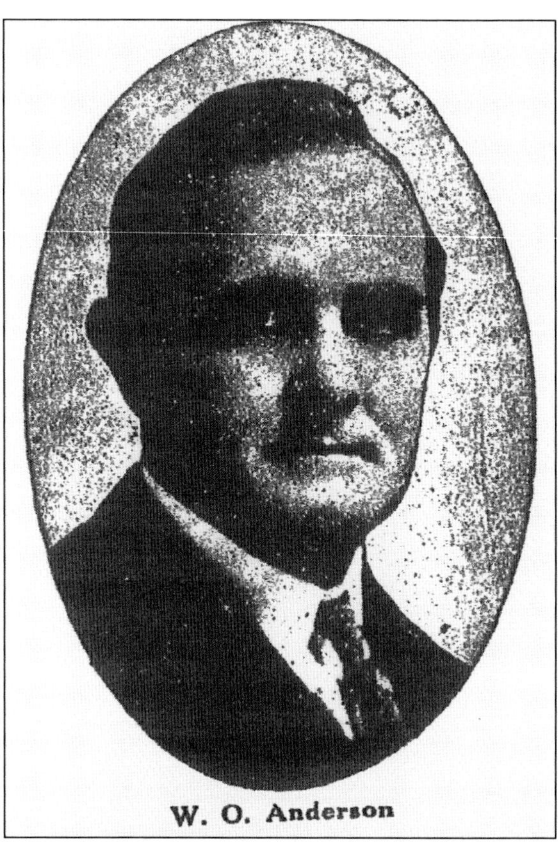

W.O. Anderson, born in Londonderry, Ireland, came to Texas and settled in Fort Worth in 1879. Arriving in Vernon in 1889, he started a coal and feed business on Wilbarger Street. Later, he moved his business to North Main Street on the corner of Main and Fannin Streets. Anderson, Robert Houssels, and Frank Kell started the Kell Milling Company. (Author's collection.)

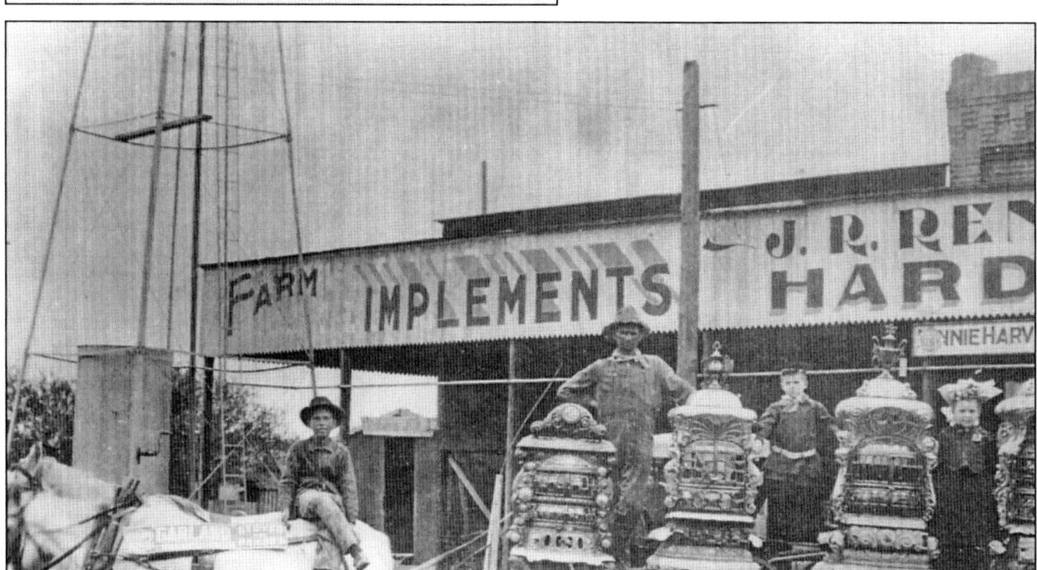

Ornate stoves are pictured in front of the J.R. Renfro hardware store. Pictured from left to right are unidentified (on horse), J.R. Renfro, Curtis Renfro, and Myrtle Renfro (Mrs. A.F. Winston). J.R. Renfro was born in Barren County, Kentucky, and came to Wilbarger County on July 3, 1890. Going into the carpentry and contracting business, he helped construct the Central School building. A few years later, he went into the hardware business. (Courtesy of Wilbarger County Historical Society.)

W.E. Johnson was in the hardware business for many years. A native of Lowden, Tennessee, he moved his family to Texas in 1883 and located to Hillsboro. In June 1886, the Johnson family came from Hillsboro to Vernon to make its home. In 1889, W.E. Johnson built this two-story brick building on the southeast corner of Wilbarger and Main Streets. (Courtesy of Wilbarger County Historical Society.)

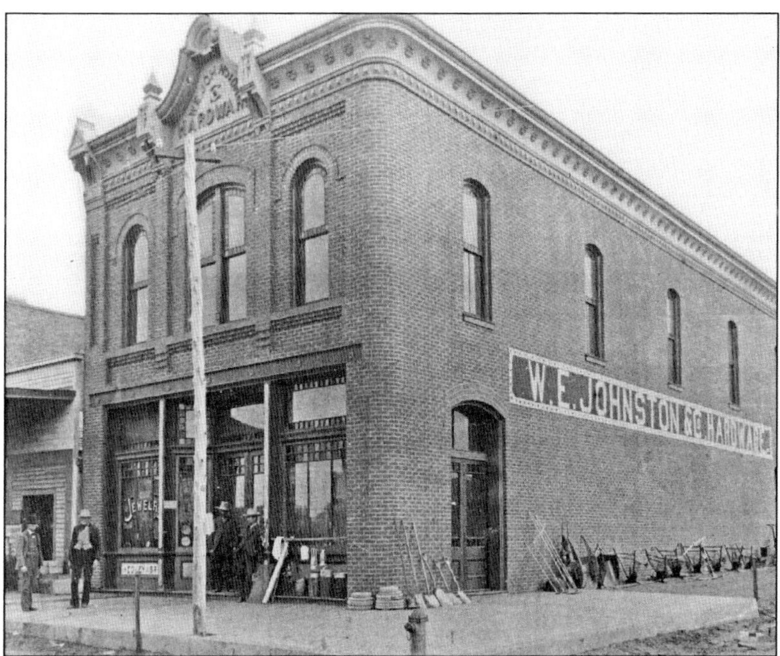

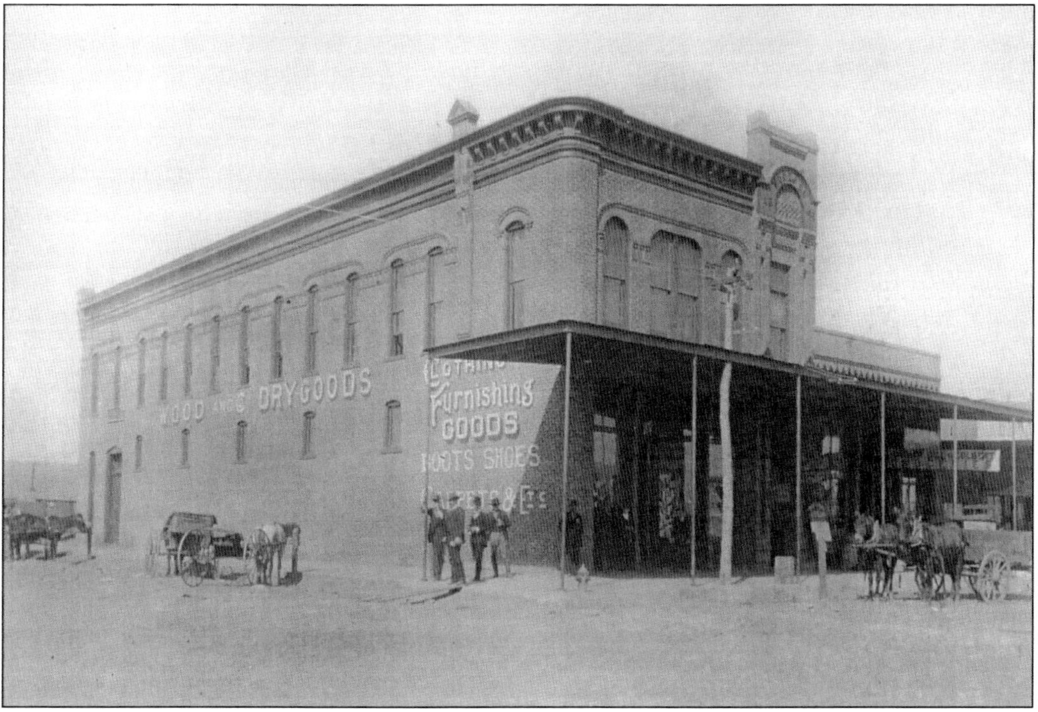

Dr. B.K. Wood came from Cincinnati, Ohio. Up until 1887, he was able to divide his time between his profession and his mercantile business, but his business had grown to such a proportion, he retired from practicing medicine and continued in the mercantile business. In 1893, it became B.K. Wood & Son until December 1896, when Wood sold his share to his son John S. Wood. It was located on the northwest corner of Main and Wilbarger Streets. (Courtesy Wilbarger County Historical Society.)

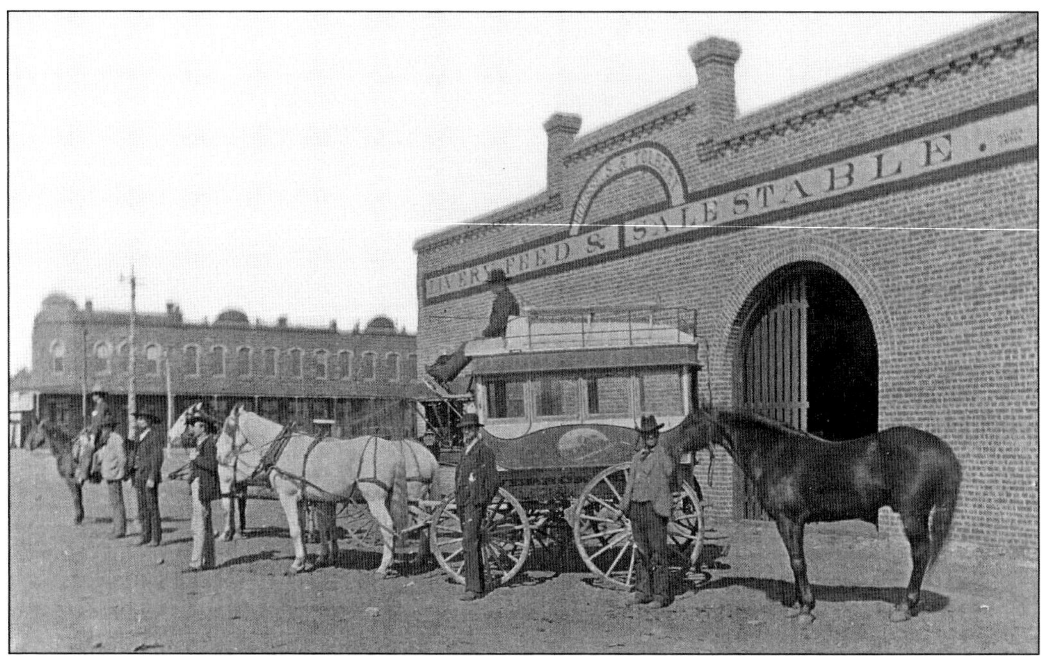

A horse-drawn coach is in front of Houssels & Tolbert livery stable on the corner of Pease and Mesquite Streets. These coaches were advertised as a taxicab service. Business statements advertised that cabs meet all trains. This picture was taken around 1892 on Pease Street, with the State National Bank in the background. (Courtesy of Wilbarger County Historical Society.)

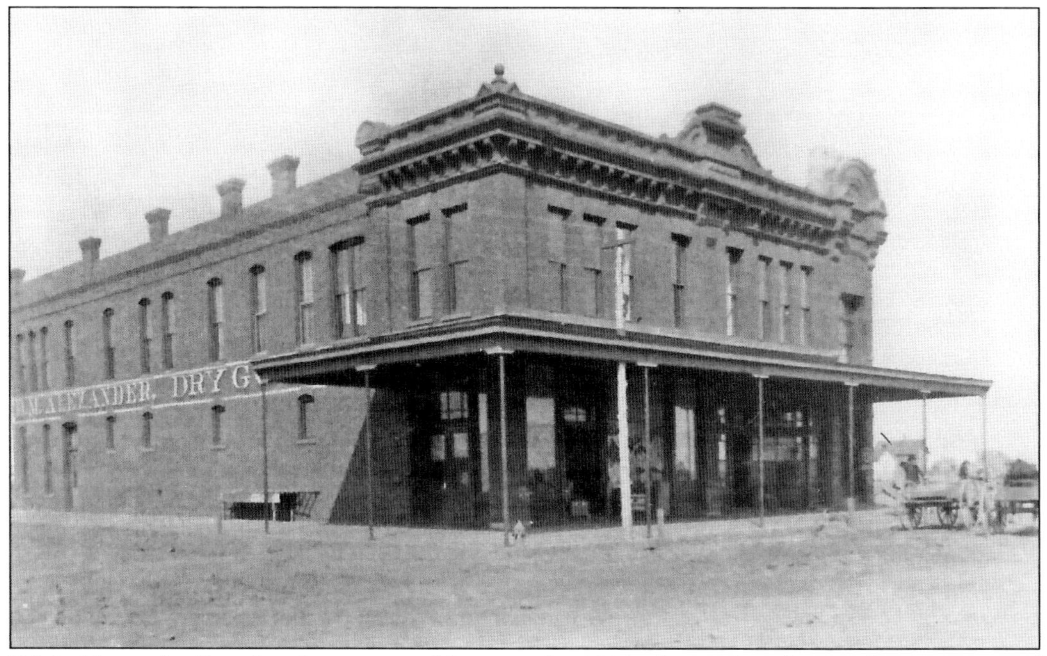

D.M. Alexander Dry Goods is pictured here in the 1890s, located at the northwest corner of Main and Olive Streets. In later years, this location housed the Coca-Cola bottling company in 1915, Parr Furniture in the 1970s, and now Provence Decorating Building, next to George's Guns. (Courtesy of Wilbarger County Historical Society.)

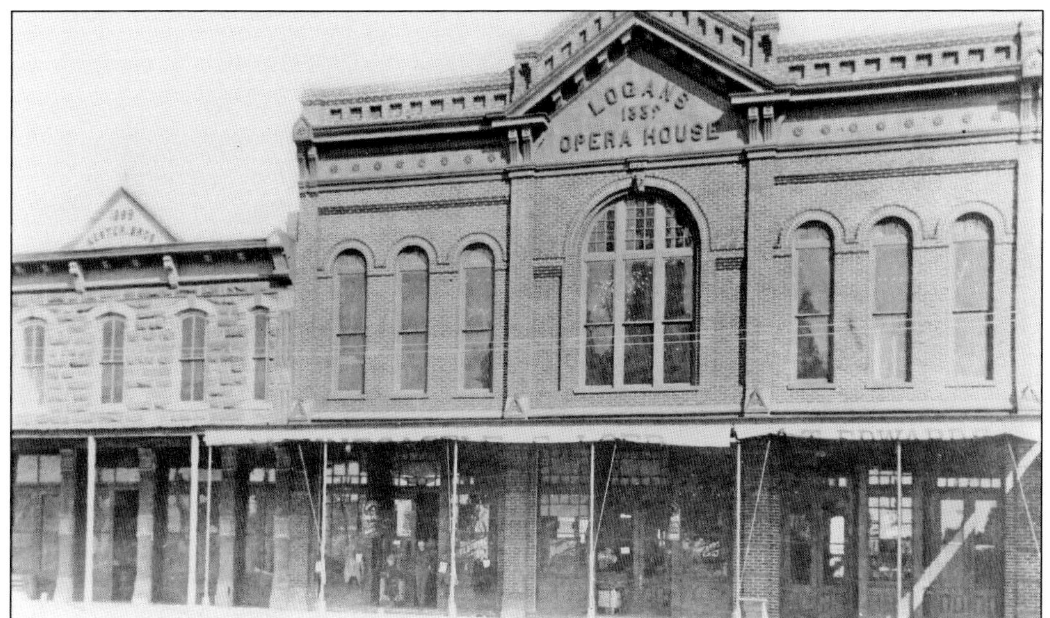

The Logan Opera House was located where the Plaza Theater now stands. It was constructed in 1889 on the east side of the square, with Dr. A.T. Edwards's drugstore and the Montcastle & Loeb hardware store on the first floor. The awning sign was damaged by a storm. Next to the opera house at 1814 Main Street is Kester Brothers Art Shop, owned by M.H. Kester and L.E. Kester. The shop sold paint, glass, and wallpaper. (Courtesy of Wilbarger County Historical Society.)

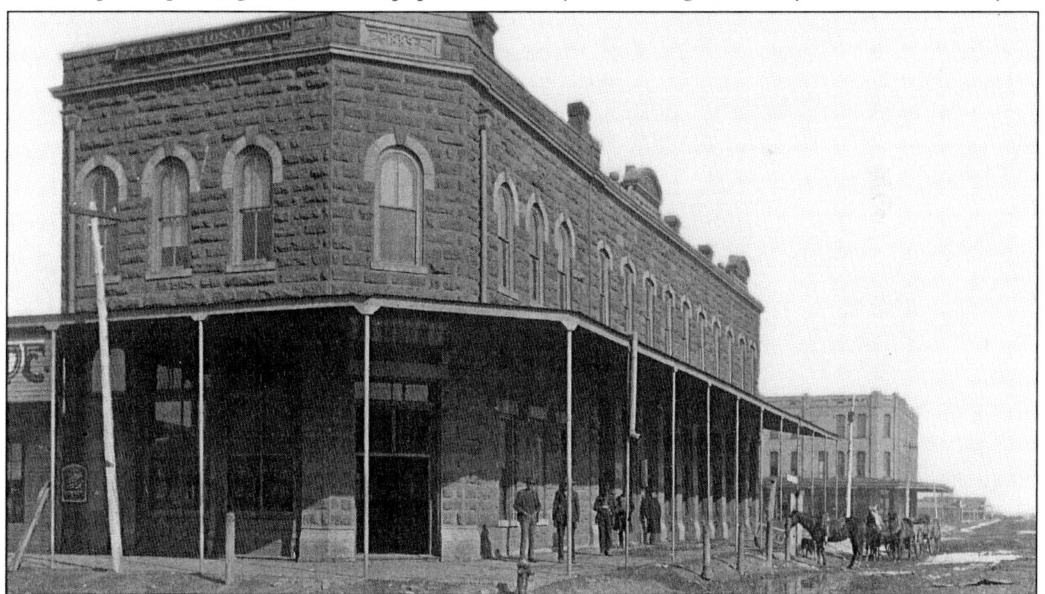

The State National Bank was built in 1889 on the northwest corner of Pease and Cumberland Streets, where the Baily Hotel was later located; it is now the postal employee's parking lot. In 1893, S.W. Lomax was the head cashier of the State National Bank and the First National Bank. These two banks failed in 1893 and went into receivership. Lomax went home and committed suicide. The Vernon Hotel can be seen in the background on Cumberland Street. (Courtesy of Wilbarger County Historical Society.)

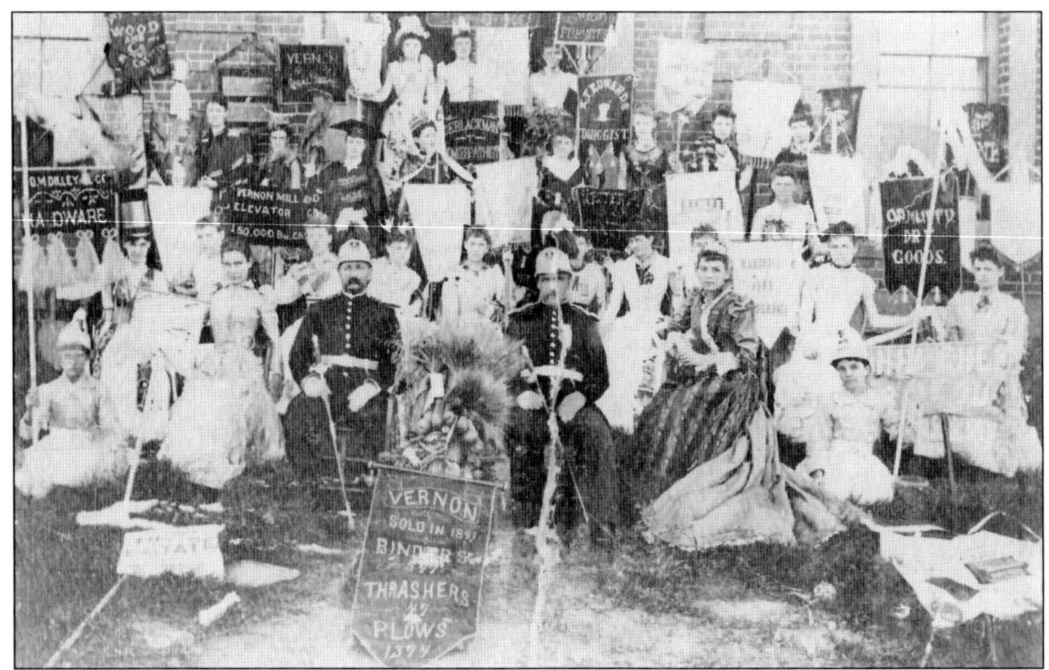

In 1891, a mercantile fair was held behind the old 1886 courthouse. The banner in front advertises the number of implements sold in Wilbarger County, including 577 binders, 47 threshers, and 1,374 plows. Other banners advertise businesses such as Vernon Mill & Elevator, Dr. A.T. Edwards's drugstore, Murry Dry Goods, Vernon Insurance Company, Wood & Company Dry Goods, and McConnie Furniture. (Author's collection.)

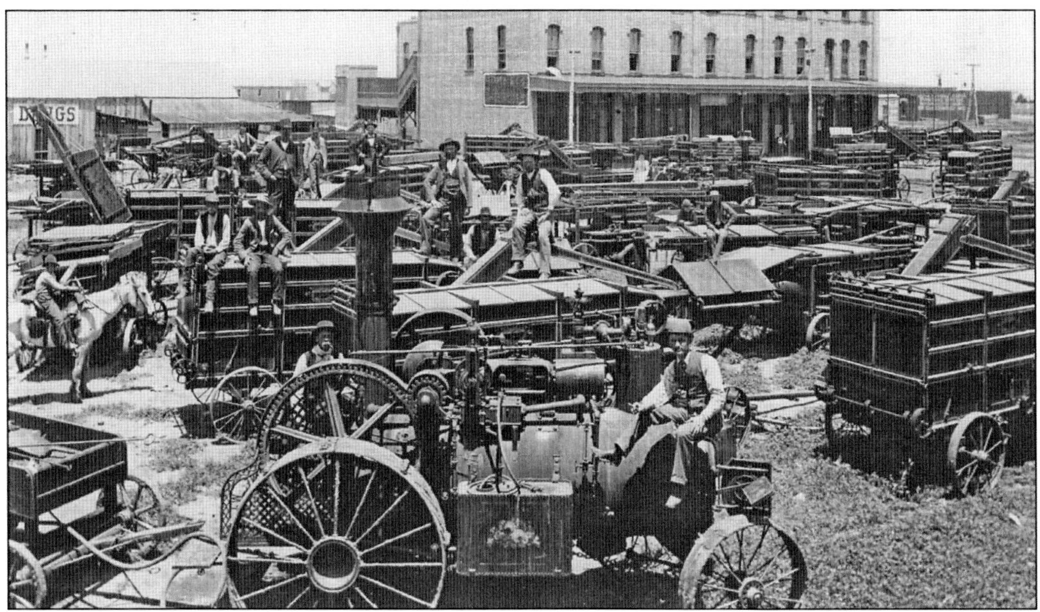

A display of farming equipment is seen in the early 1900s on an empty lot located where the post office now stands. The post office was built in 1917. The pieces of equipment in the foreground are threshers, binders, wagons, and plows. The large building in the background is the Vernon Hotel. (Courtesy of Wilbarger County Historical Society.)

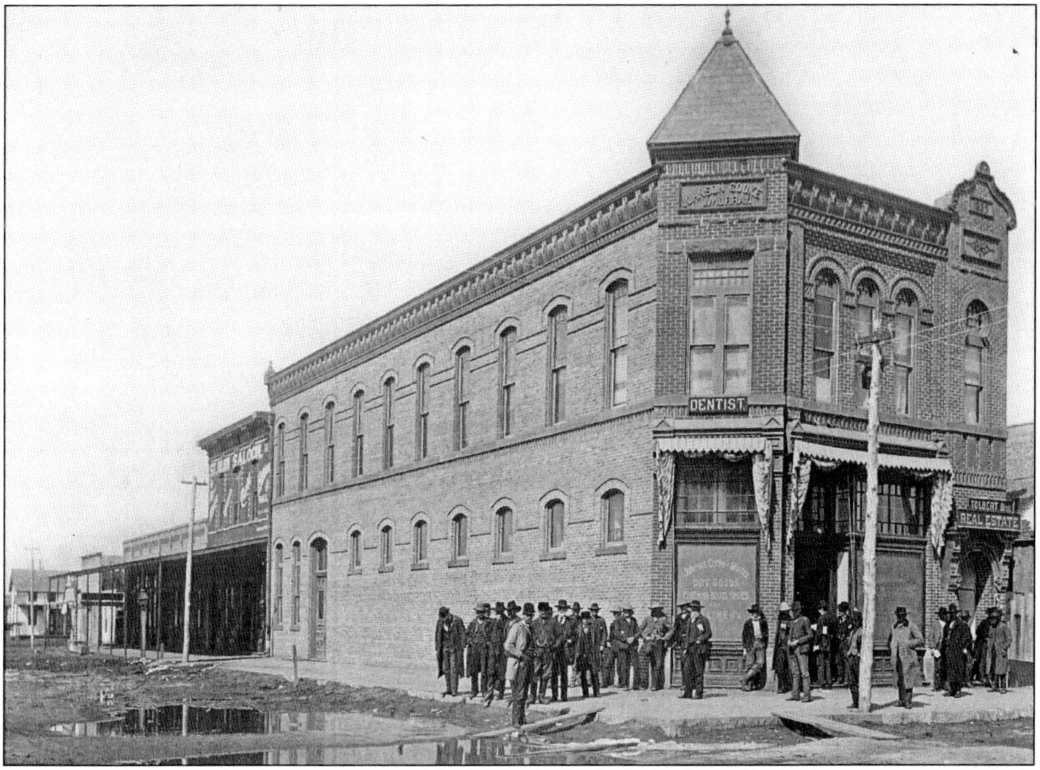

The northwest corner of Main and Pease Streets is known as "Cooke's Corner." This was the location of Johnson, Cooke & Murray Dry Goods, which sold clothing, boots, shoes, and millinery. Tolbert Brothers Real Estate was to the left, and a dentist office was upstairs. The building to the south is St. Julian's Saloon. (Courtesy of Wilbarger County Historical Society.)

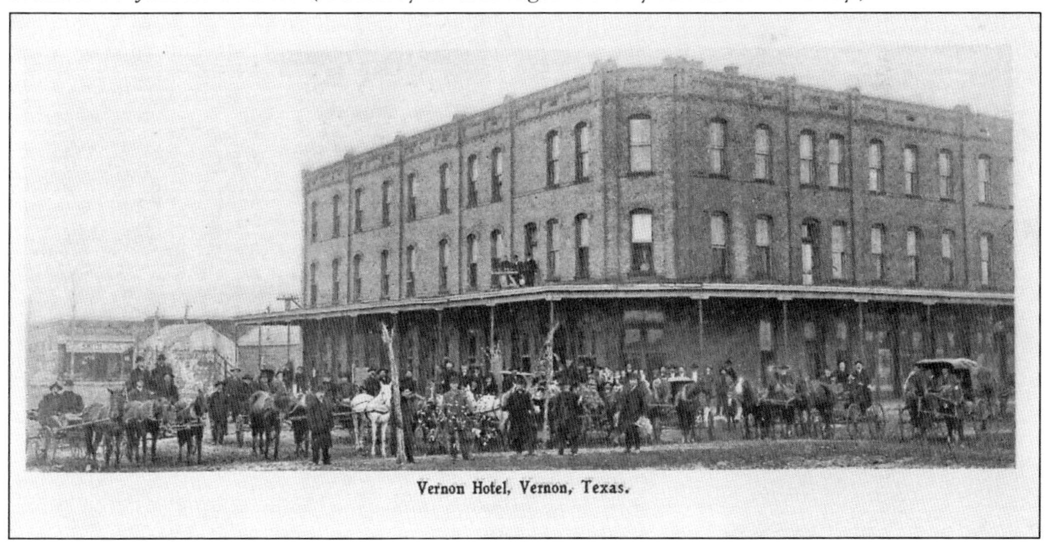

The Vernon Hotel was built in 1885. This was one of the first hotels in Vernon to serve a meal on real china dishes. This two-story hotel was in business until 1938, when it was destroyed by fire. After the fire, this lot stayed vacant until 1946, when a single-story building was constructed for the Popular Furniture Company. Popular Furniture was in this location until 1985. (Author's collection.)

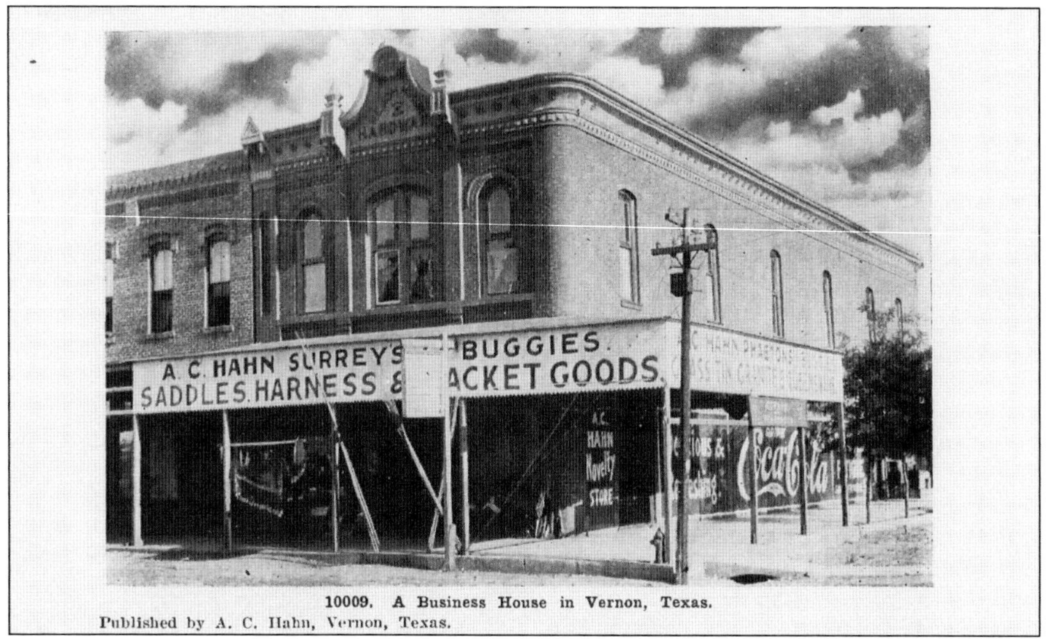

A.C. Hahn Hardware was located on the southeast corner of Main and Wilbarger Streets in W.E. Johnson's old hardware building, which is now the drive-through for city hall. A.C. Hahn not only sold saddles, buggies, and cooking ware but also sold novelty pieces, including postcards published with pictures of Vernon businesses on them, in his novelty shop. (Author's collection.)

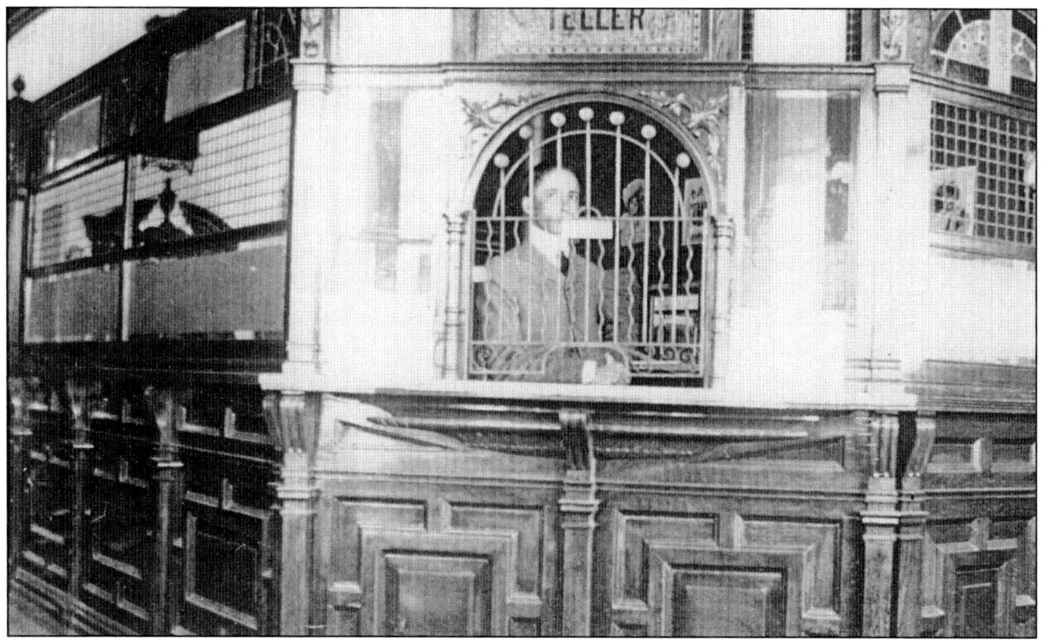

The interior of the C.T. Herring Banking Company was photographed in 1902. Col. C.T. Herring was born in Smith County, Texas. In the early 1880s, he came to this part of Texas and started in the cattle business. In 1893, he established his home in Vernon and continued to carry on his cattle business in Texas and Oklahoma. In 1899, he organized the C.T. Herring Banking Company. (Courtesy of Herring National Bank.)

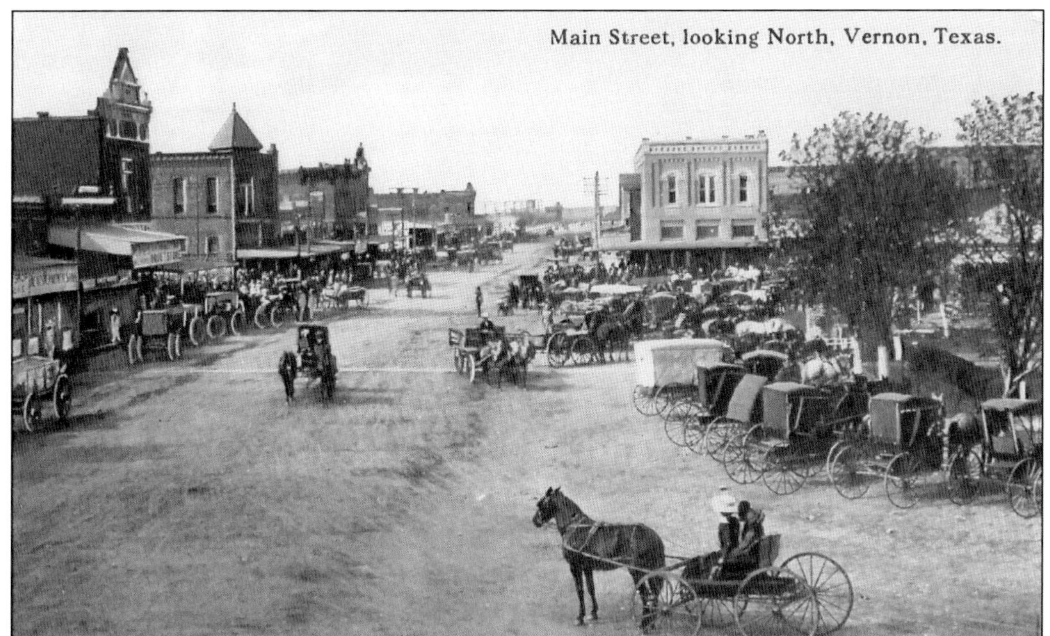

The two-story building in the top center of the picture is the C.T. Herring Banking Company, organized in 1899. This bank operated as a private bank until 1903, when a charter was secured and the Herring National Bank was formed. Looking north from the courthouse, the bank building is on the northeast corner of Pease and Main Streets. (Author's collection.)

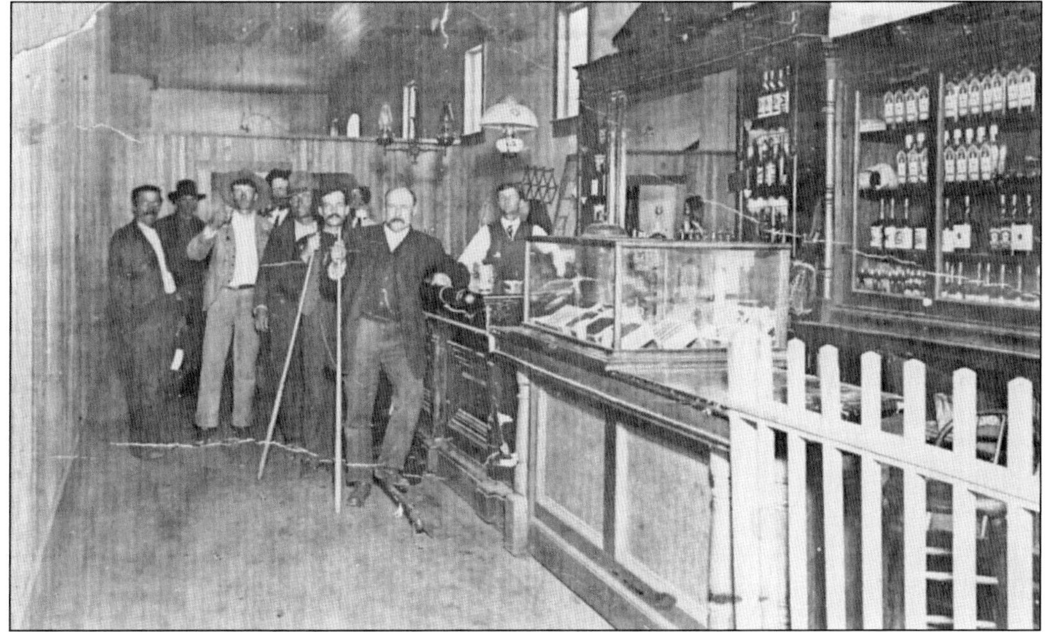

The man at front holding the cue stick is H.C. Justin, known as Uncle Charlie, the owner of the saloon. Justin came to Vernon in 1882 after working as a buffalo hunter and cattle drover as well as selling buffalo hides. Justin was tax assessor of Wilbarger County from 1886 to 1892. In 1894, he was appointed deputy US marshal and worked among the Indians in Oklahoma. In 1898, he returned to Vernon and was a city officer for nine years. (Author's collection.)

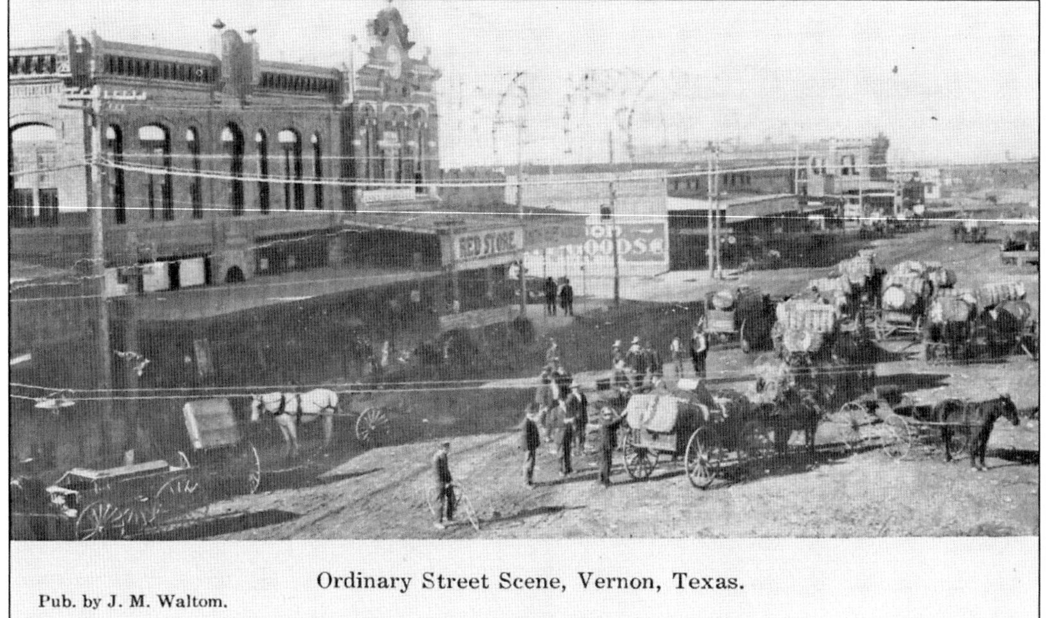

A street scene in Vernon, around 1905, shows wagonloads of cotton going to market. Looking north on Main Street are the Waggoner National Bank, the Red Store, Smith-Huff, and Collins (boys' clothing store). Norwood Dry Goods is on the northeast corner of Main and Fannin Streets. (Author's collection.)

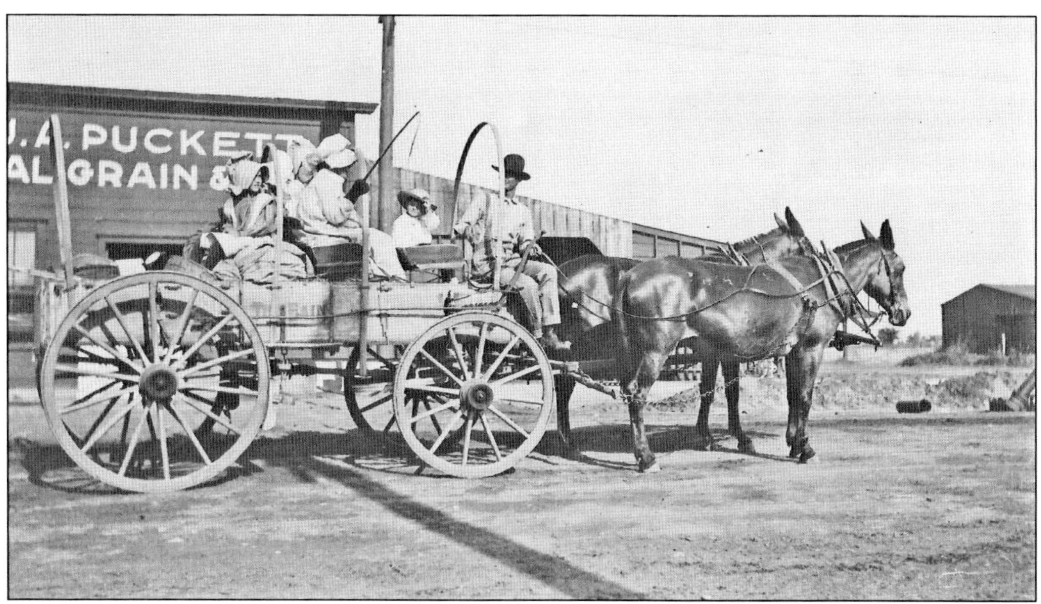

A mule-drawn wagon is parked in front of J.A. Puckett Coal, Grain & Feed. J.A. Puckett came to Wilbarger County in 1891 from Travis County with his wife and daughter and settled west of Vernon in what was known as the Kincheloe Community. After 15 years of farming, the Puckett family moved to Vernon, and in 1905, J.A. Puckett entered the wagon yard, coal, and feed business. (Author's collection.)

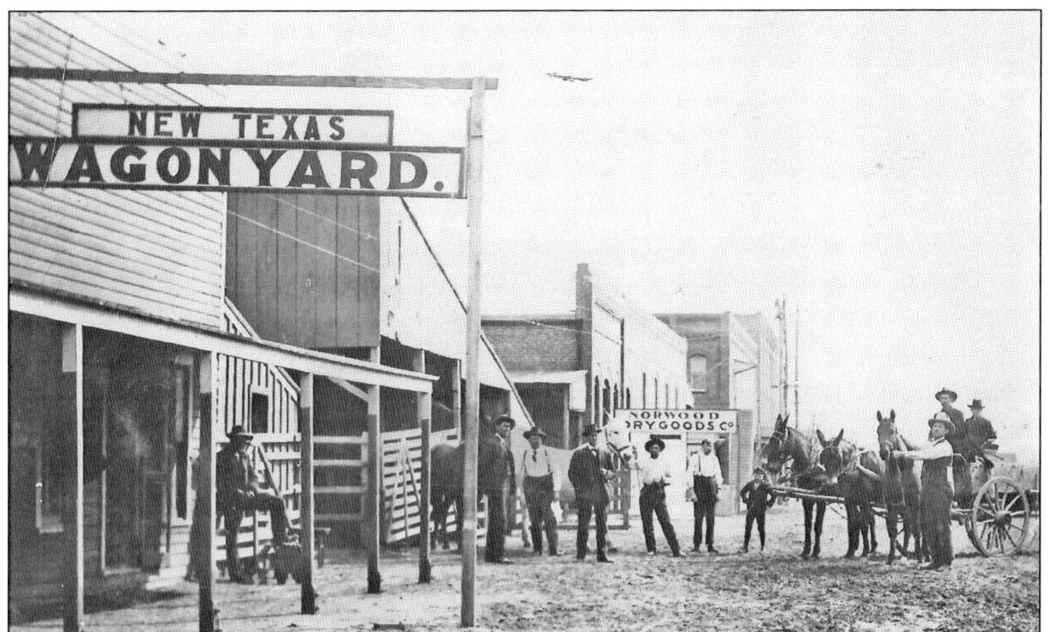

The New Texas Wagon Yard, located on the northwest corner of Texas and Fannin Streets, is now the location of the Waggoner National Bank. Looking east on Texas Street, one can see the south side of Norwood Dry Goods, which faces east on Main Street. The far building on Texas Street is the Vernon Hotel, on the corner of Texas and Cumberland Streets. (Author's collection.)

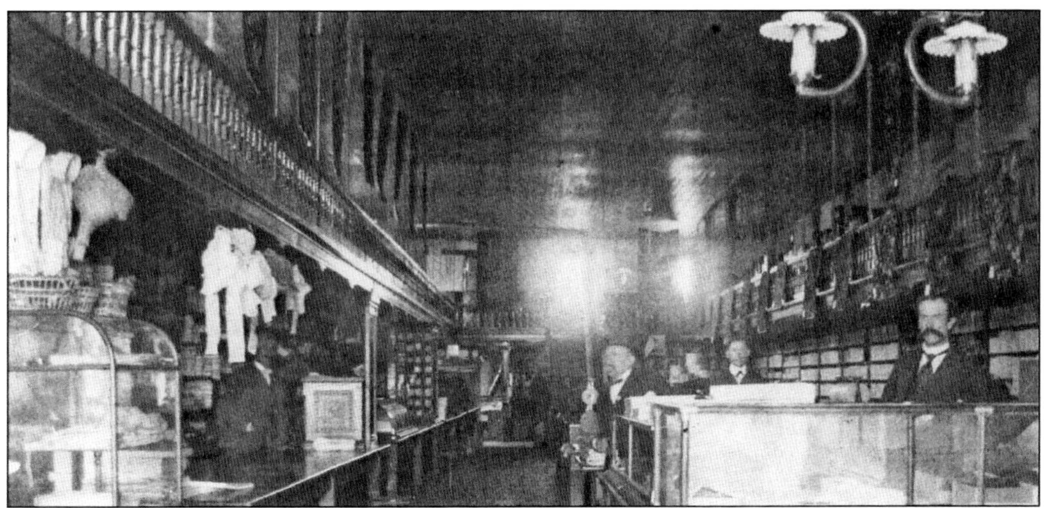

Denny Brothers Dry Goods & Clothing was established by William and Ben Denny in 1886 on the west side of the square, where a large cottonwood tree and a public water pump were located. Another brother, J.N. "Jake" Denny, came to Vernon later and bought Ben's interest, continuing until 1919, when the business was sold to Perkins-Timberlake, a popular store in Vernon until its closing in early 1980s. (Courtesy of Wilbarger County Historical Society.)

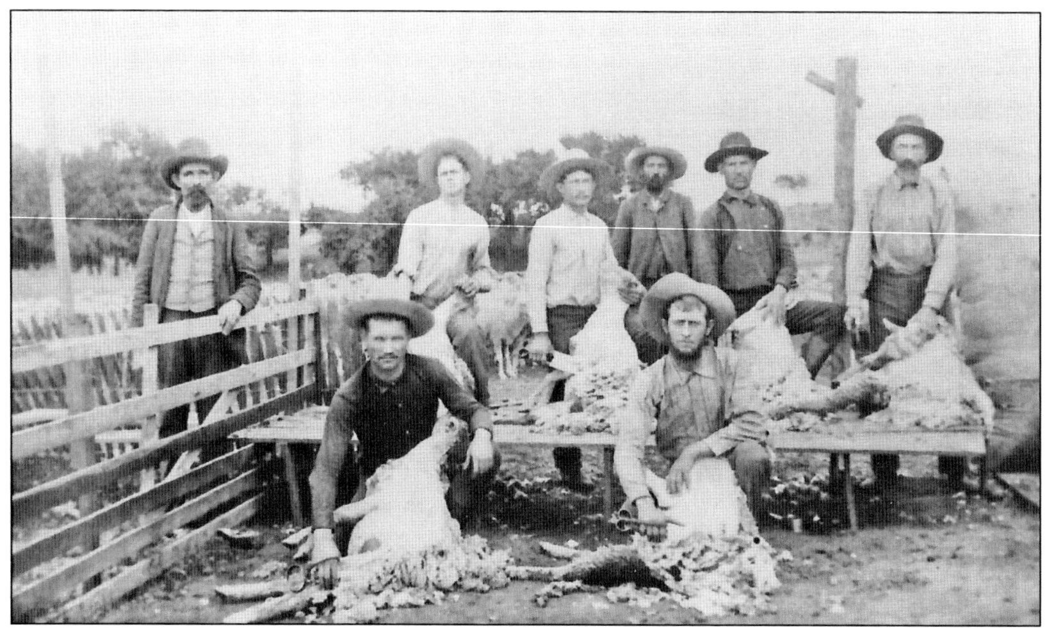

Here is a sheep-shearing scene on an early-day sheep ranch in Wilbarger County. In 1881, an Irish adventurer, Thomas Boyle, along with his brother David and cousin Ed Beare, established the county's first sheep ranch on Lily Creek, located 16 miles south of Vernon. After David died in 1889, two other brothers, Robert and Samuel, along with their families, came from Ireland to join the ranching business. (Courtesy of Wilbarger County Historical Society.)

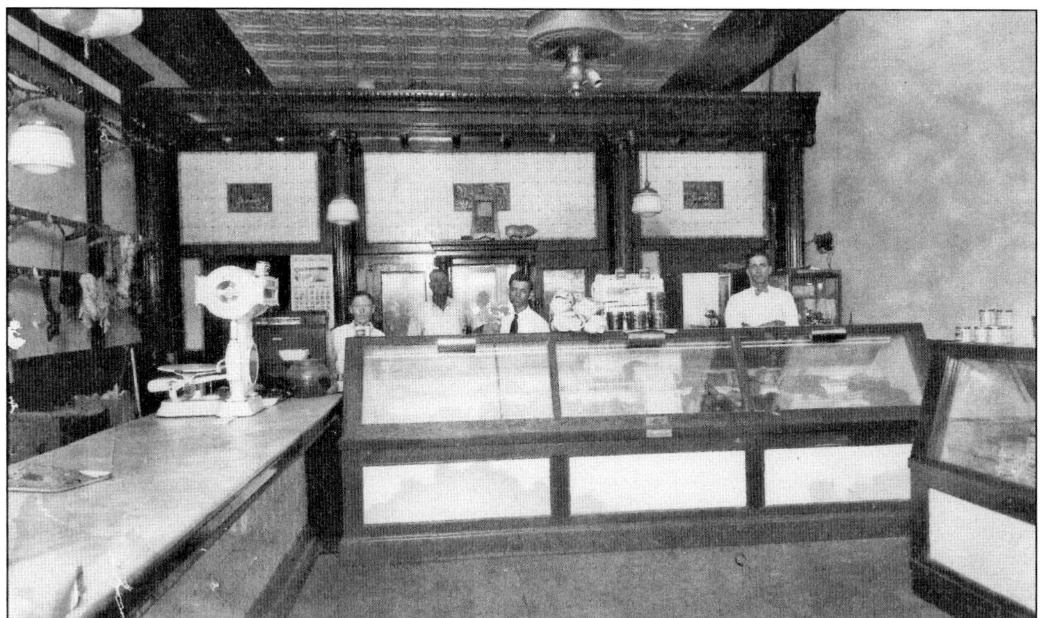

Pictured is the interior of Minarik Grocery & Market around 1950. After arriving in the United States from Zlyn, Austria, Frank Minarik and his family settled in West Texas. After a few years in that location, they came to Wilbarger County in 1888 when he went to work for Carl Zipperle in the meat market business, learning the butcher trade. In later years, Minarik went into business for himself as Minarik Grocery & Market. (Courtesy of Jack Minarik.)

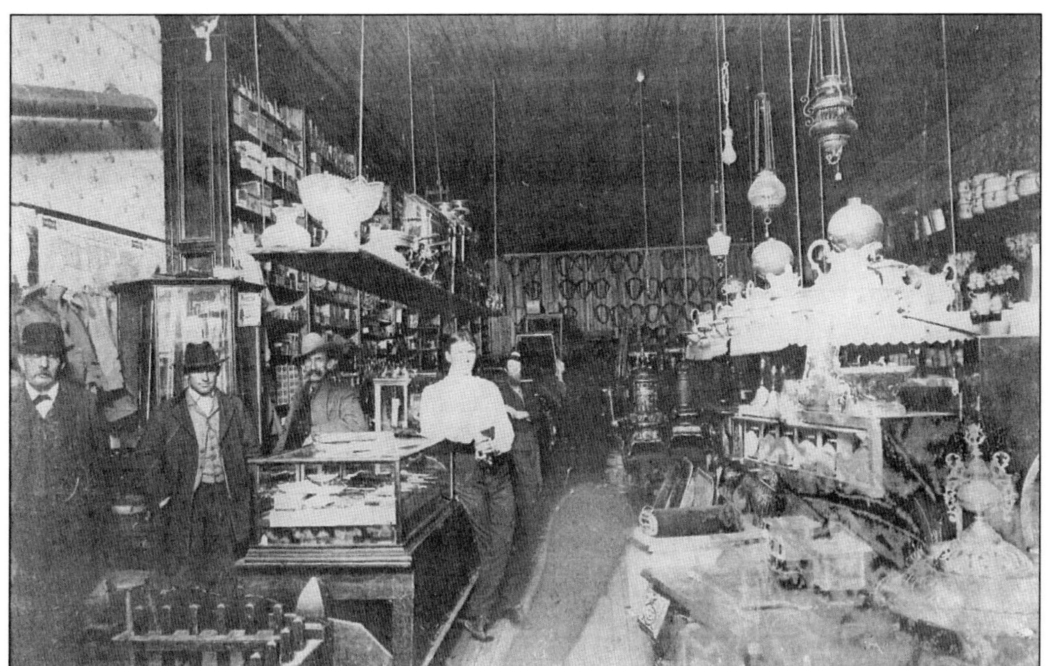

Born in Alabama, R.S. Kelly came to Texas as a child with his family and settled near Rusk. Coming to Vernon in 1883, he was in many different businesses, including a hardware business known as Vernon Hardware Company. Vernon was incorporated in 1889, and James R. Tolbert was appointed mayor. R.S. Kelly was the first elected mayor in 1890 and served until resigning in 1892. (Courtesy of Wilbarger County Historical Society.)

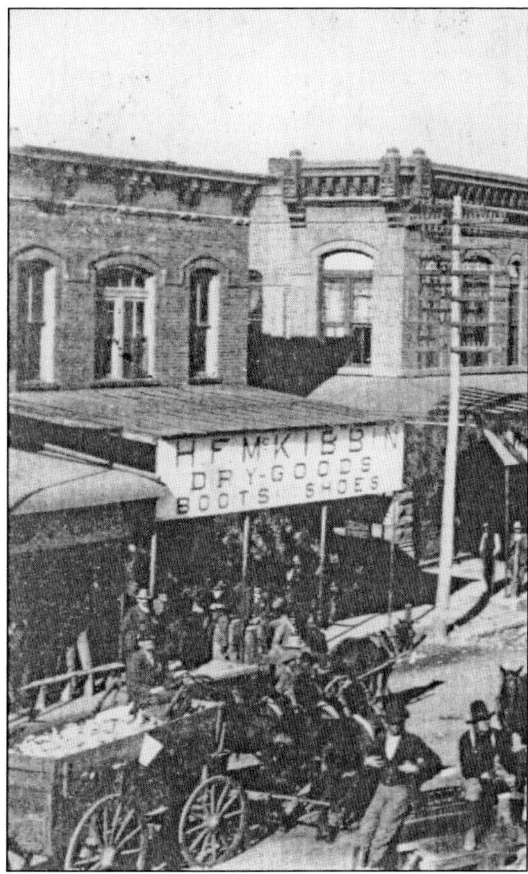

H.F. McKibbin and his family moved to Vernon in 1893. Shortly after his arrival in Wilbarger County, he entered the mercantile business, located around 1614 Main Street, selling boots, shoes, and dry goods. McKibbin was one of Vernon's substantial merchants, and he took an active interest in the growth of Vernon and Wilbarger County. He passed away in 1928 (Author's collection.)

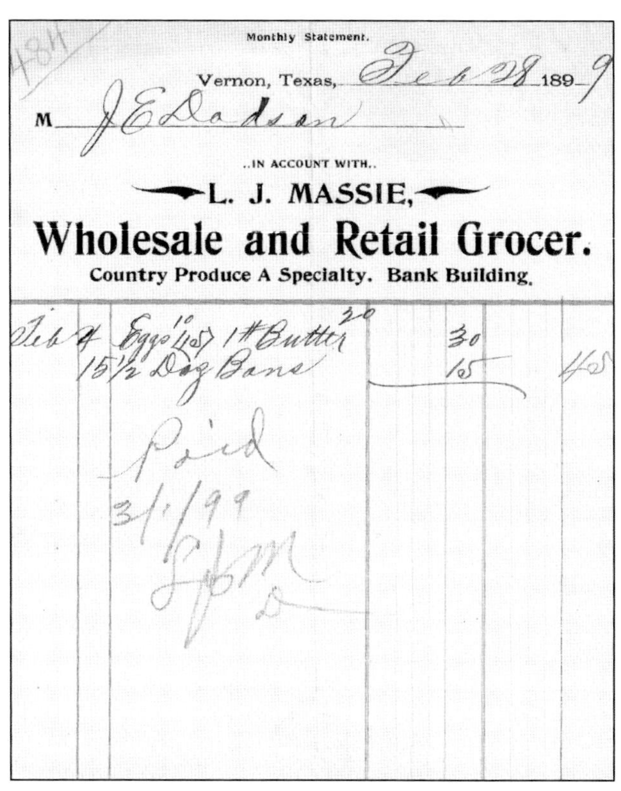

Monthly Statement.

Vernon, Texas, Feb 28 1899

M J E Dodson

..IN ACCOUNT WITH..

L. J. MASSIE,

Wholesale and Retail Grocer.

Country Produce A Specialty. Bank Building.

Feb 4 Eggs 10 1# Butter 20 — 30
15½ Doz Bans — 15 — 45

Paid 3/1/99 LJM

L.J. Massie was born in Kentucky and settled in McKinney, Texas, in 1877. After arriving in Vernon, on May 10, 1888, he bought into a small grocery business on the west side of the square. In 1892, S.L. Mallow and Massie opened the Massie-Hogsett grocery store. After 1896, he had several different partners in the grocery business. Massie stores were located in Texas and southern Oklahoma. (Author's collection.)

Pictured are J.H. Pendleton and his daughter Anna Jo in Pendleton Drugstore around 1910. J.H. Pendleton came to Vernon in 1884 and became partners with Dr. H.H. Rhodes a few years after his arrival. They bought out W.T. Dickey & Co. Drugstore. After a short while, Dr. Rhodes sold his part of the company to T.M. Fergeson, and it became Pendleton & Fergeson Vernon Drug. (Courtesy of Jo Jones.)

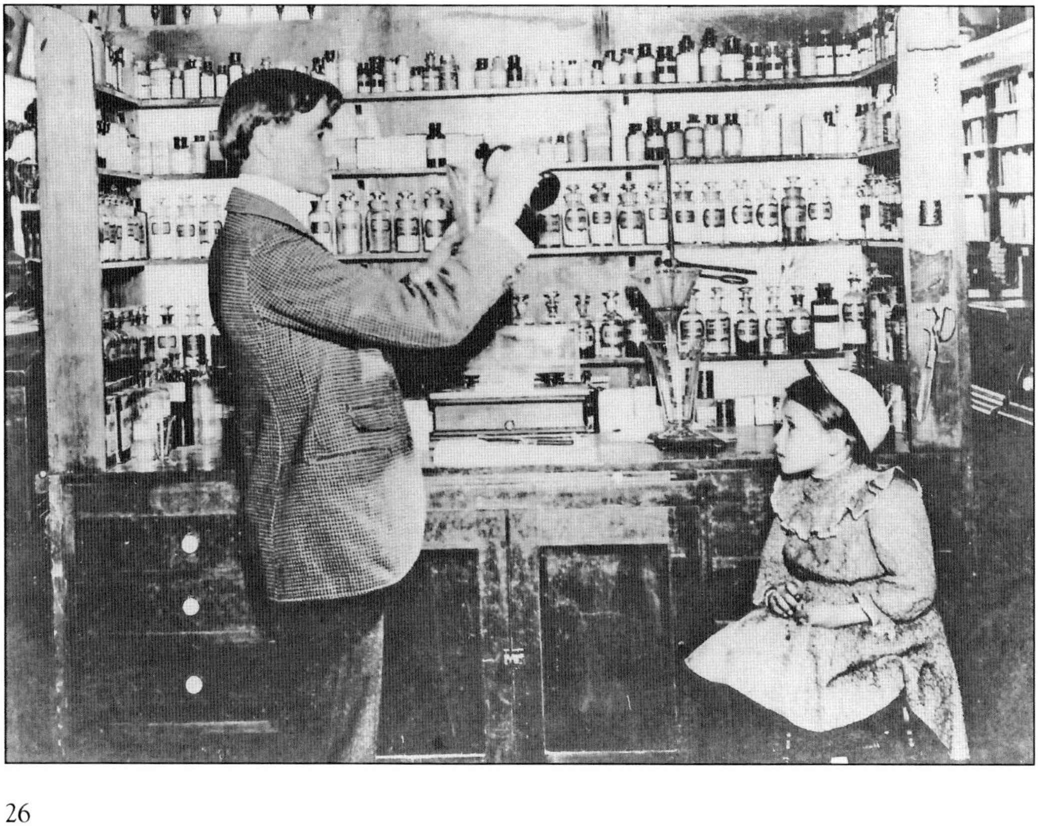

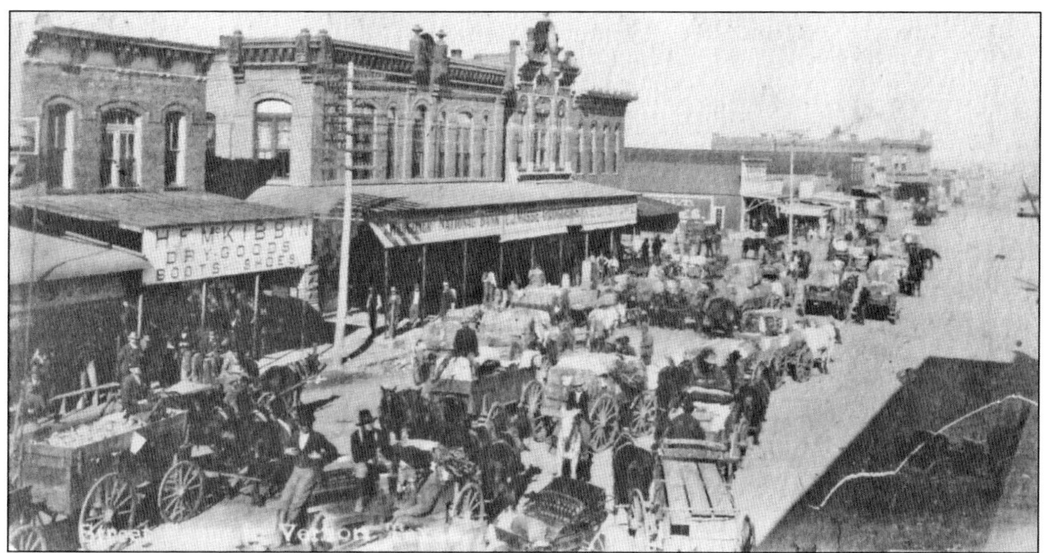

This street scene, taken in early 1890s looking north on Main Street, shows H.F. McKibbin Dry Goods; the Waggoner National Bank, with L.J. Massie grocery store on the first floor; the Red Store; and Smith, Huff & Collins. Across Texas Street is T.M. Holt Grocery Store. (Author's collection.)

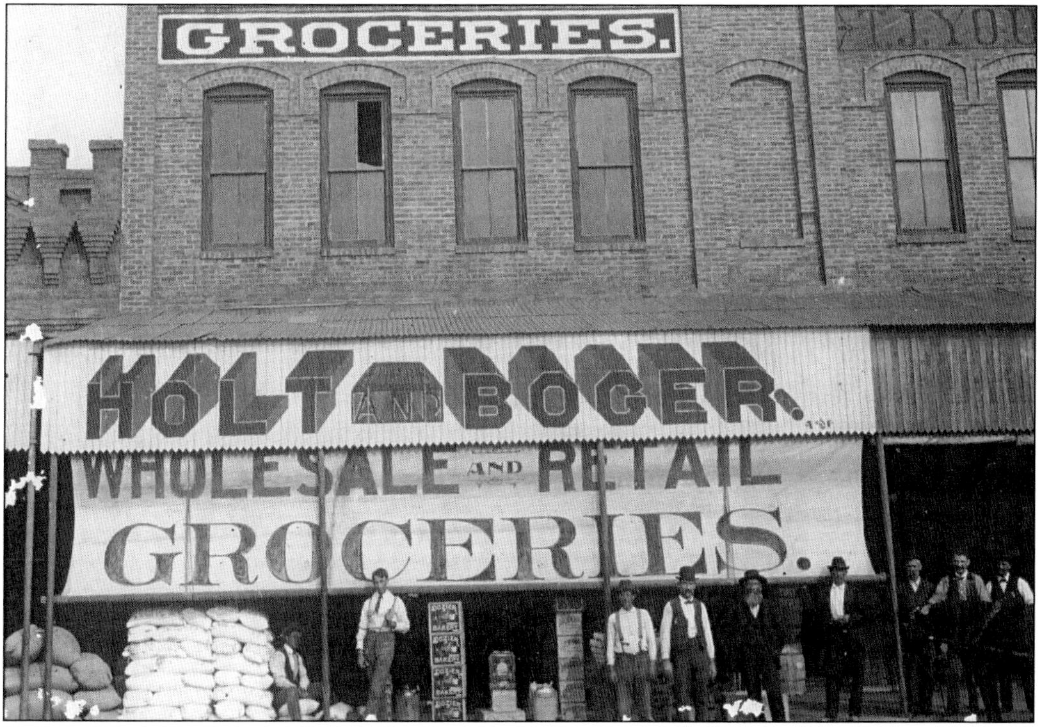

Holt & Boger grocery store, located in the 1500 block of Main Street next to the T.J. Youngblood furniture store, sold wholesale and retail groceries. Grocery stores placed some of their goods in front of the business to entice customers into their store. This entire block was destroyed by fire but was later rebuilt. This location is now occupied by Yesterdaze Antiques, at 1519 Main Street. (Author's collection.)

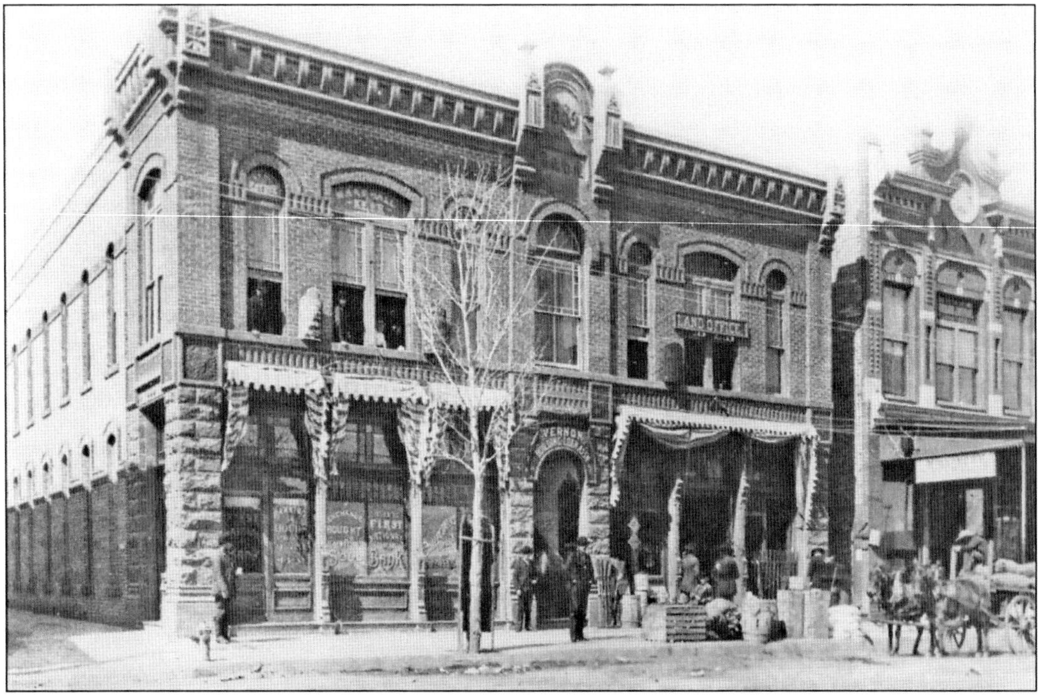

The First National Bank, built in 1889 at 1614 Main Street, was forced to close due to financial circumstances. In 1893, Dr. R.C. Neal organized a private bank called the R.C. Neal Banking Company in the same location. Dr. Neal was president, W.T. Waggoner was vice president, and John A. Henry was cashier. Later known as the Merchants and Cattlemen's Bank, it merged into Waggoner National Bank in 1899. (Courtesy of Waggoner National Bank.)

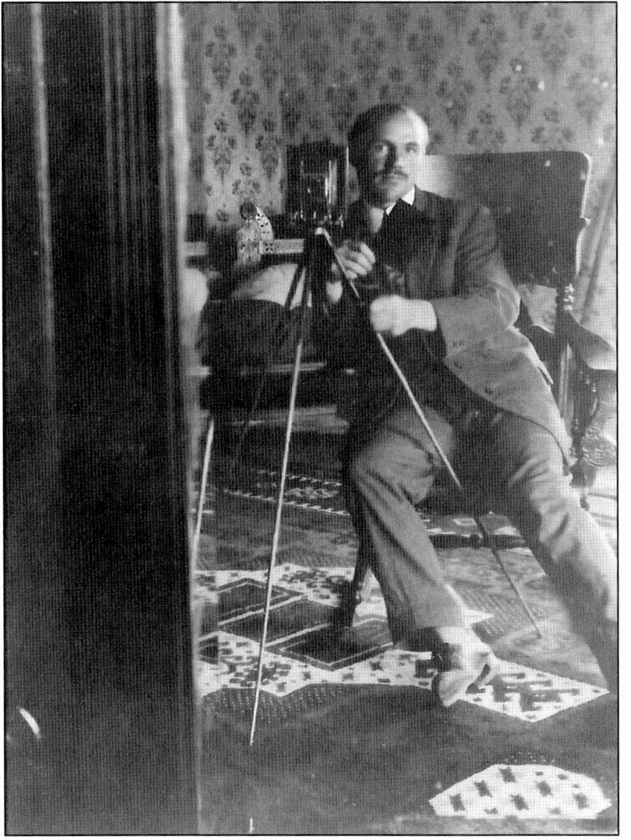

D.P Sink came to Vernon in 1889. A few days after his arrival, he erected a tent for his first photographic studio on the location now occupied by the old city hall. He photographed two celebrities that came to Vernon, Quanah Parker, one of the last chiefs of the Comanche tribe, and Pres. Theodore Roosevelt. He sold his studio in 1919 to R.B. Clifton. (Author's collection.)

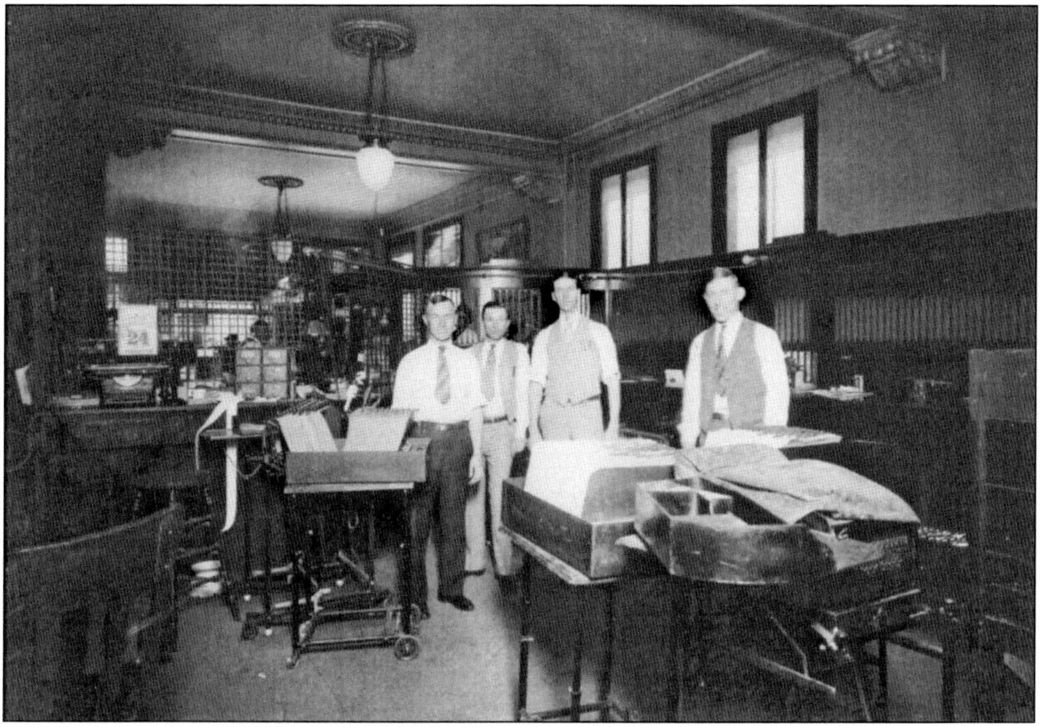

Pictured in early 1890s is the interior of the Waggoner National Bank, located at 1614 Main Street. Among the first officers of the Waggoner National Bank were W.T. Waggoner, president; L.G. Hawkins (for whom Hawkins Elementary School was named), vice president; C.E. Basham, cashier; and S.C. Hogsett, assistant cashier. (Courtesy of Waggoner National Bank.)

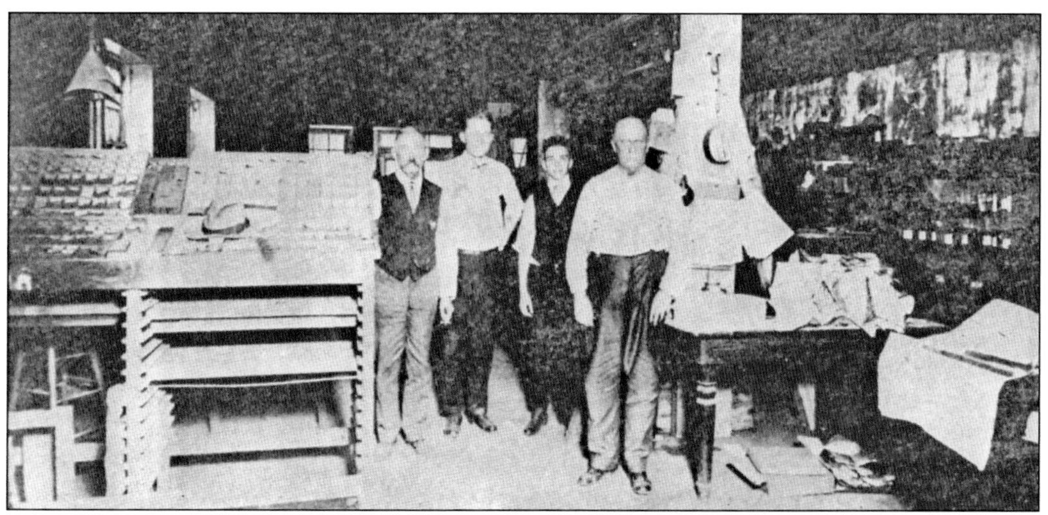

Pictured is the interior of the *Vernon Guard* newspaper office, established January 19, 1883. The office was located on the northeast corner of the courthouse square. The editor for the paper was B. Wilson Edgell, and the office staff consisted of a Mr. Tschiffley, Bob Stone, Dora Capps, and a Mr. Hendrick. Turning on the press on publication day was a Mr. Capps and a Mr. Haney. (Courtesy of Jo Jones.)

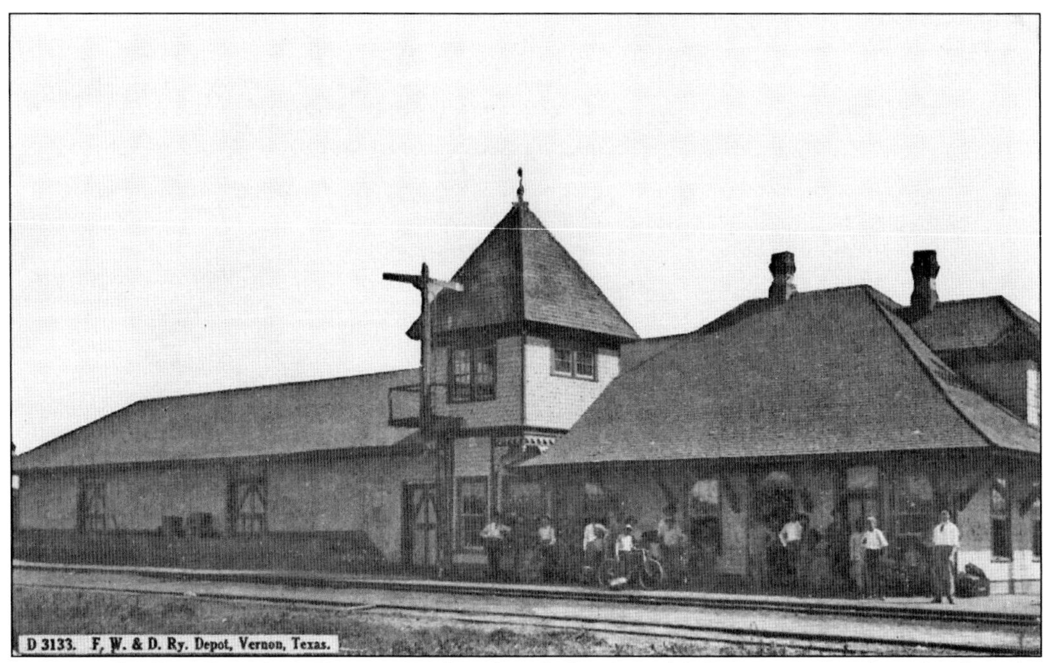

In 1886, the Fort Worth & Denver Railroad ended at Harold, Texas. It was thought that the railroad would extend its tracks north through Oklahoma (Indian territory), but instead it went west to Vernon on October 15, 1886. The depot pictured was originally an old wooden freight house built around 1901 and used as passenger depot until 1910, when it was replaced by a brick structure. (Author's collection.)

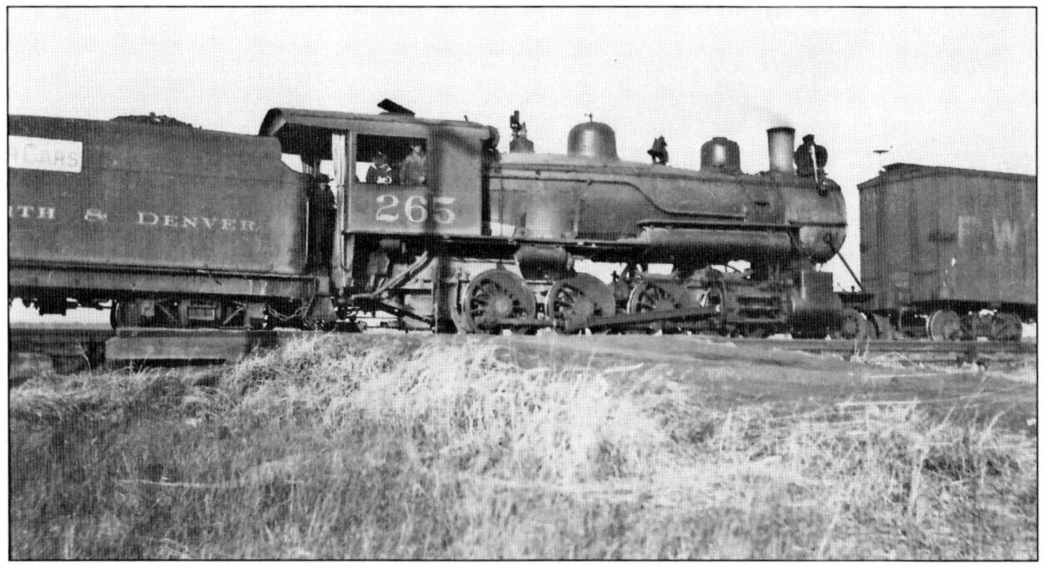

The iron horse brought the greatest change to Vernon with an ever-increasing number of settlers. When the first train arrived, everyone in town went out to see it in Tom Jones's pasture where it stopped. The great iron horse was a marvel to the Indians. They would climb all over the coaches and under them trying to figure out what made them go. (Author's collection.)

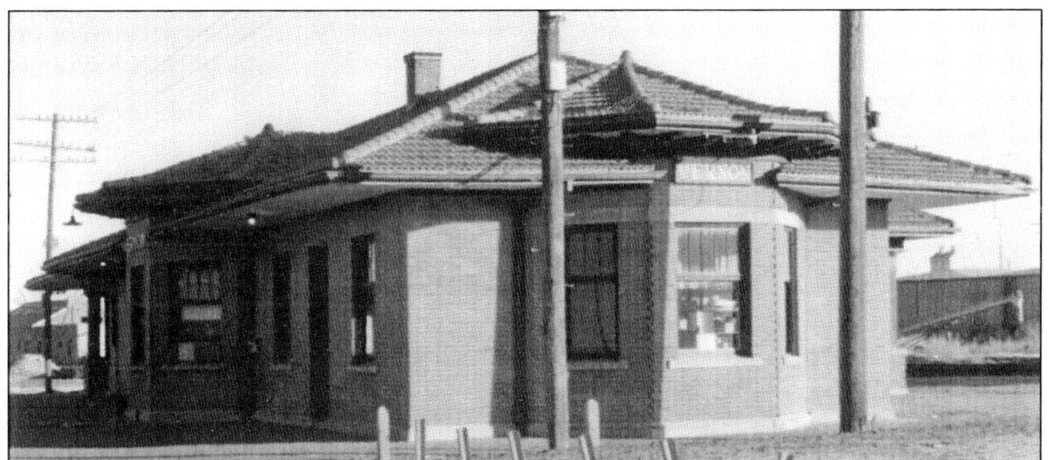

This redbrick depot was the last passenger station built by the Fort Worth & Denver Railroad; it was completed in November 1910 at 70 North Main Street. The Fort Worth & Denver merged with the Burlington Railroad system in 1952 and eventually became the Burlington Northern Railroad. This building with its terrazzo floor and red tile roof stood until January 16, 1986, when it was torn down by Burlington Northern workmen. (Author's collection.)

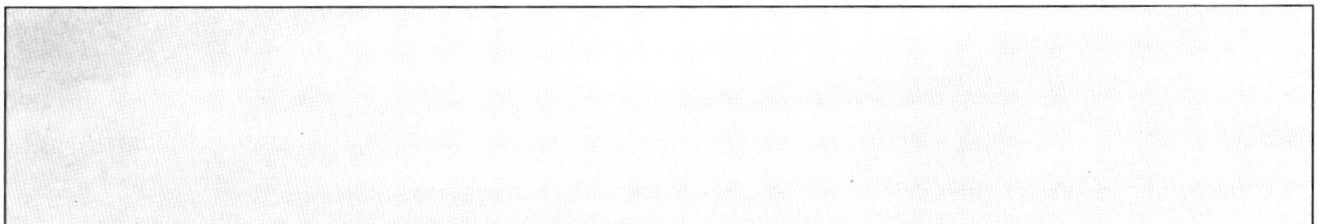

This photograph was taken from the top of the courthouse at the turn of the 20th century, looking north at the corner of Main and Pease Streets. On the west corner is Mittenthal Dry Goods, and on the east corner is the clothing store located on the first floor of the old C.T. Herring Bank Building. The Pease River can be seen in the far background. (Author's collection.)

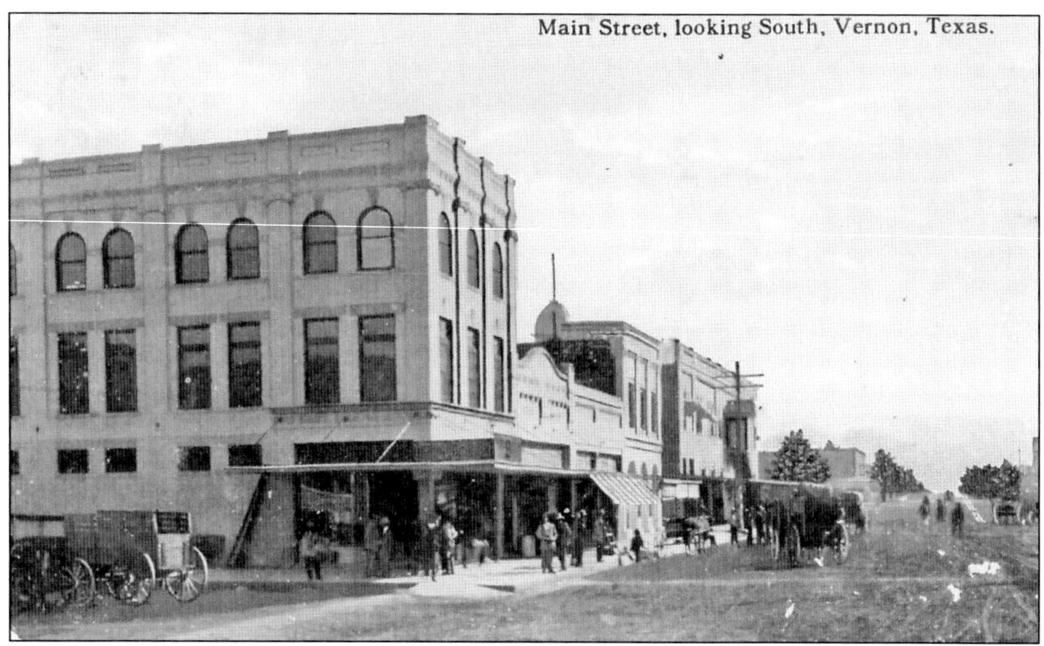

Looking south from the corner of Main and Texas Streets, one can see the Lutz Building. Next to the Lutz Building is the Peoples Dry Goods, then Freeman's barbershop with a red-and-white-stripped awning. The next building is the First Guaranty State Bank, with the Herring National Bank on the corner of Main and Pease Streets. The Lutz Building was better known as Hill's Youth Center in the 1950s and 1960s. (Author's collection.)

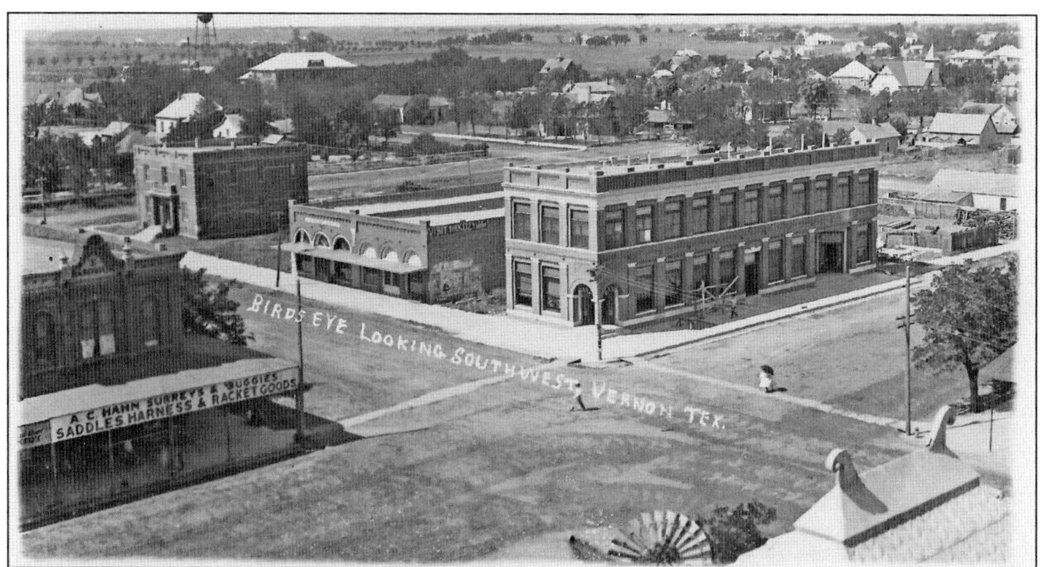

This photograph was taken from the top of the courthouse at the corner of Main and Wilbarger Streets around 1909. A.C. Hahn Hardware is on the northwest corner, and the Farmers State Bank is on the southwest corner. The next building to the south is Pendleton Music Store and then the American Railway Express Company. The last building to the south is the first city hall. (Author's collection.)

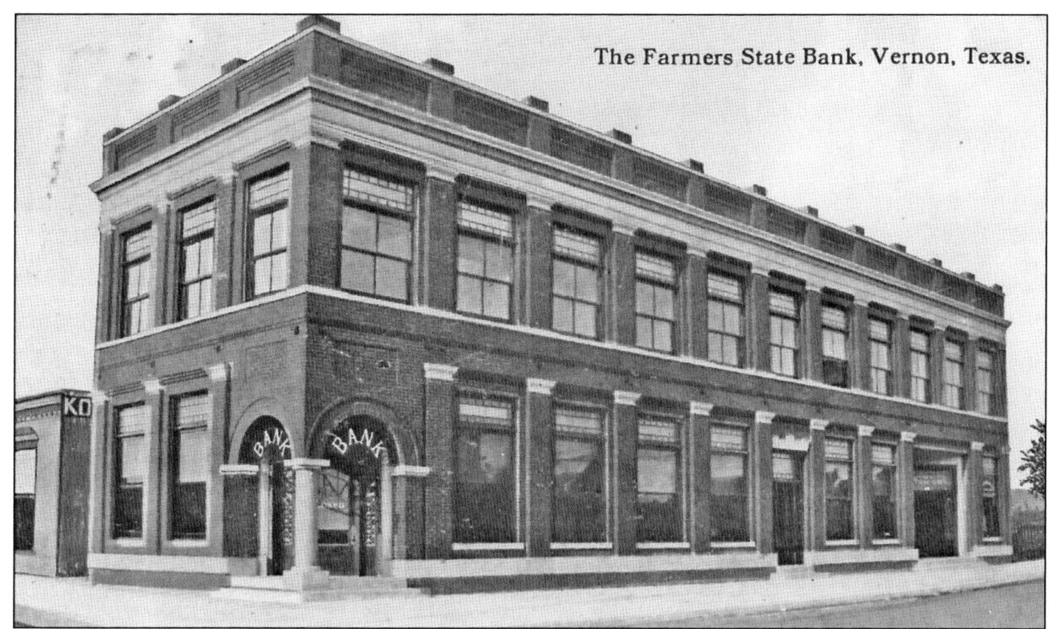

The Farmers State Bank in early 1910 was located on the corner of Main and Wilbarger Streets, with H.H. Rhoads as president, F.L. Massie and Emory Rhoads as active vice presidents, A.M. Bourland as vice president, R.B. Gibson as cashier, and A.A. Hingst and R.E. Martin as assistant cashiers. KVWC radio station occupied the top floor from early 1940s until the mid-1950s, when fire destroyed the building. Now, a single-story building is the location of Bunch-Norris Insurance Agency. (Author's collection.)

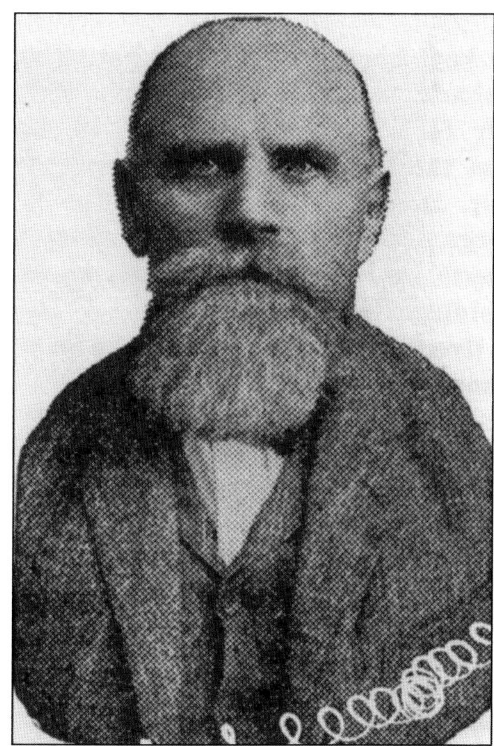

The first icehouse was built by Joseph Schmidt, who also owned a hotel. Ice was cut from a lake near town and stored in sufficient amounts to furnish his hotel during the summer months. Joseph Schmidt donated ice for the first picnic to celebrate the county's 10th birthday in 1891. (Author's collection.)

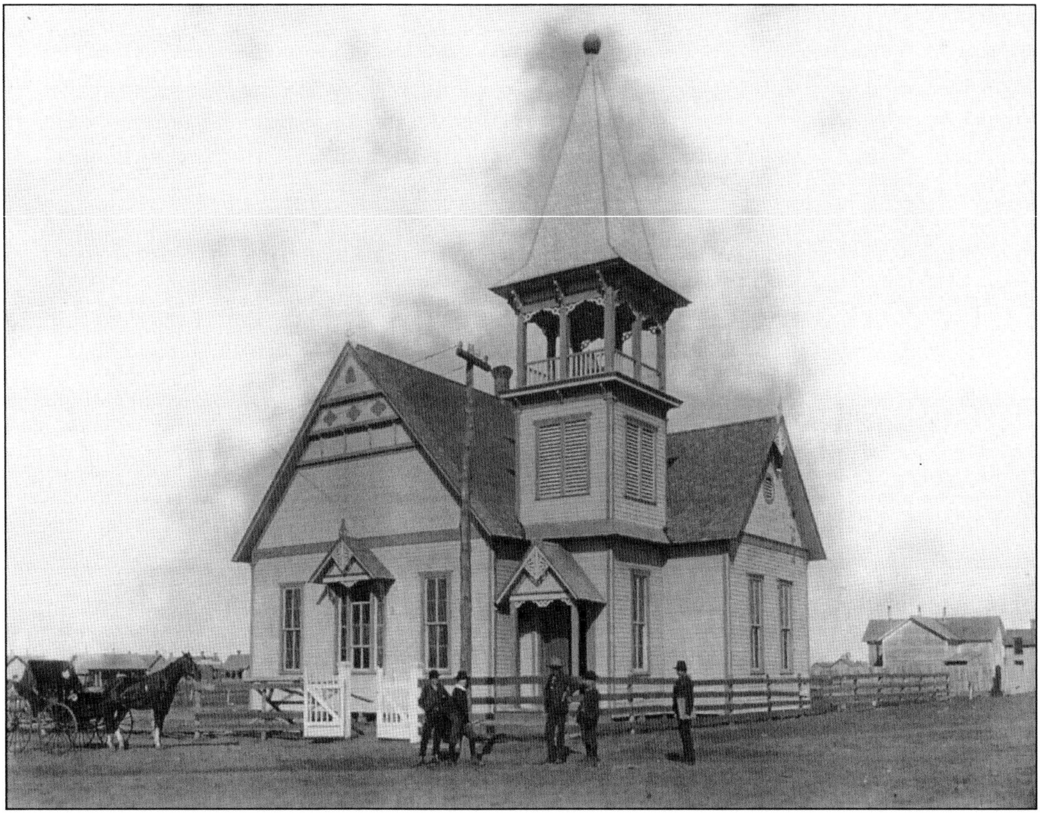

Pictured is the first First Baptist Church, built in 1888, on the corner of Mesquite and Marshall Streets under the leadership of the Rev. J.H. Cason. The First Baptist Church was organized on July 17, 1884, with charter members listed as Ella Jones, Mr. and Mrs. A.T. Boger, Mr. and Mrs. E. Lowe, and Mr. R.S. Kelly. The first Sunday school was organized by J.A Gilliland in June 1889. (Author's collection.)

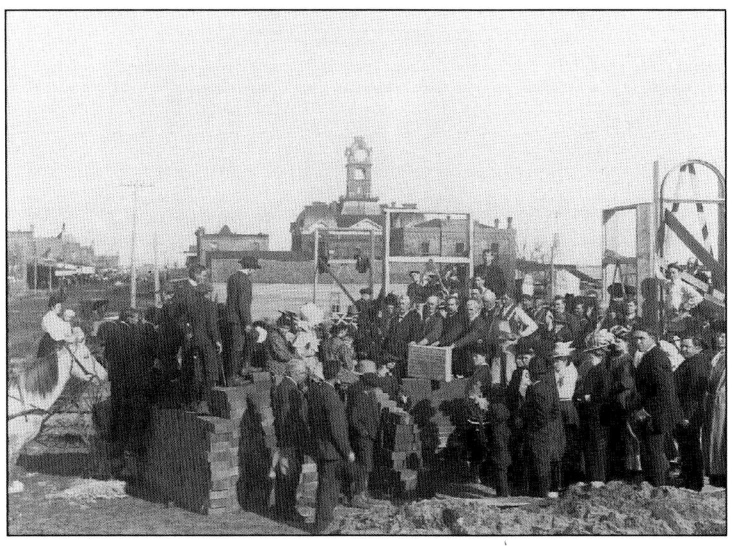

This picture shows the laying of the cornerstone for the second First Baptist Church on the corner of Main and Paradise Streets in 1906. This church building was used from 1907 until 1927. The first services were held on May 20, 1907. An addition was made on two adjoining lots in 1917. The courthouse, built in 1886, can be seen in the background. (Courtesy of the First Baptist Church.)

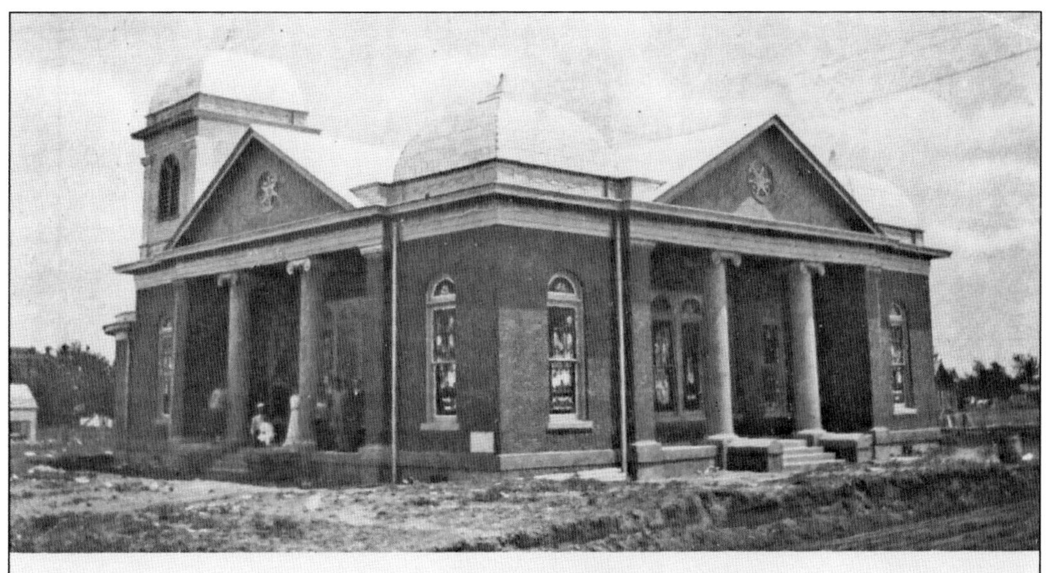

First Baptist Church, Vernon, Texas.

Pub. by J. M. Waltom.

The second First Baptist Church was built on the corner of Main and Paradise Streets in 1906. This building was used until 1926, when it was sold to S.A. Castlebury. The front of the building was resurfaced in stucco with the name S.A. Castlebury embossed on the front. Castlebury leased this building to different businesses, such as Gray & Laxton Funeral Home and car dealerships, including Dodge and Hudson. (Author's collection.)

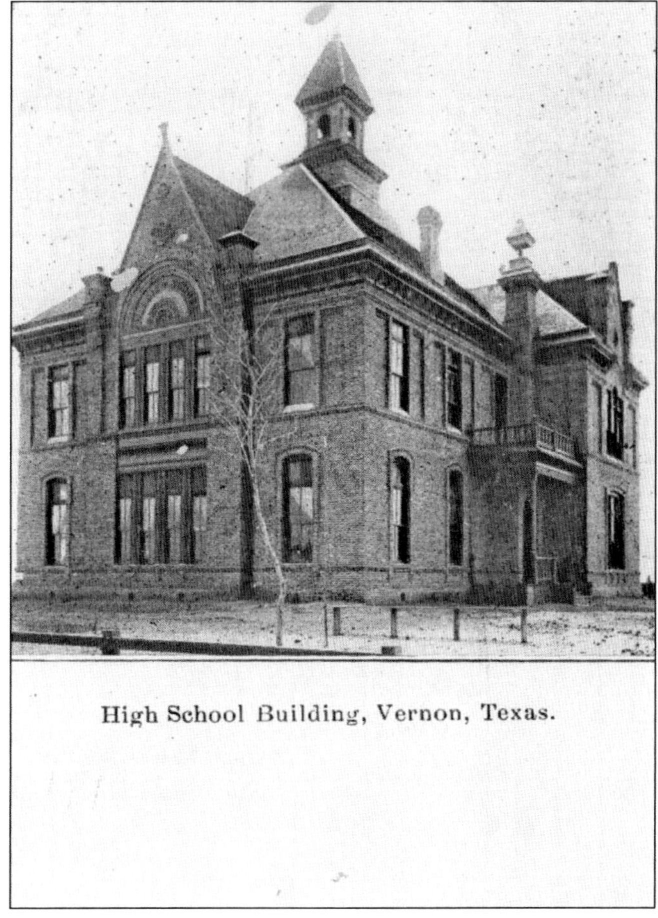

High School Building, Vernon, Texas.

Pictured is the old Central High School in Vernon, as seen in 1910. According to the early history of Wilbarger County, the first school in Vernon was in a house west of the public square in what is now the 170 block of Main Street. L.N. Perkins was the teacher in 1880. (Author's collection.)

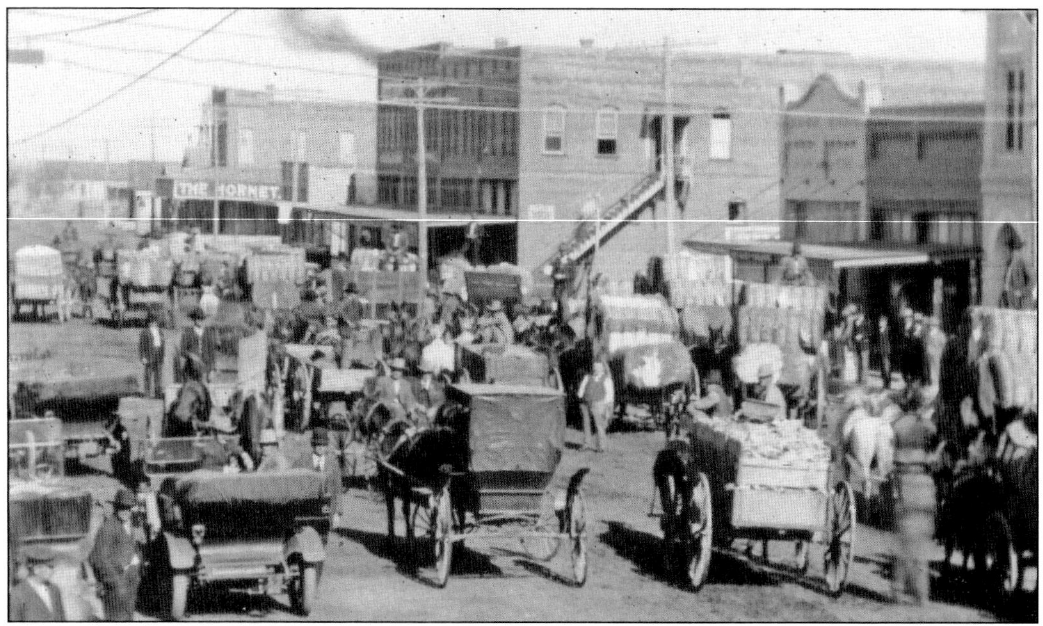

Pictured is trade day in Vernon around 1907 with wagonloads of cotton and other farm-grown produce. Looking north on Main Street, one can see the *Hornet* newspaper office, located in the old Masonic Building, now occupied by Pat Bryant Enterprise's. This picture shows the change in transportation; note the early automobile to the left and the buggy to the right. (Courtesy of Jo Jones.)

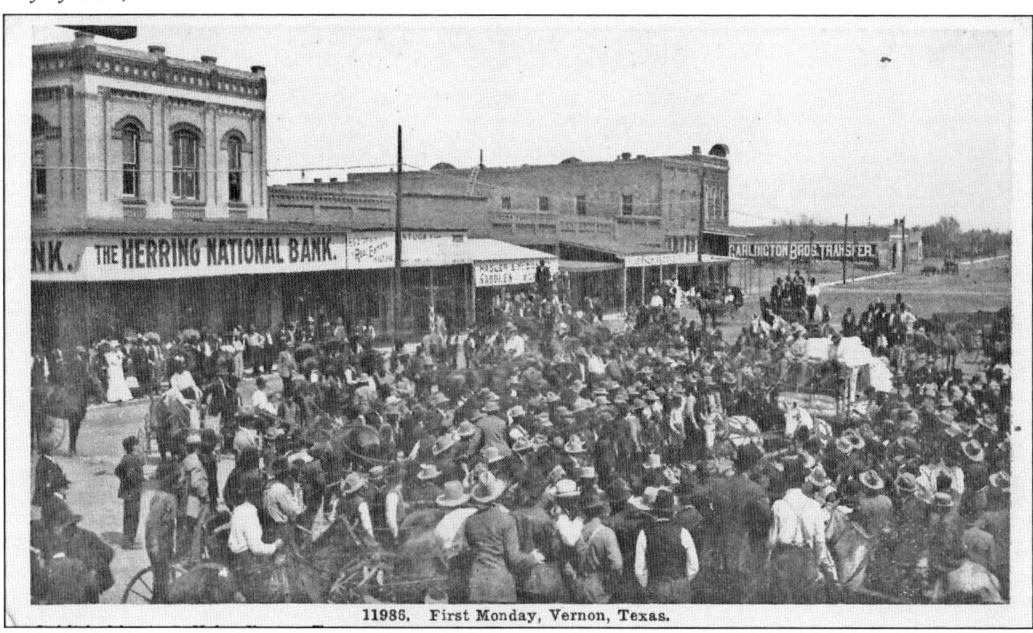

This postcard, published by A.C. Hahn, shows First Monday in Vernon around 1907. Looking east down Pease Street from Main Street, one can see the Herring National Bank, Kentucky Real Estate, Hagler & McKibbin Saddle Shop, the first location of the *Vernon Daily Record*, Baily Hotel, and the State National Bank, located on the corner of Pease and Cumberland Streets. After crossing Cumberland Street is Garlington Brothers Transfer. (Author's collection.)

Pictured is Fletcher Bright getting a drink from the same watering hole as his horse in 1910. The city well was located on the courthouse square, with a windmill, a large holding tank, and a watering trough. The barbed-wire fence around the courthouse was to keep livestock off the courthouse lawn. (Author's collection.)

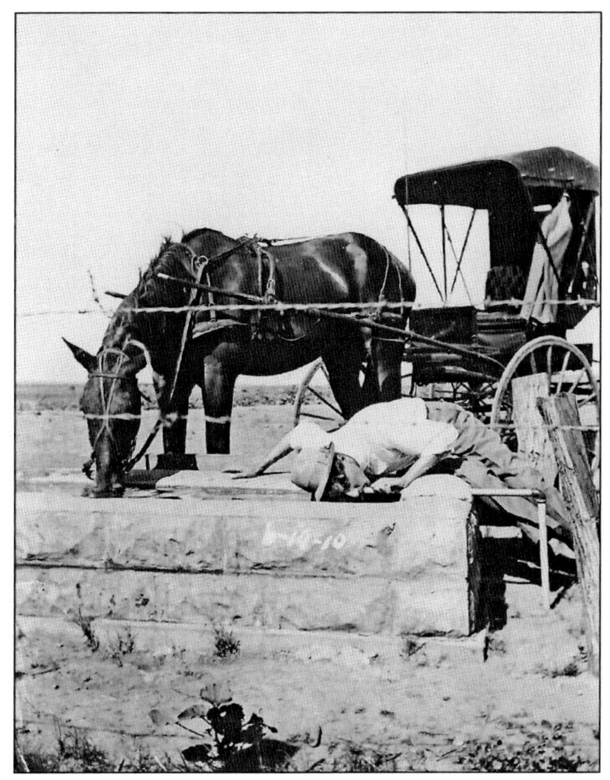

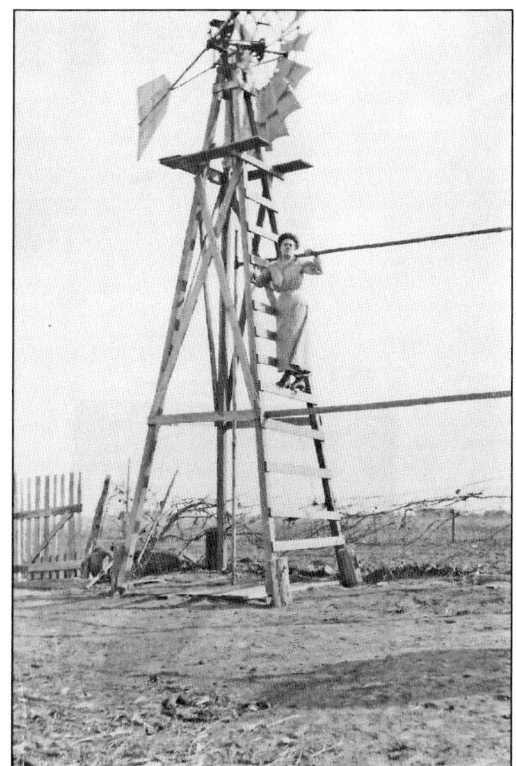

Marie Gilliland is seen posing on a wood-framed windmill in 1910. Medal-framed windmill stands could be bought at hardware stores such as Lowke Brothers Hardware, Swartwood & Company, William Cameron, J.R. Renfro, and others. (Author's collection.)

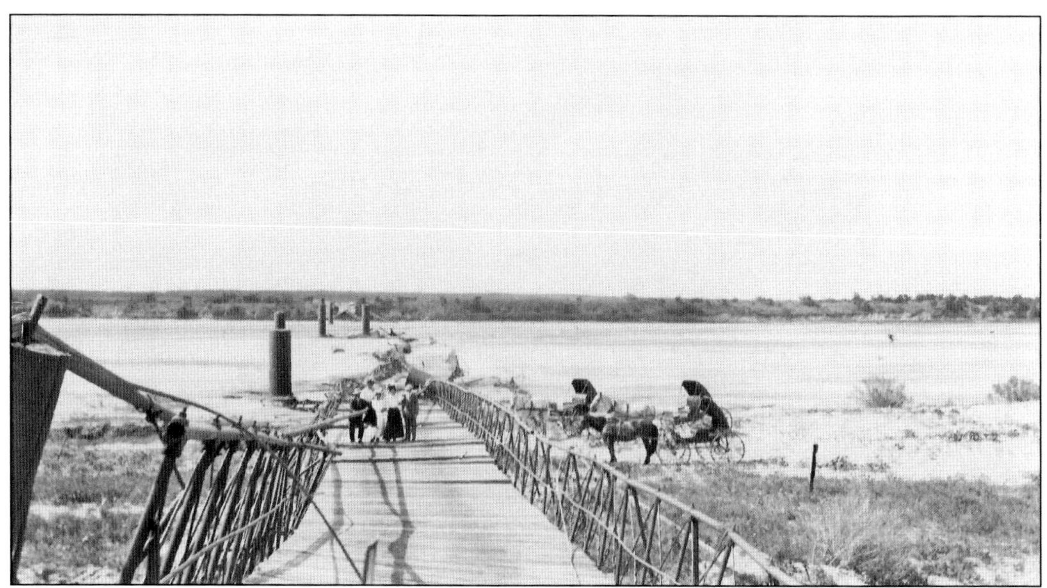

This was the first bridge built crossing Pease River, about a half a mile downstream from the one that is there today. This suspension bridge was completed in 1889 and lasted a few years before it was destroyed by a tornado in early 1907. The people on the bridge are sightseeing and getting pictures taken on the washed-out bridge. (Author's collection.)

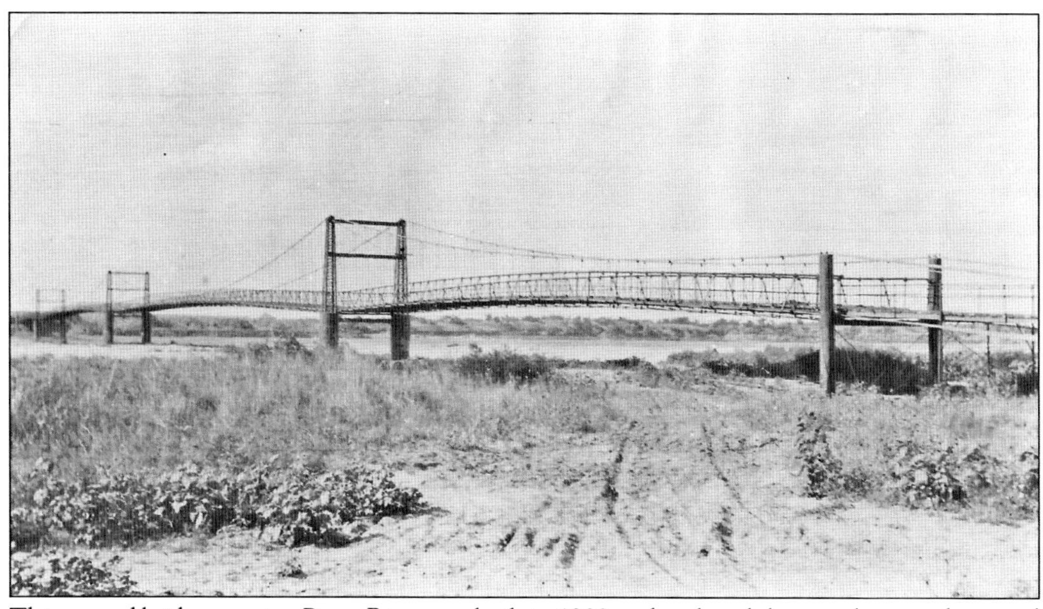

This second bridge crossing Pease River was built in 1909 and replaced the one that was destroyed by a tornado. This suspension bridge was built just west of today's southbound lanes of the Highway 287 Bridge and was used until February 1927, when it collapsed. One metal support remains today next to the present concrete highway bridge. (Author's collection.)

This picture of the 1906 bridge has signs on the top of the support. The top one made of cast iron is embossed with the following: "Wfd Mch & Fdry Co. / Builders 1909 / Weatherford, Texas / . . . / J.A. Nabers, judge / C.A. Allingham / J.N. Parsley / J.S. Archer / J.N. Richardson / Comr's." The white sign says, in part, "$500 fine to drive on or across this bridge any traction engine with lugs on wheels or seperator with out using skids not less than three inches thick 12 inches wide and 16 feet long or to drive more than 23 head of stock on or across this bridge at one time." (Author's collection.)

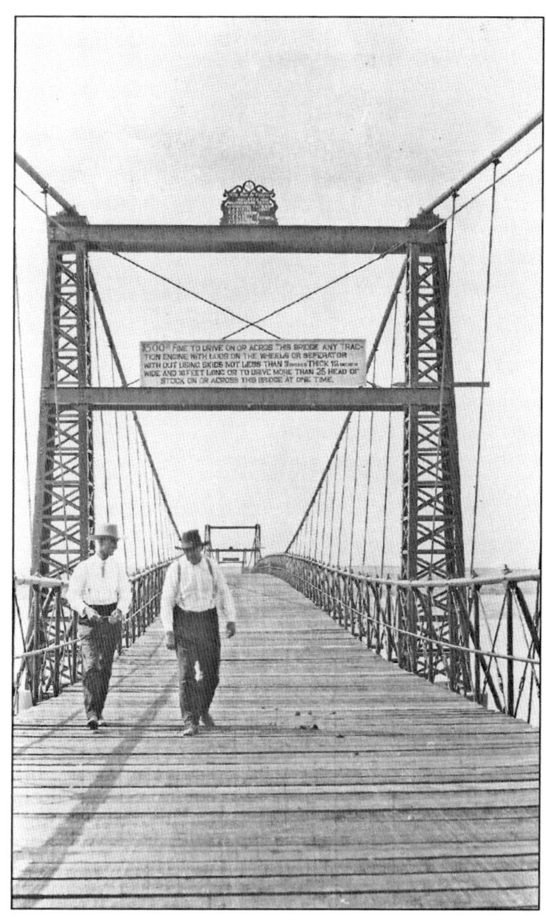

This bird's-eye view taken around 1909 shows the corner of Main and Pease Streets. The building at center right is the Vernon Hotel with an empty lot across from it, which is where the post office was constructed in 1917; it still stands in that location today. W.O. Anderson's icehouse and the Pease River can be seen on the horizon. (Author's collection.)

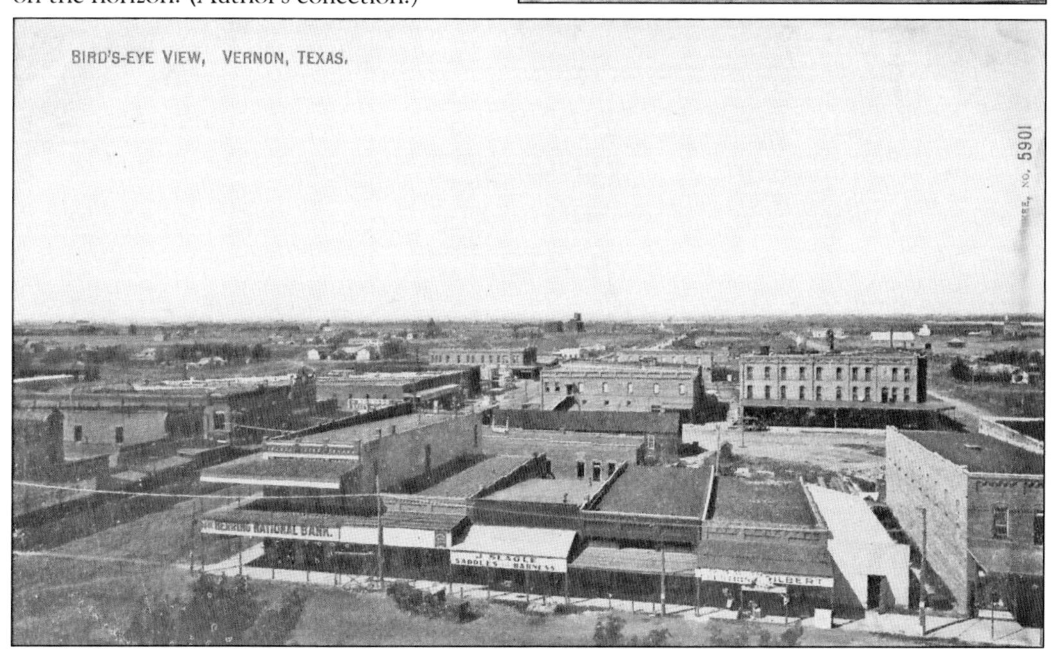

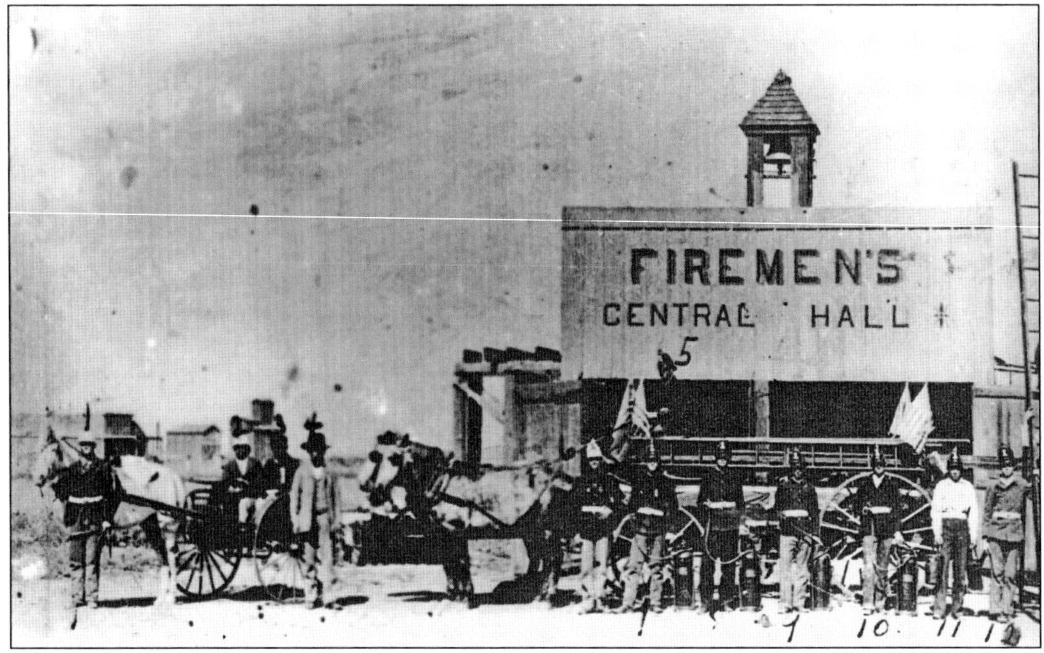

The Vernon Fire Department was organized in 1889, the same year that the city was incorporated. The firemen's central hall was built in east Vernon on Pease Street, between Mesquite and Cumberland Streets. The men in the picture are, from left to right, Charlie Mabry, Chief A.M. Hiatt Sr., city marshal A. Malvern, C.F. Lanter, driver A.B. Boyd, Chess Naylor, Charlie Hogsett, Earnie Creager, Joe Creager, Sam Ponder, Earl Plummer, and Milton McConell. (Courtesy of Jo Jones.)

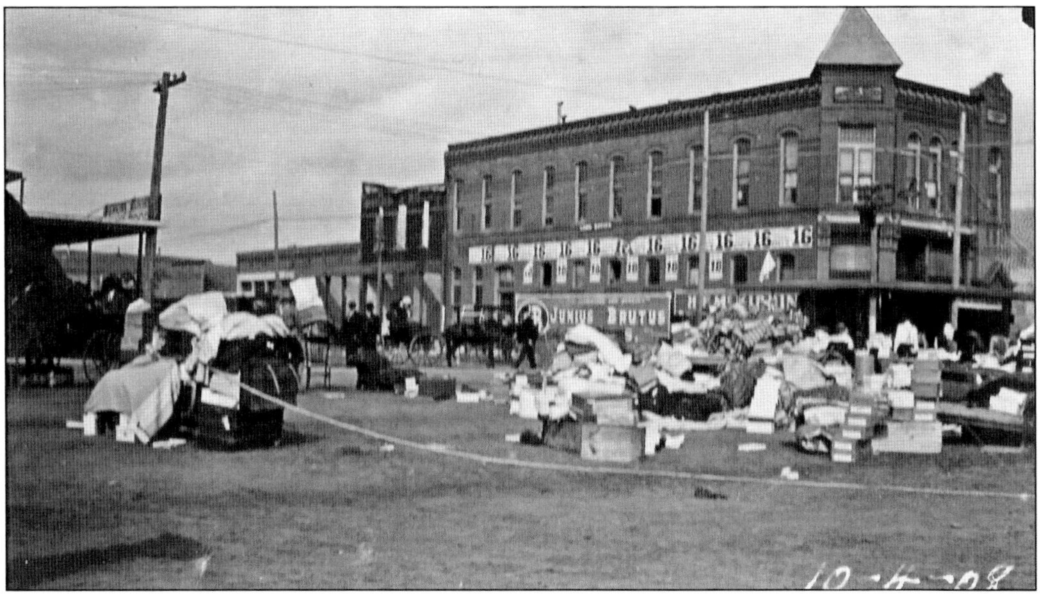

Damage can be seen after the fire on October 4, 1908, at an unidentified grocery store, behind H.F. McKibbin on the corner of Main and Pease Streets. Note the groceries were moved to the middle of the street. This building once housed St. Jullians Saloon in the late 1890s. (Author's collection.)

In this image dated April 26, 1910, the Keltz brothers are on a delivery wagon with the following words written on the side: "Busted By-God Keltz Bros." Benjamine (left) was a cotton farmer, and Eugene was manager of a cotton gin. It is not known what the wording "Gloria-Lights," written across the top of the buggy, means. (Author's collection.)

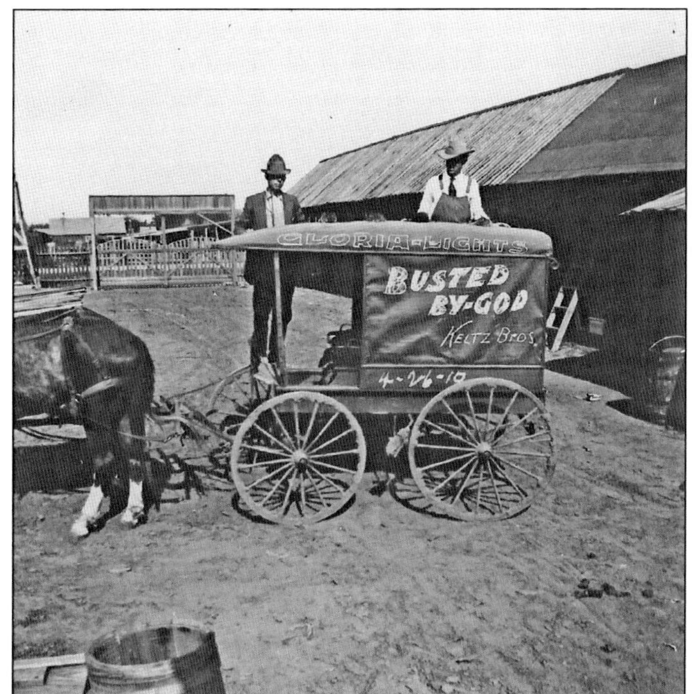

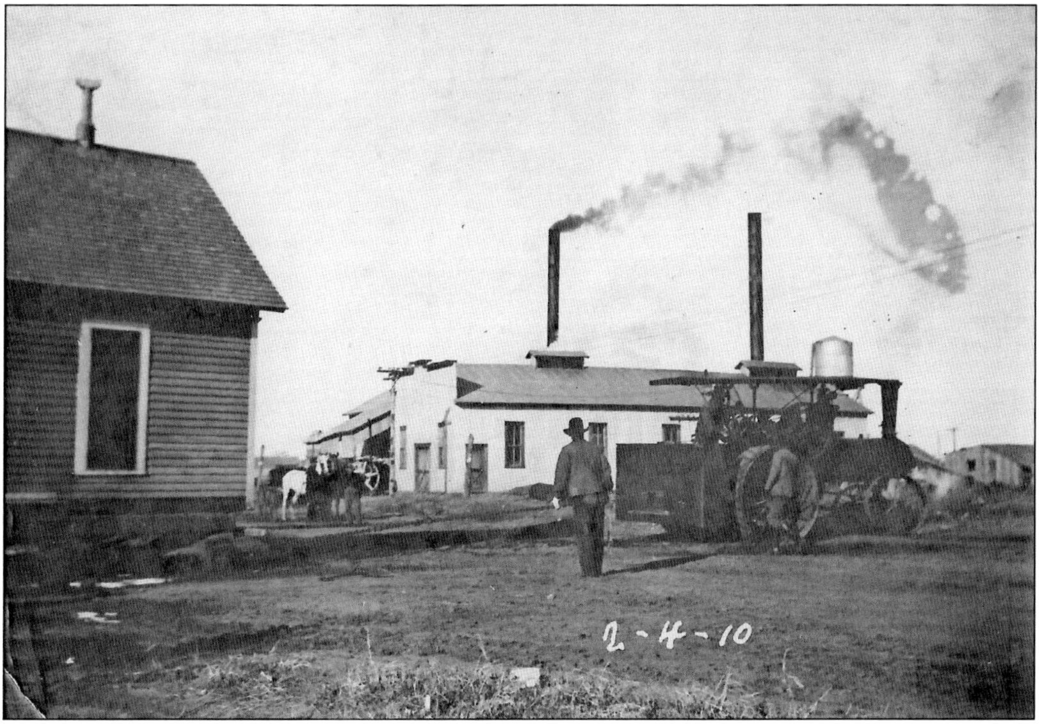

This icehouse was located where the old West Texas Utilities power plant was located in north Vernon on the Fort Worth & Denver tracks. After two icehouses had already failed in Vernon and the equipment shipped out to other places, W.O. Anderson bought the building and started another one in the early 1900s. (Author's collection.)

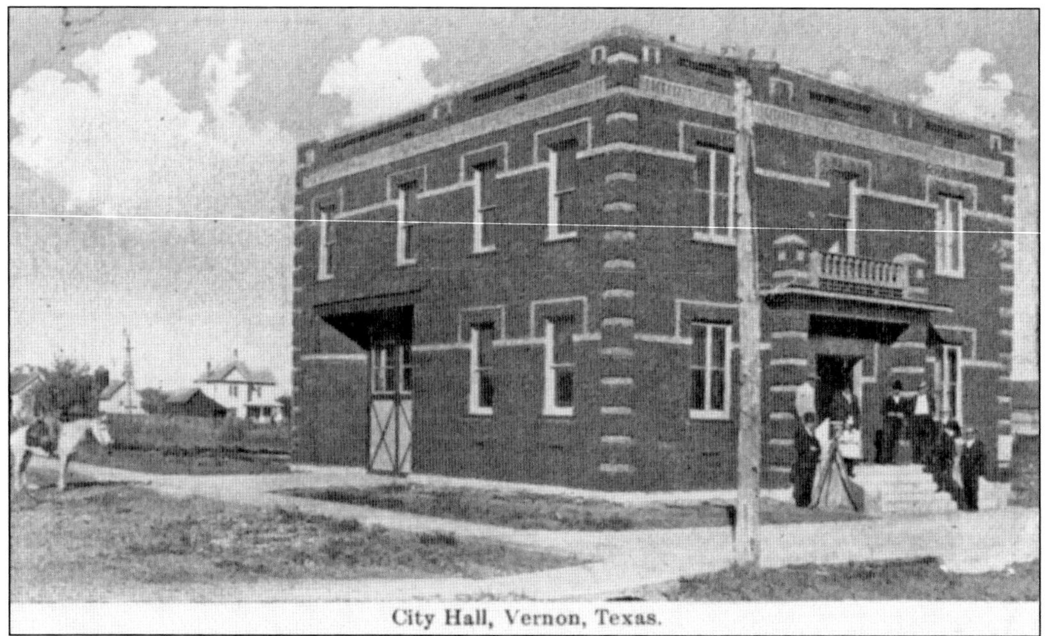

City Hall, Vernon, Texas.

For many years, the town did not have a city hall but used various buildings in the district for this purpose. This building was used in the early 1890s after Vernon was incorporated in 1889. The location of this structure is where the last city hall built still stands vacant at the corner of Main and Marshall Streets. (Author's collection.)

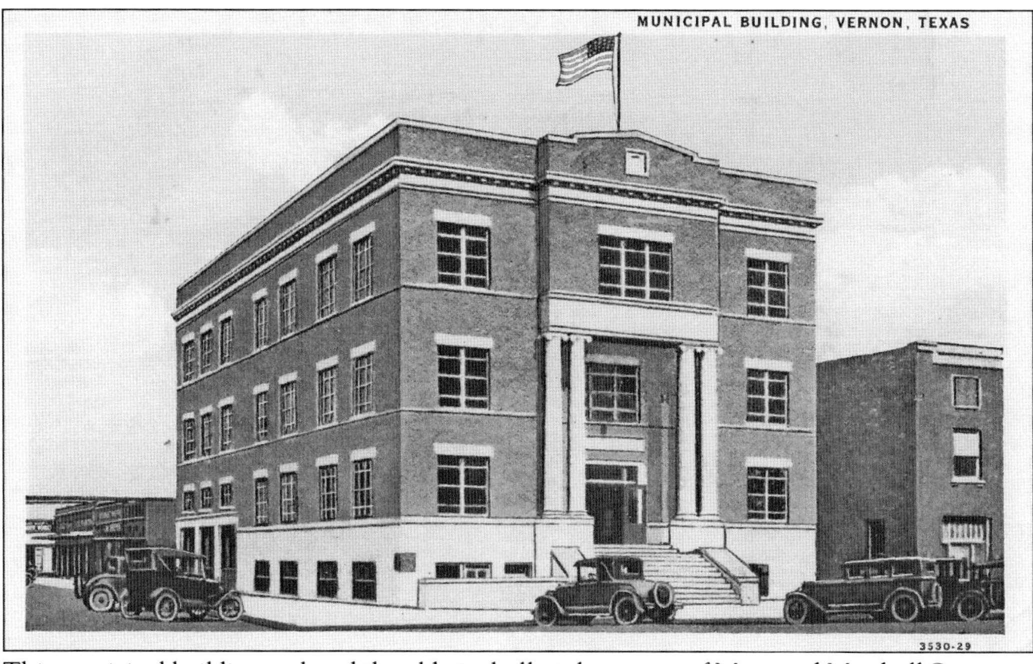

MUNICIPAL BUILDING, VERNON, TEXAS

3530-29

This municipal building replaced the old city hall at the corner of Main and Marshall Streets in 1929. R.H. Stuckey was the architect, with the Taylor Brothers & Co. as the building contractors. The city police station was in the basement along with the jail cells. The upper floors housed the city offices and the Lion's Den, a place for teens to get together after games. (Author's collection.)

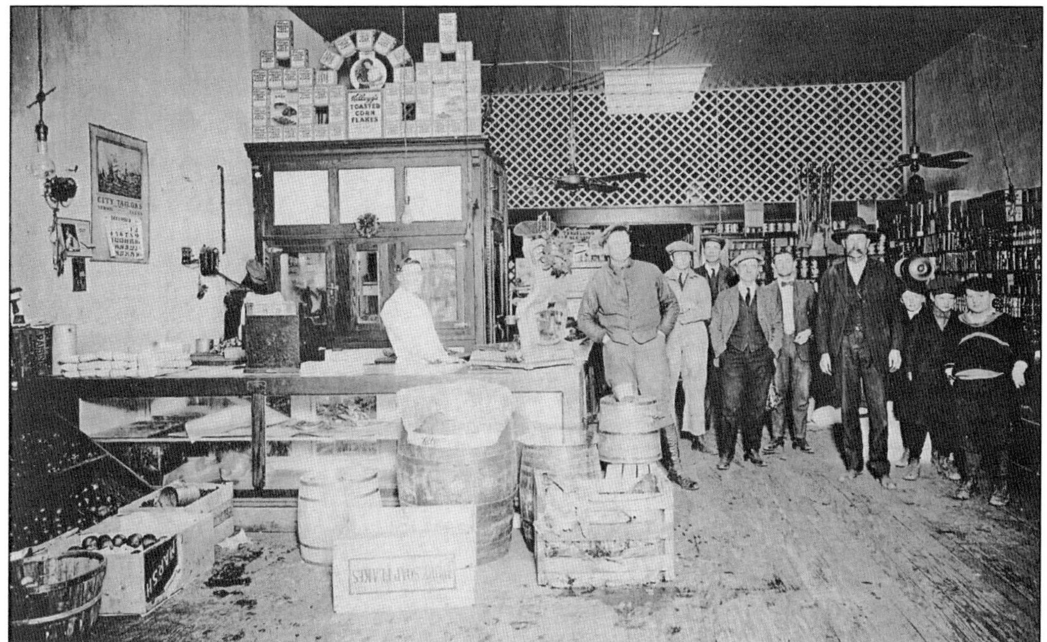

This is the interior of the B.J. Parker grocery store in 1905. B.J. Parker came to Vernon in 1889 and was in the wholesale and retail grocery business. He took an active interest in the advancement of the city. Parker served on the school board for 14 years, and the Ward Building in the northeast part of town was named Parker School in his honor. (Courtesy of Wilbarger County Historical Society.)

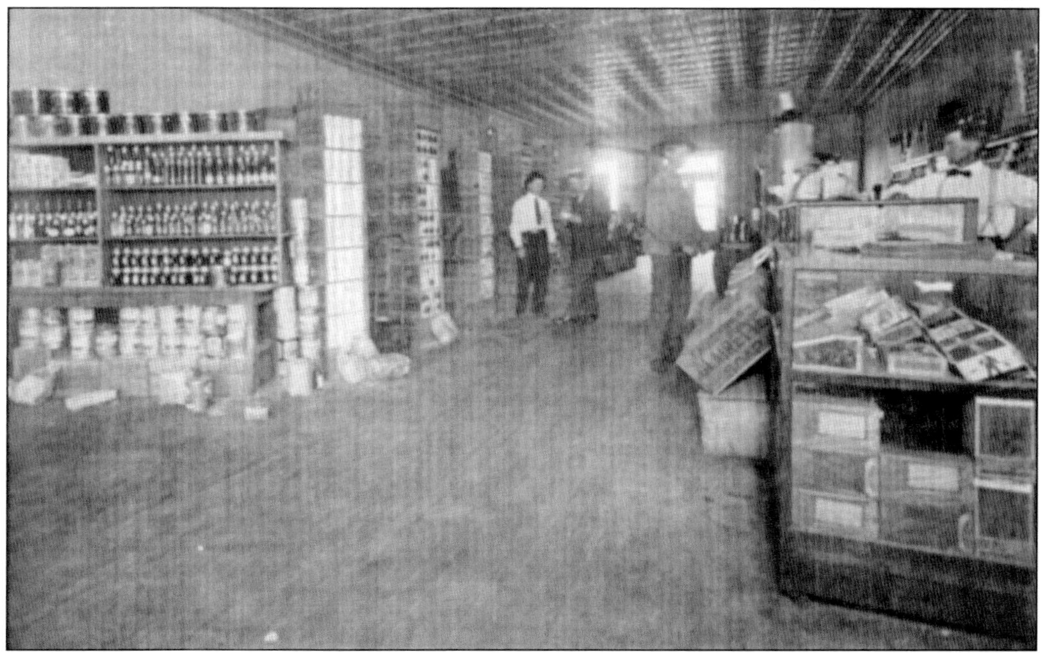

Shive, Piper & Wright grocery store was in the 1800 block of Texas Street at the turn of the 20th century. E.F. Piper is pictured at left, and J.O. Wright is at far right. Early on, Piper was associated with L.J. Massie in the firm of Massie, Shive & Piper. After that partnership was dissolved, he and R.D. Shive were in business together. (Courtesy of Wilbarger County Historical Society.)

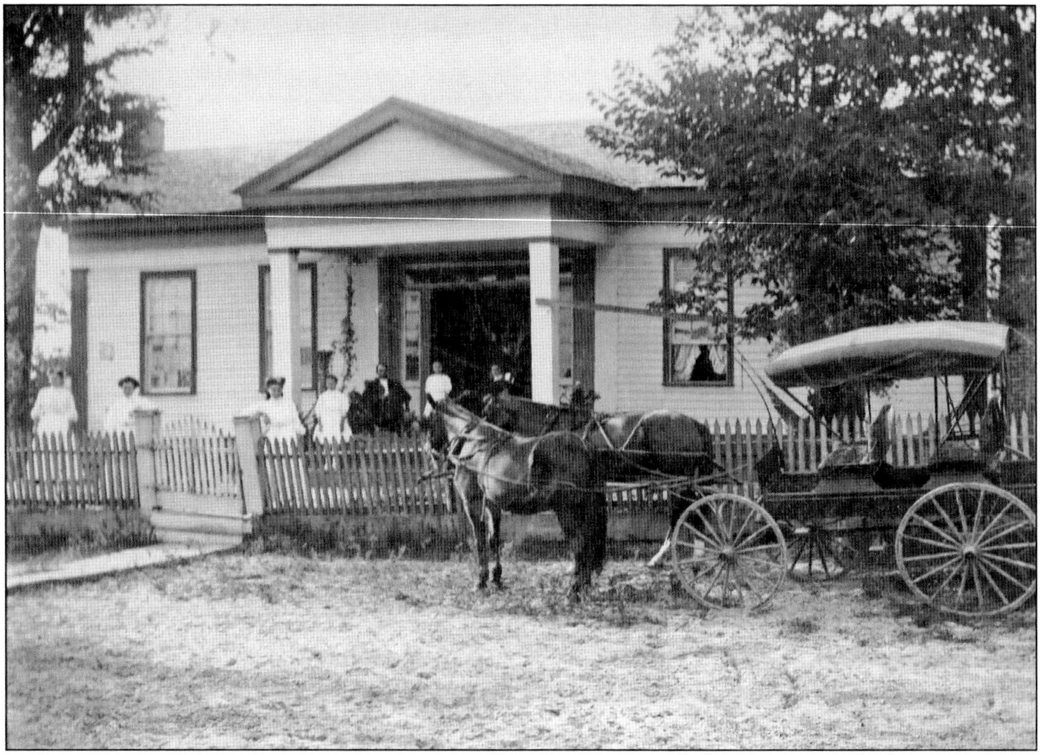

Pictured is Dr. J.E. Dodson's buggy sitting in front of an unidentified home in Vernon. Born in Tennessee, Dodson enlisted in the Confederate army at the age of 14. In 1887, he came to Wilbarger County from the Indian territory, where he was in the governmental service. For a number of years, he was the only surgeon in Vernon and this section of the state. (Author's collection.)

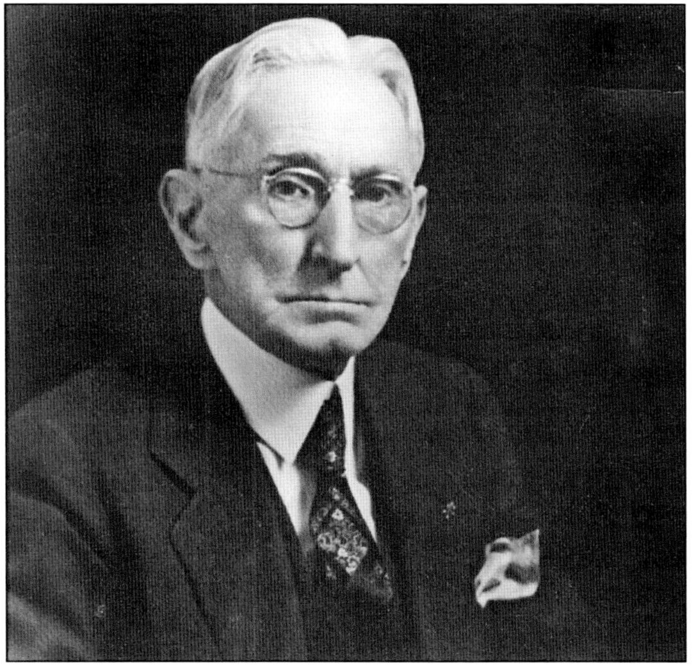

L.G. Hawkins came to Vernon in 1892 as a cashier for the Fort Worth & Denver City Railroad. Later, he was made station agent and in 1897 was transferred to Bowie, Texas, where he stayed until 1900, when he returned to Vernon to become cashier of the Waggoner National Bank. Several years later, he was made vice president and, after the death of Robert Houssels, the president, he was elected to that office. (Author's collection.)

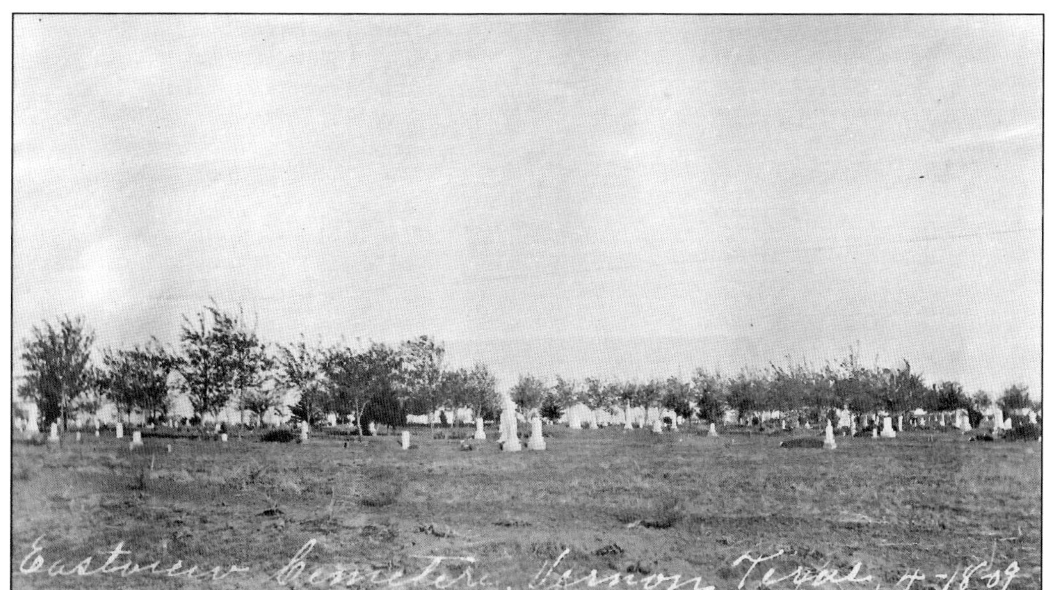

This picture of East View Cemetery was taken in 1909. The original graveyard, established in the late 1880s, was located north of where the old Frisco freight house once stood, close to where the last depot was located. The coffins were dug up and moved by horse-drawn wagons to the new East View Cemetery in 1889. The citizens of Vernon had purchased this site and made a contract for the graveyard to be relocated. (Author's collection.)

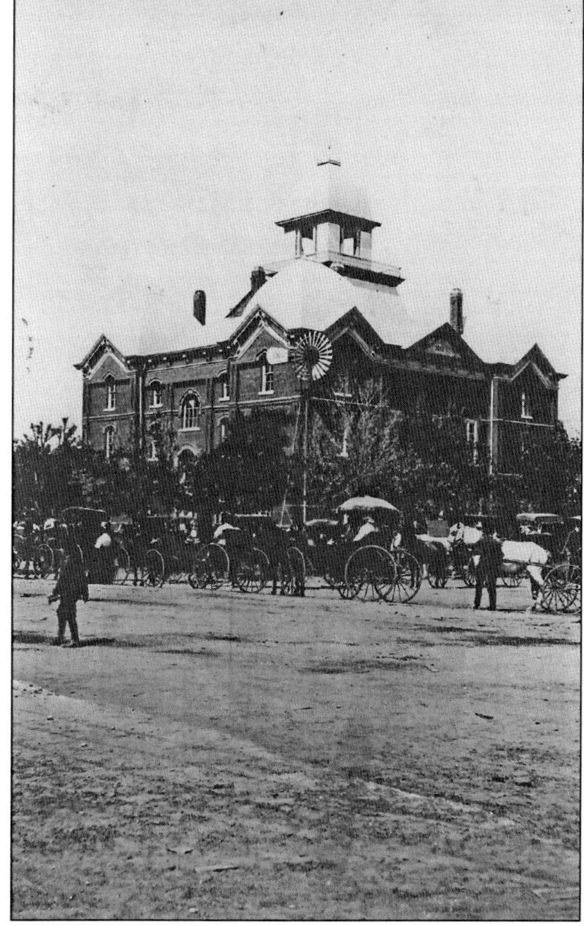

Pictured is the Wilbarger County Courthouse, built in 1886, as it looked after a tornado had destroyed the clock tower. The top was lowered down, and the clock was never replaced; this structure was demolished to make room for the new one in 1928. (Author's collection.)

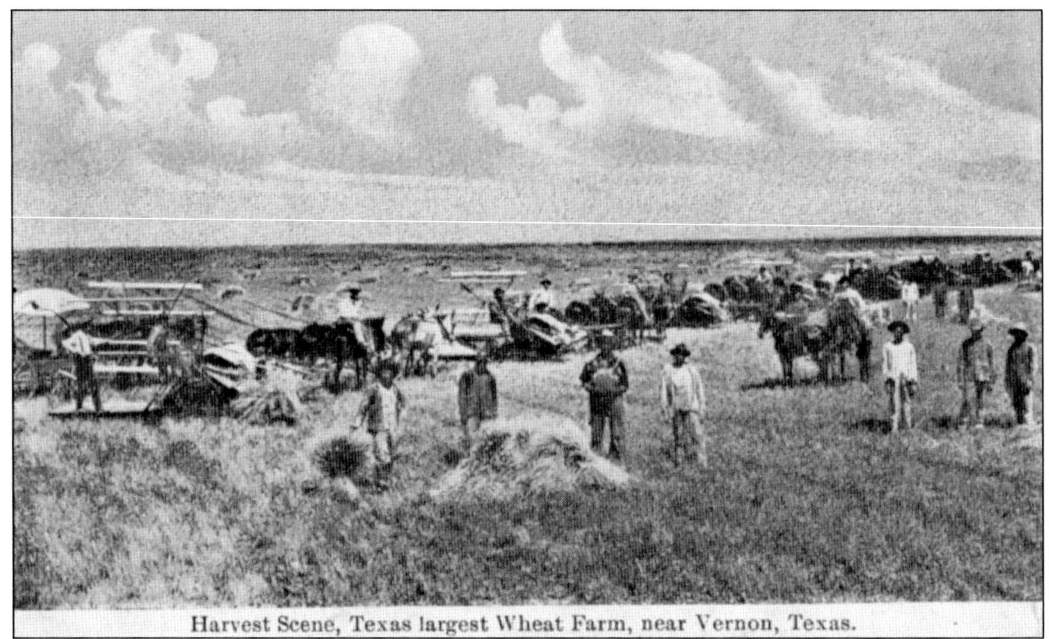
Harvest Scene, Texas largest Wheat Farm, near Vernon, Texas.

This postcard states, "Harvest scene, Texas largest wheat farm, near Vernon, Texas." The wheat field pictured was on the Waggoner Ranch. In the 1890s and early 1900, a lot of oxen were used for harvest time as well as horses and mules. Pictured are horse-drawn threshers being used in this wheat field. Farming is still an important part of the Waggoner ranch today. (Author's collection.)

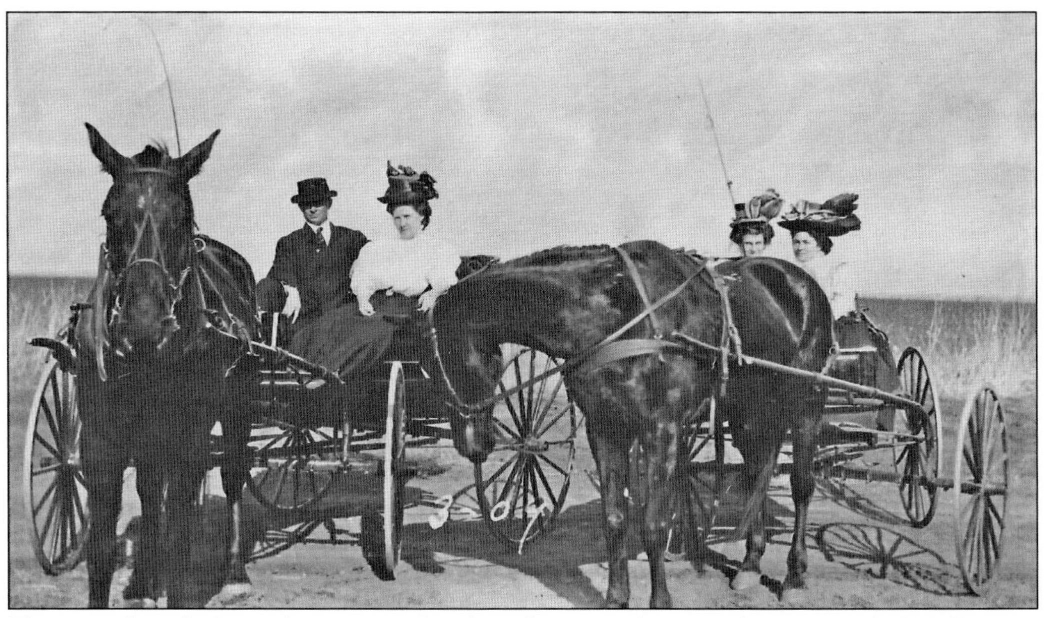

These unidentified people are on a Sunday afternoon drive in the spring of 1909. Buggies and wagons like these could be bought at local dealers, such as Swartwood & Co., Vernon Hardware & Implement Co., Herring-Bennett lumber company, and Lowke Brothers Hardware. (Author's collection.)

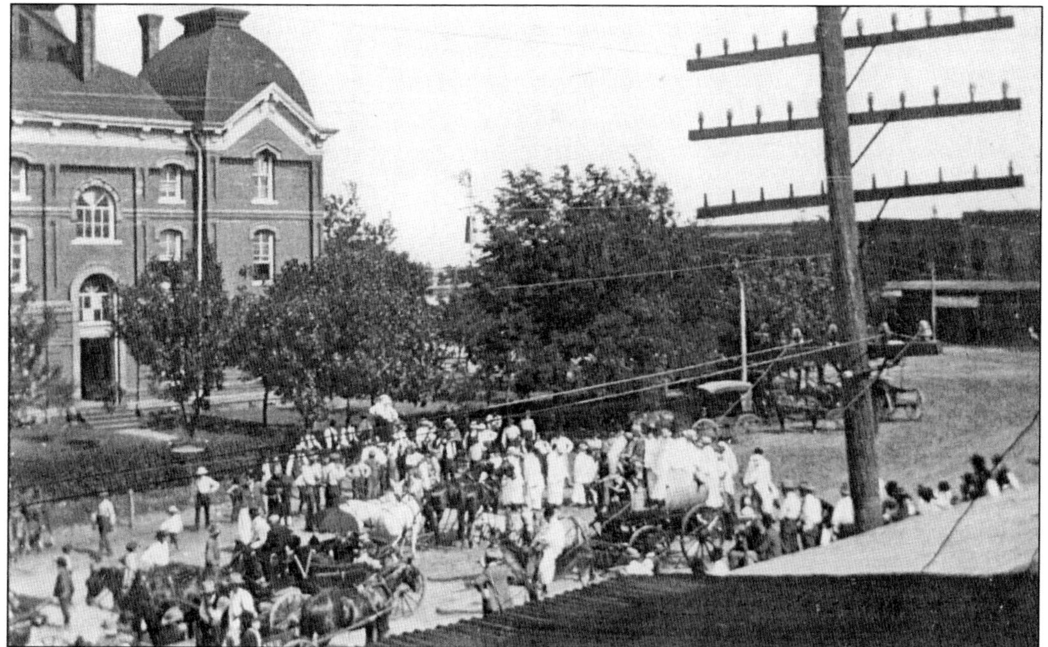

This picture in the early 1890s seems like just another parade, but a closer look shows men wearing white robes. The Ku Klux Klan sprang up in Texas in the late 1860s and became stronger in the early 1920s. A notice was printed in the *Vernon Times* on October 27, 1921, that stated Vernon Klan No. 148 was making their presence known. (Courtesy of Wilbarger County Historical Society.)

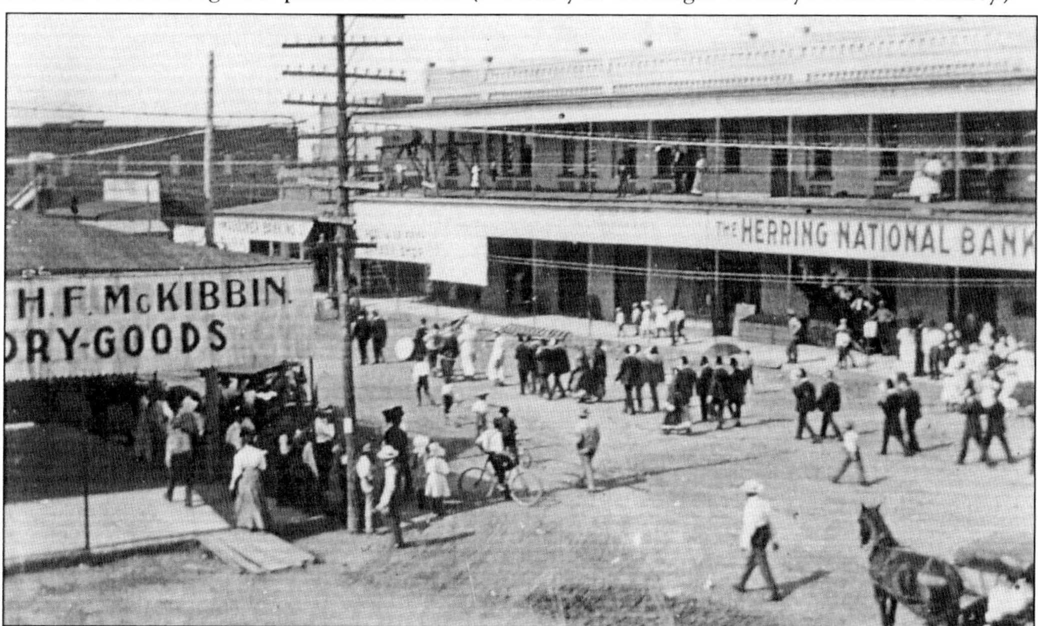

This picture, taken from the top of the Timberlake Building on the corner of Main and Pease Streets, shows men heading north on Main Street after leaving the courthouse in the early 1890s. After passing the Herring National Bank on the right and H.F. McKibbin on the left, the last business that can be seen in the picture is the Waggoner Banking Company on the right. (Courtesy of Wilbarger County Historical Society.)

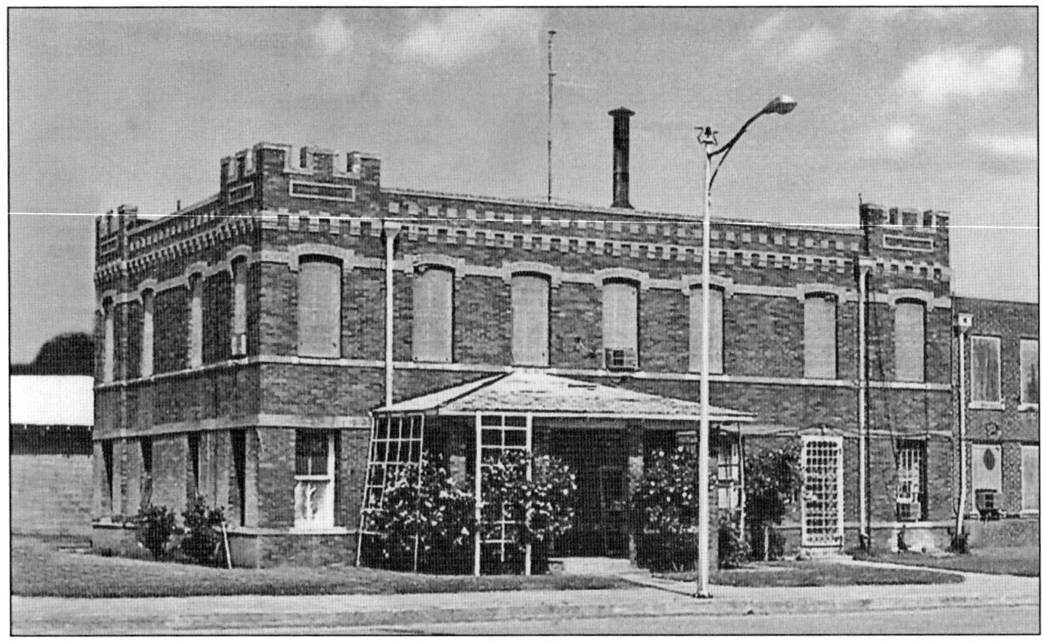

The first jail, built in 1883, was located about where the county courthouse now stands. That jail was torn down to make room for the courthouse, built in 1886. The second jail was built of brick in 1885 on Marshall Street. The jail pictured was built in 1912 by J.A. White and located on Cumberland Street. A contract for an annex to the jail was awarded to J.K. Stuckey on July 13, 1935. It is now the location of the Wilbarger County Historical Museum. (Courtesy of Stewart Studio.)

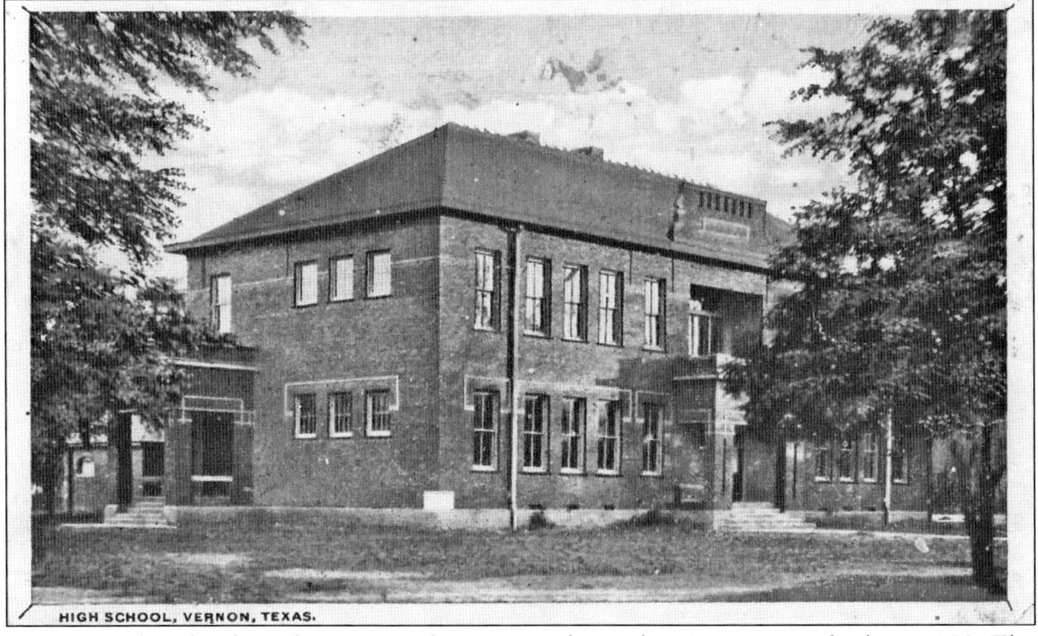

Vernon High School, at the corner of Fannin and Paradise Streets, was built in 1909. The high school annual at this time was not called the *Yamparika*, but *The Roundup* instead. After several face-lifts and different uses, this is now the location of the First Baptist Church Youth Center. (Author's collection.)

The first First Methodist Church was a simple one-room frame building, erected in 1889, and was used until 1909. It was stated that it was the community and Methodist church working together. Although the Reverend Emmit Hightower was pastor at this time, the Reverend Hosmer assisted greatly with the financial problems by taking subscriptions from among his wide acquaintances. (Author's collection.)

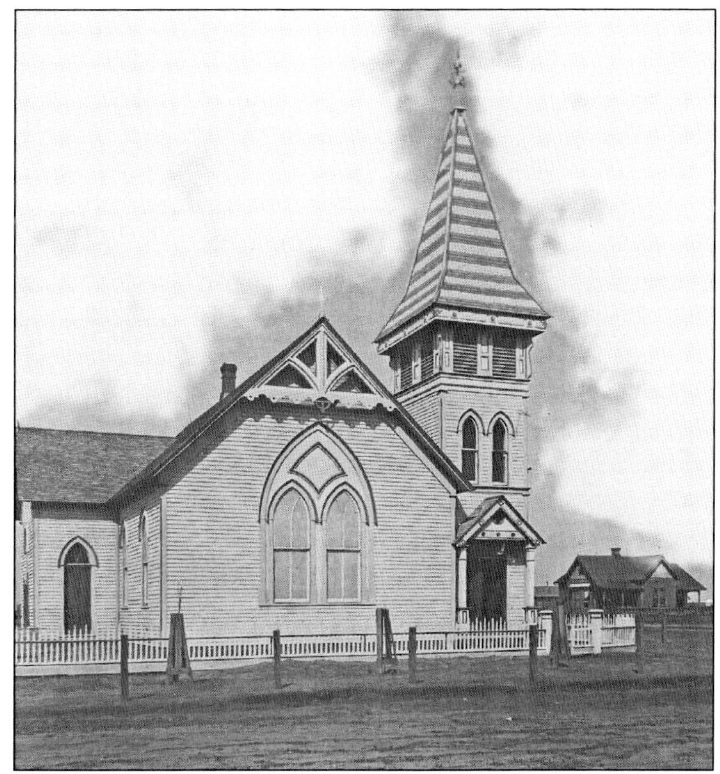

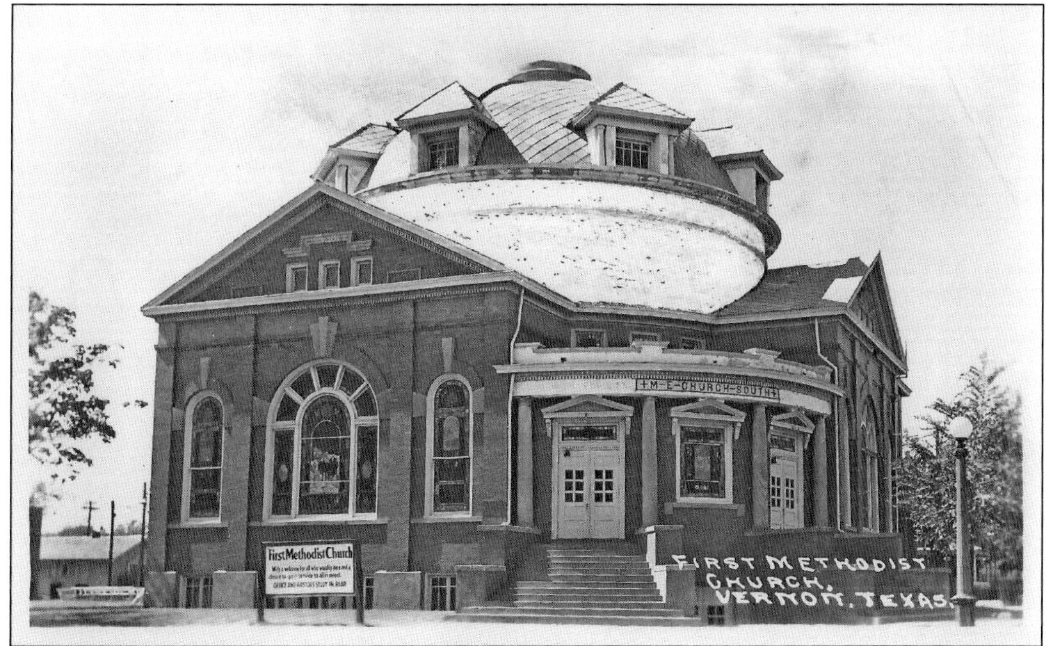

The second First Methodist Church, built on the corner of Pease and Deaf Smith Streets, was built in 1910. This location for the church was used until 1949. In 1948, the W.T. Waggoner Estate purchased the church and parsonage property. The Waggoner Estate Building was constructed on this location and still stands there today. (Author's collection.)

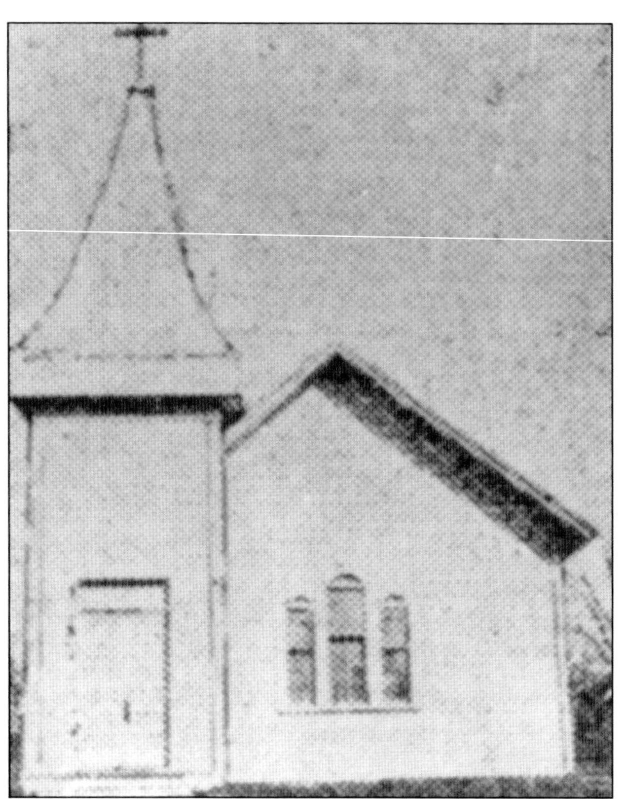

Records show that the organization of the Central Christian Church dates back to 1893. The Christian Church was formally organized in 1902. At that time, they purchased their first building, located on Cumberland Street, from the presbytery. (Courtesy Jo Jones.)

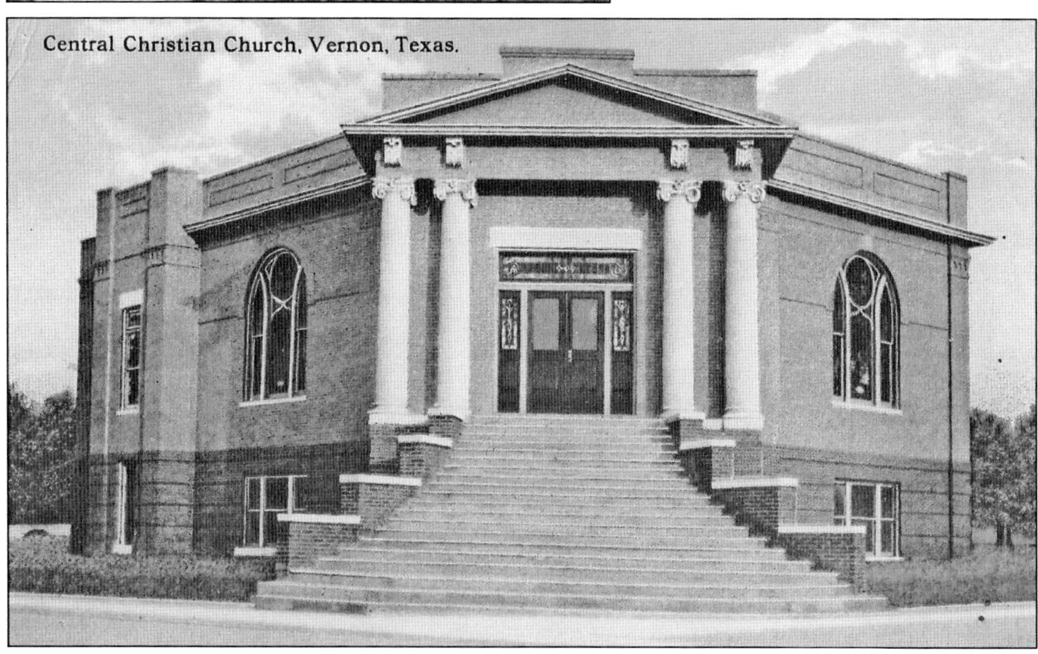

While Rev. L.H. Humphries was pastor, plans were made and construction was completed on this fine looking church building on the corner of Mesquite and Wilbarger Streets. Its dedication was celebrated on May 13, 1913. At that time, the building on the corner of Mesquite and Marshall Streets was torn down and a parsonage was built. (Author's collection.)

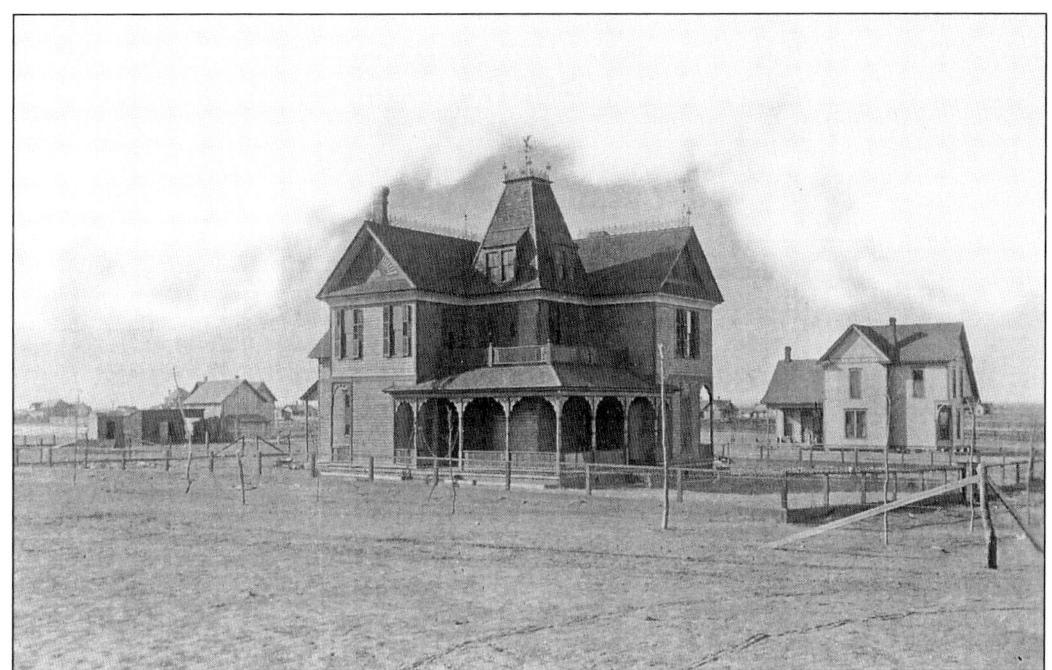

Pictured is the home of E.T. Murchison, who came to Vernon from Terrell in 1888. Murchison was born in North Carolina and moved to Texas in 1880. After coming to Vernon, Murchison entered the implement business. Later, he disposed of this store and went into the life insurance business, until his death in 1908. (Courtesy of Wilbarger County Historical Society.)

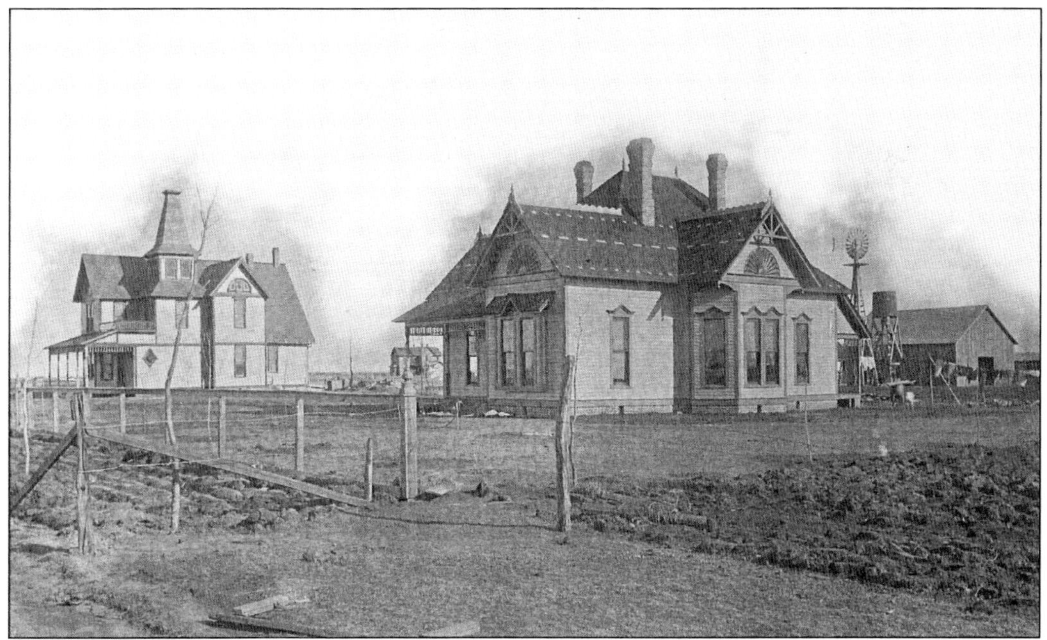

This was the home of Robert Houssels, who came to Wilbarger County in 1891. The Waggoner National Bank was organized in 1899. Tom Waggoner was elected president and served until 1906. When he resigned, Houssels succeeded him as president and served in that position until his death in 1921. (Courtesy of Wilbarger County Historical Society.)

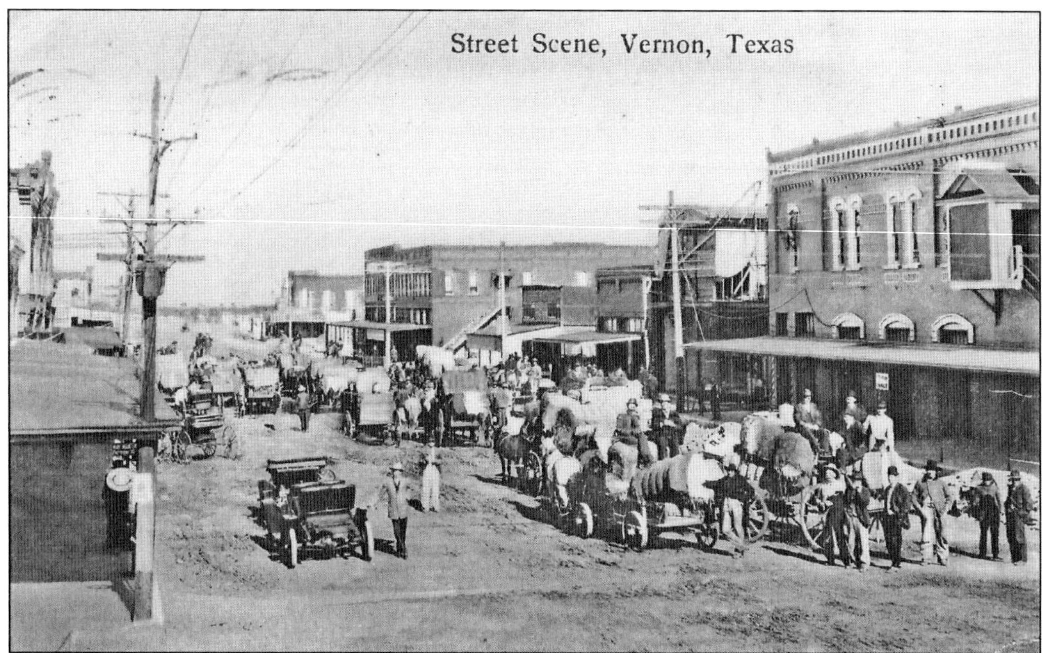

Unidentified men are seen posing with their wagonloads of cotton, heading north on Main Street to W.O. Anderson's Gin; the Red Store is on the left-hand side of the picture and the Herring National Bank is at right. Even though horse and buggies were still the majority, early automobiles can be seen in this scene from 1908. (Author's collection.)

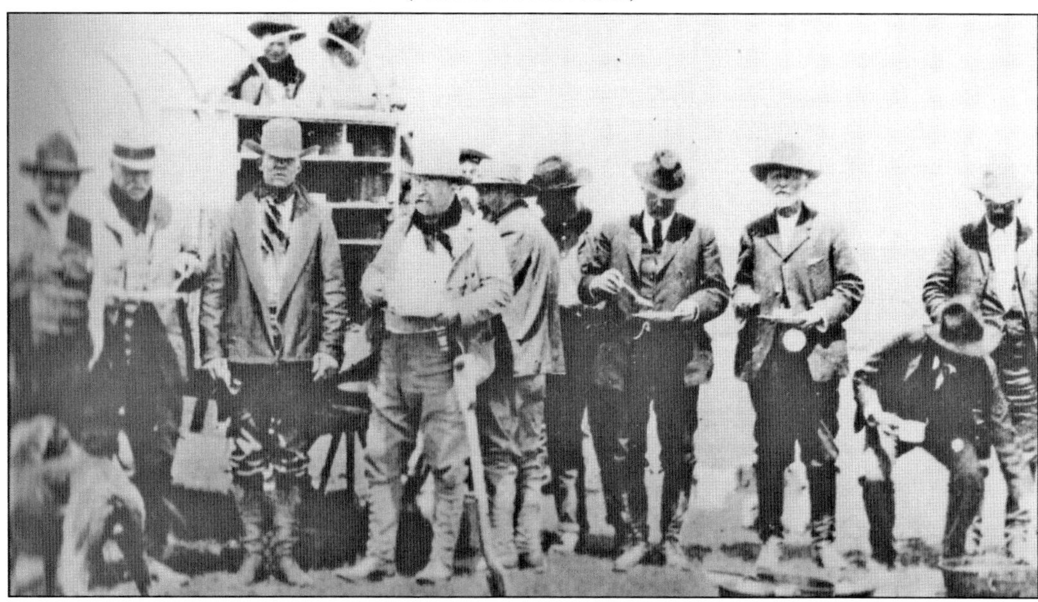

Theodore Roosevelt gave a speech from the Frisco train station in Vernon on April 9, 1905, when on his way to a six-day wolf hunting trip with S.B. "Burk" Burnett and W.T. Waggoner. The hunting party from left to right are W.T. Waggoner, Maj. S.B. Young, Tom L. Burnett, Pres. Theodore Roosevelt, Cecil Lyons (in the background), Dr. Lambert, Bonnie More, Capt. S. Burk Burnett, Capt. Bill McDonald, Chief Quanah Parker, E.M. Gillis, and Guy Waggoner. (Courtesy of Wilbarger County Historical Society.)

Two

1915–1930s

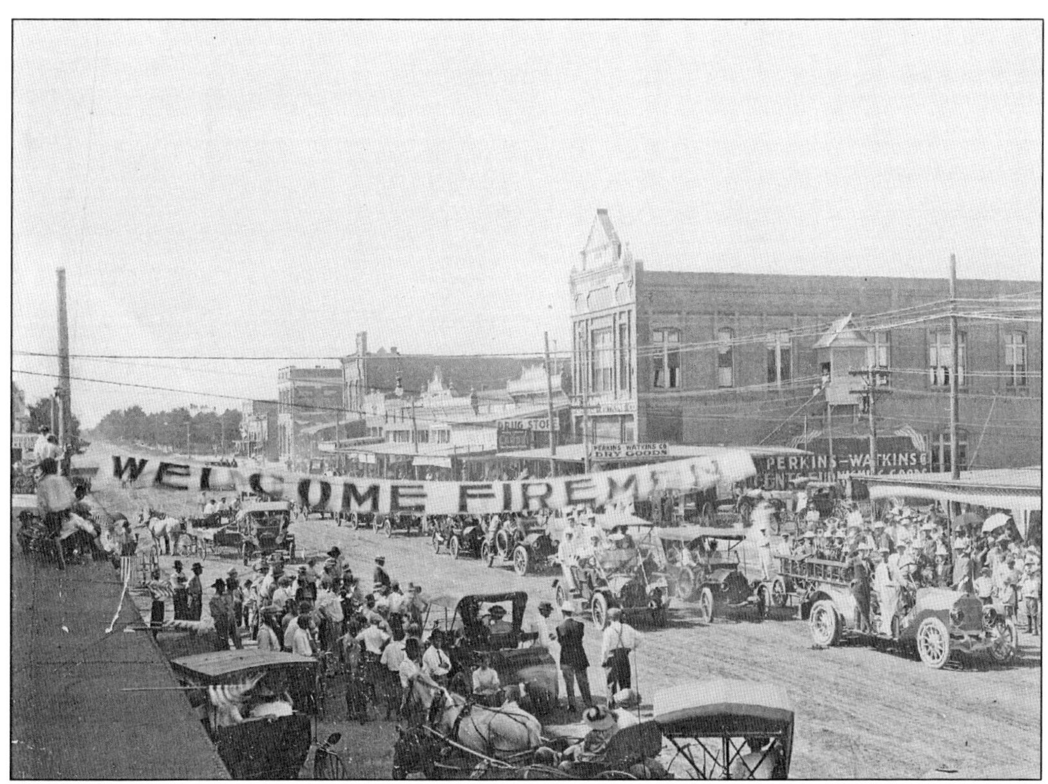

This was a great turnout for the firemen's convention in 1915. Note the early fire truck in the lead of automobiles to the right, heading north on Main Street. The large building to the right on the southwest corner of Main and Pease Streets is the Perkins-Watkins Dry Goods Store, which will later become Perkins-Timberlake. (Courtesy of Wilbarger County Historical Society.)

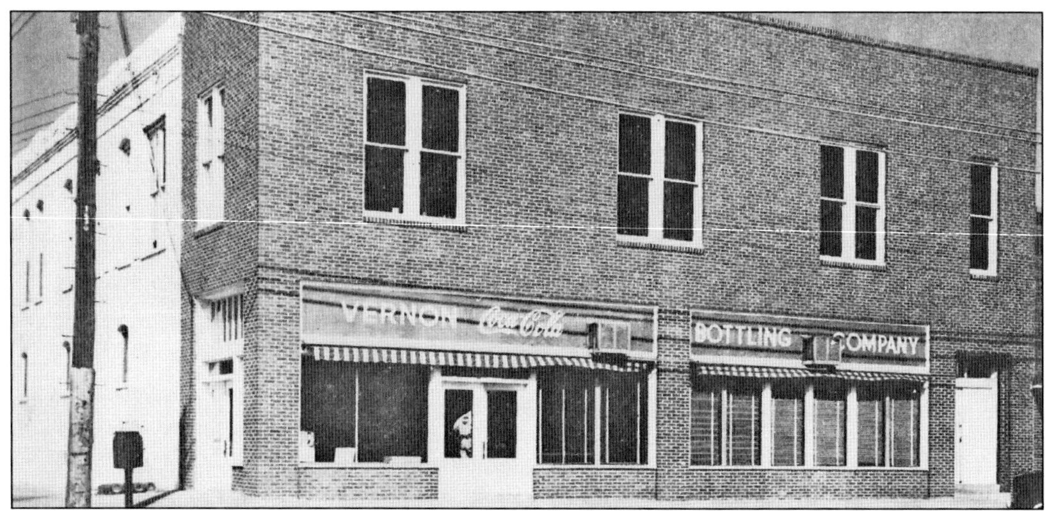

Eunice Wilson, a native of Bastrop County, moved to Vernon in 1908. After several years with William Cameron and as manager of the J.S. Mayfield Lumber Company, he went into the bottled drink business in 1915 as a partner with L.E. Key, the owner of Crown Bottling Works. In that same year, it became Key & Wilson Coca-Cola Bottling Company in this location at the northwest corner of Main and Olive Streets. (Author's collection.)

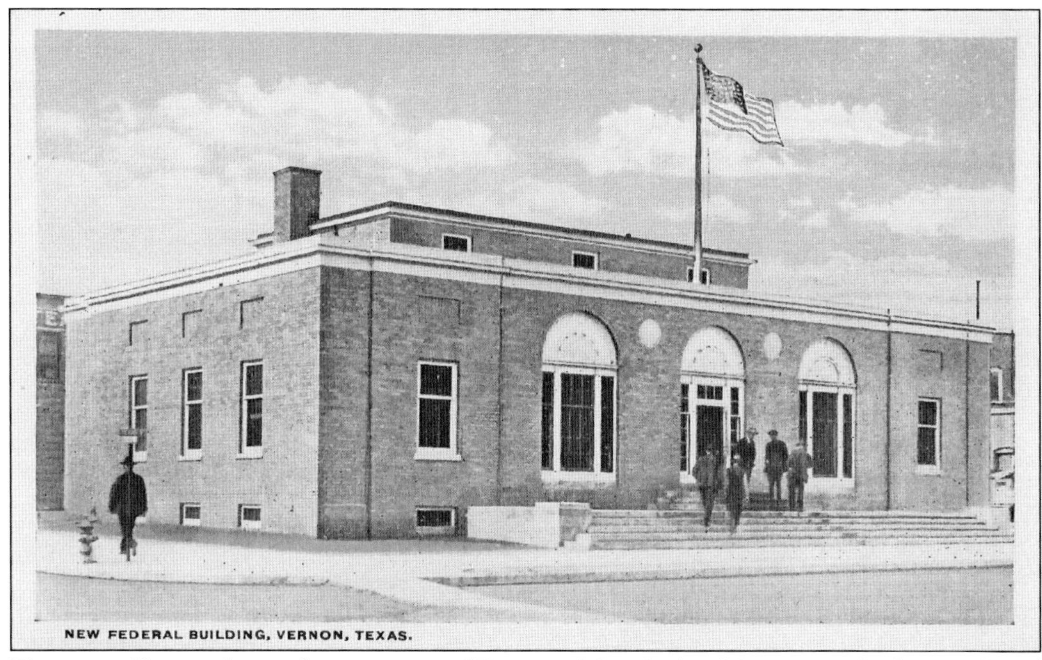

This post office on the southwest corner of Texas and Cumberland Streets was built in 1917 and opened in 1918. The building was remodeled and enlarged in 1936, and an entrance was placed on the Cumberland Street side, in addition to the entrance on Texas Street. This building still serves as the local post office today. (Author's collection.)

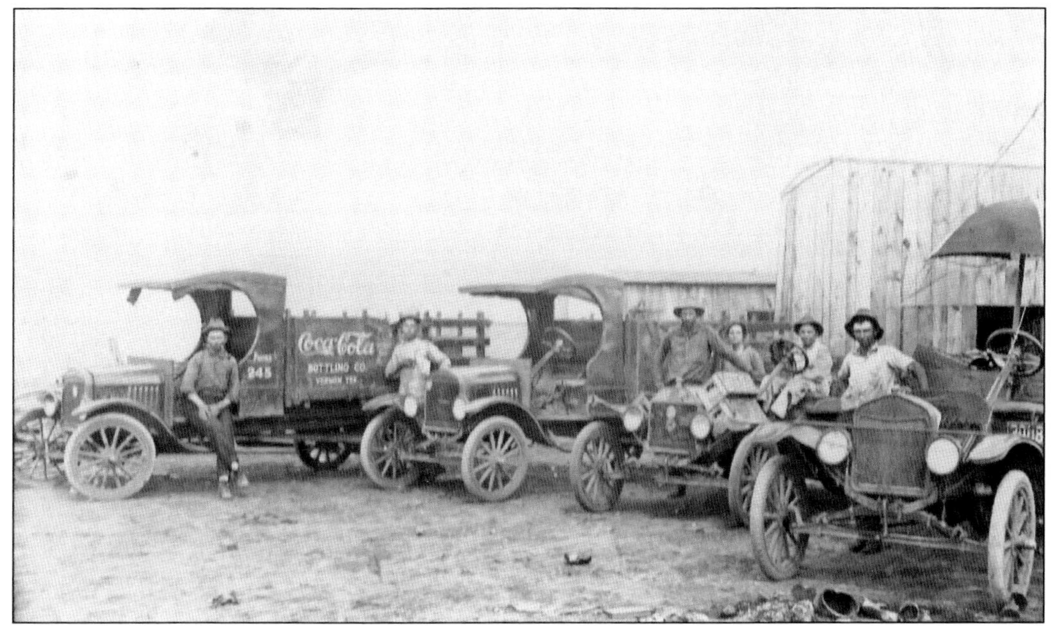

Four Coca-Cola delivery trucks are seen with their drivers and crew in 1915. The advertising on the truck doors has the three-digit phone number 245. This was also the phone number for ice delivery, which was added in 1916. This business was known as Key & Wilson Coca-Cola Bottling & Ice Company. The familiar curved bottle for Coca-Cola was also introduced in 1915. (Author's collection.)

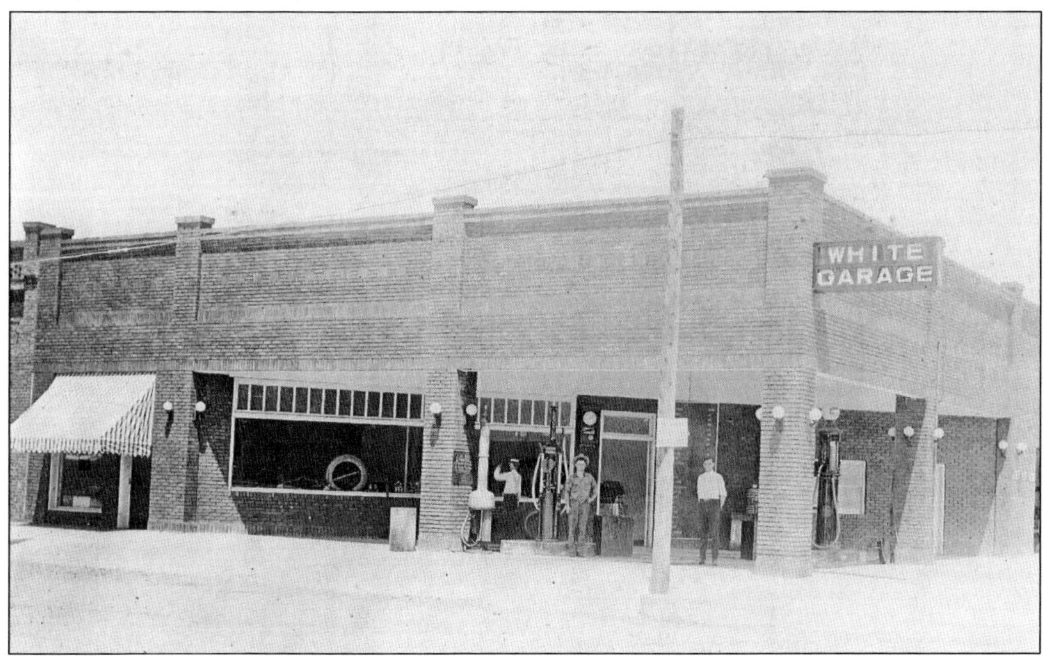

Around 1916, White Garage was located on the northwest corner of Cumberland and Wilbarger Streets. This business was owned by R.W. Ferrell and A.B. Swartwood. In 1917, it was the Cooperative Garage. It was better known in the 1950s as the Buck Horn Texaco gas station, and the last business in this location was the Tire Shop. (Author's collection.)

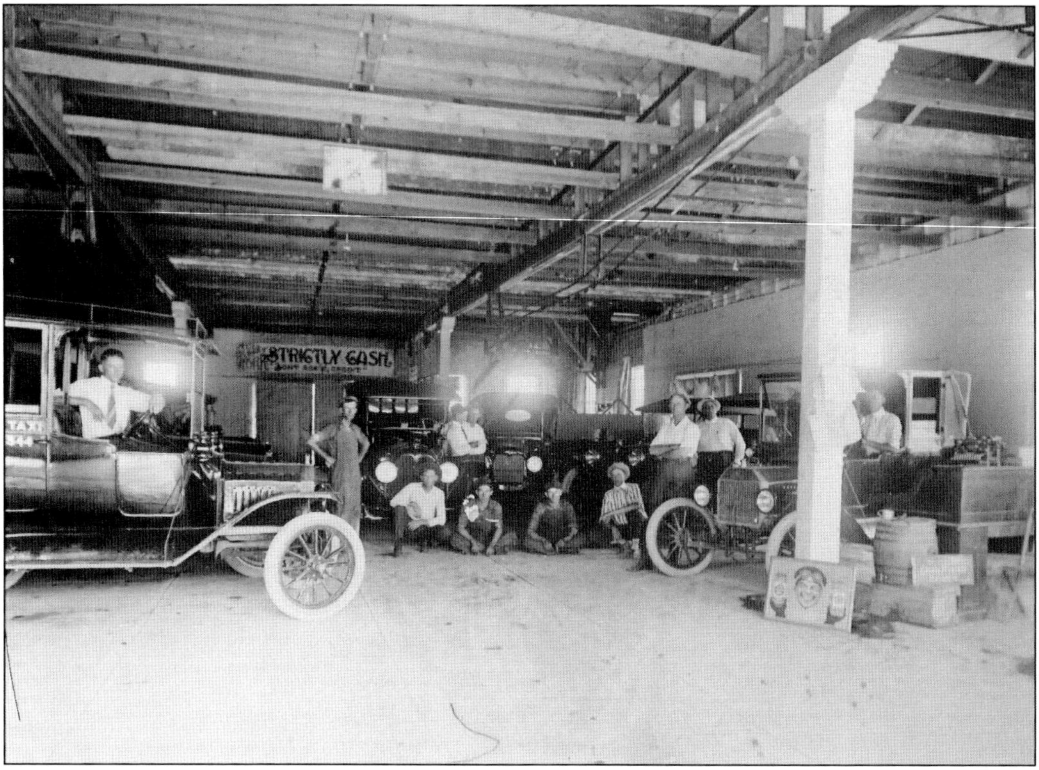

The interior of the White Garage shows a group of unidentified men with a taxicab and the mechanic standing (second from left). The large white sign states, "Strictly Cash. Don't ask for credit." The advertising sign on the floor to the right has a guy wearing driving goggles. (Author's collection.)

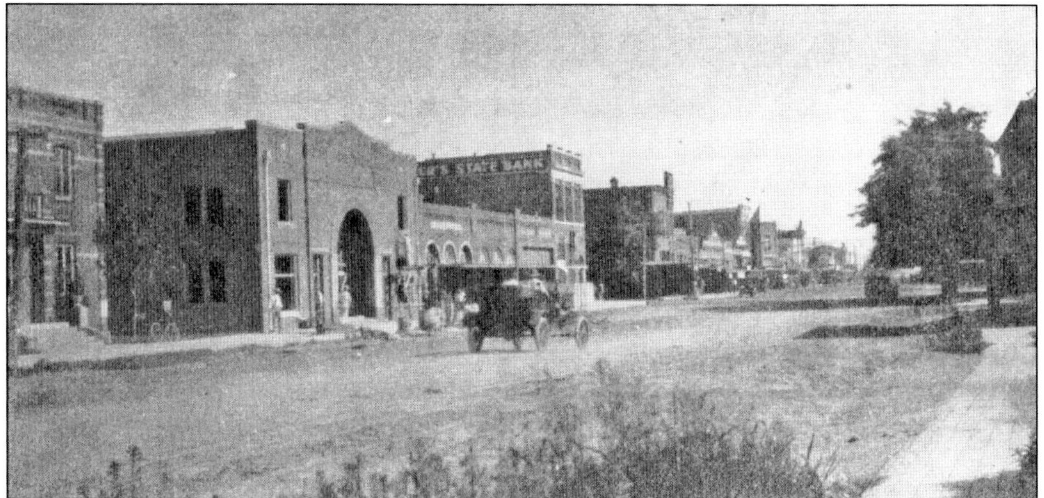

Looking north on Main Street, one can see the edge of the municipal building, followed by the More Theater, in 1917. The More Theater would later become the Vernon Theater. On the north side are Pendleton Music Store and then the Wright Grocery Store, owned by W.W. Wright, with the phone number 356. On the corner is the Farmers State Bank, the location of Bunch Norris Insurance today. (Author's collection.)

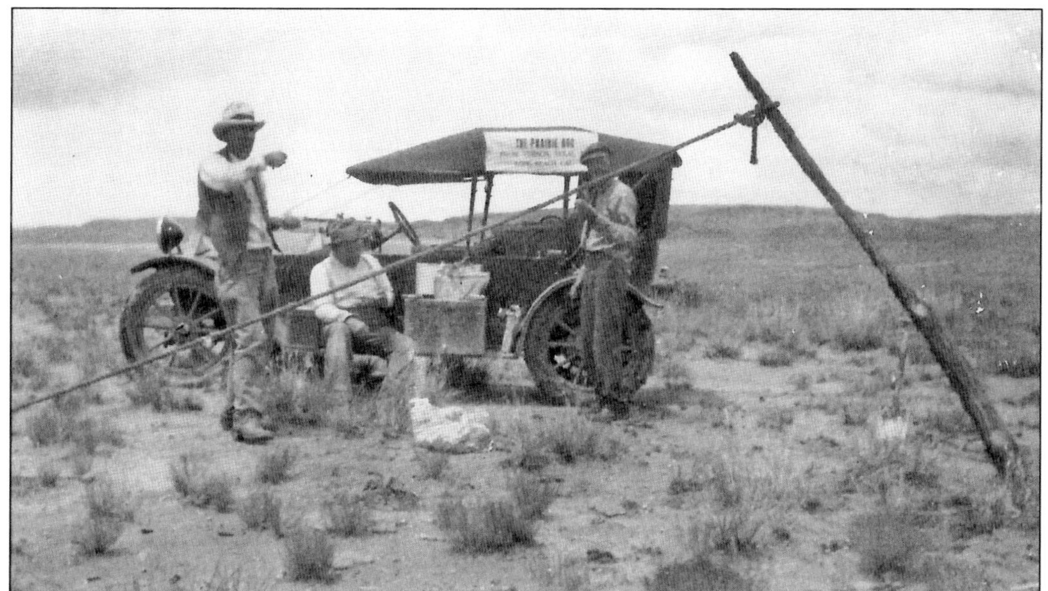

An unidentified group of men is preparing to cross the desert on their way to California. The sign across the top of the car says, "The Prairie Dog from Vernon, Texas, to Long Beach, California." Canvass water bags carried extra water for the trip. Automobiles usually crossed the desert at night when it was cooler to keep from overheating. (Author's collection.)

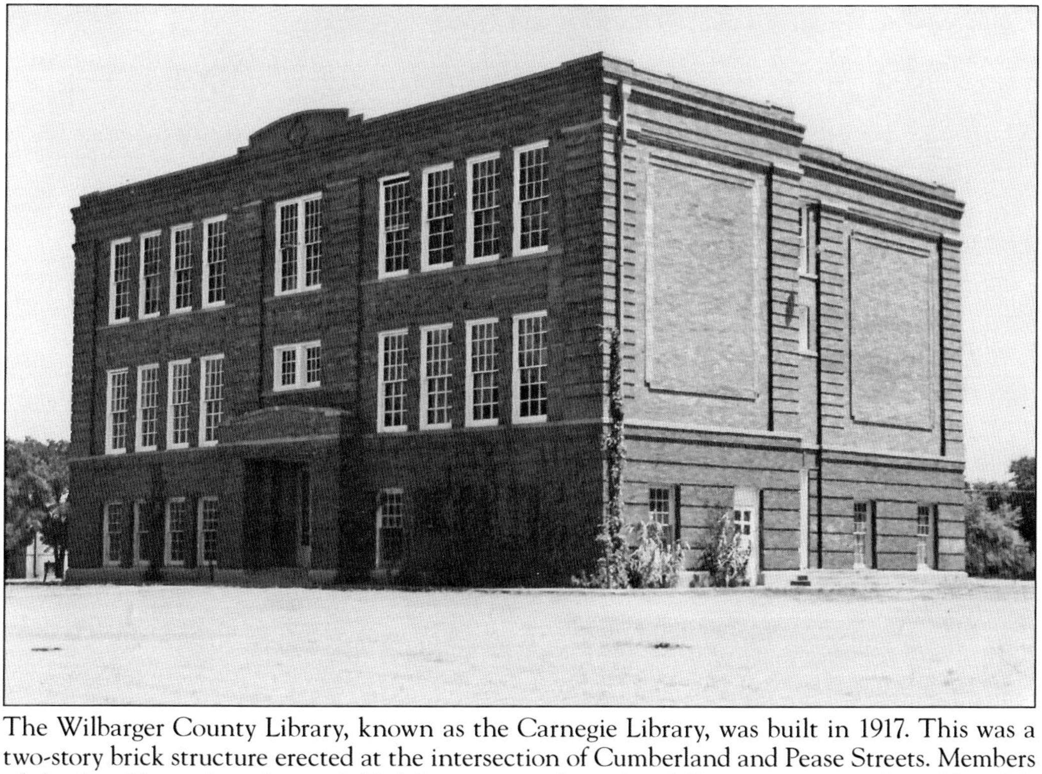

The Wilbarger County Library, known as the Carnegie Library, was built in 1917. This was a two-story brick structure erected at the intersection of Cumberland and Pease Streets. Members of the first library board were L.K. Johnson, president; Cecil Storey, vice president; Mrs. C.J. Farrell, secretary; and Mrs. Harry Mason, treasurer. (Author's collection.)

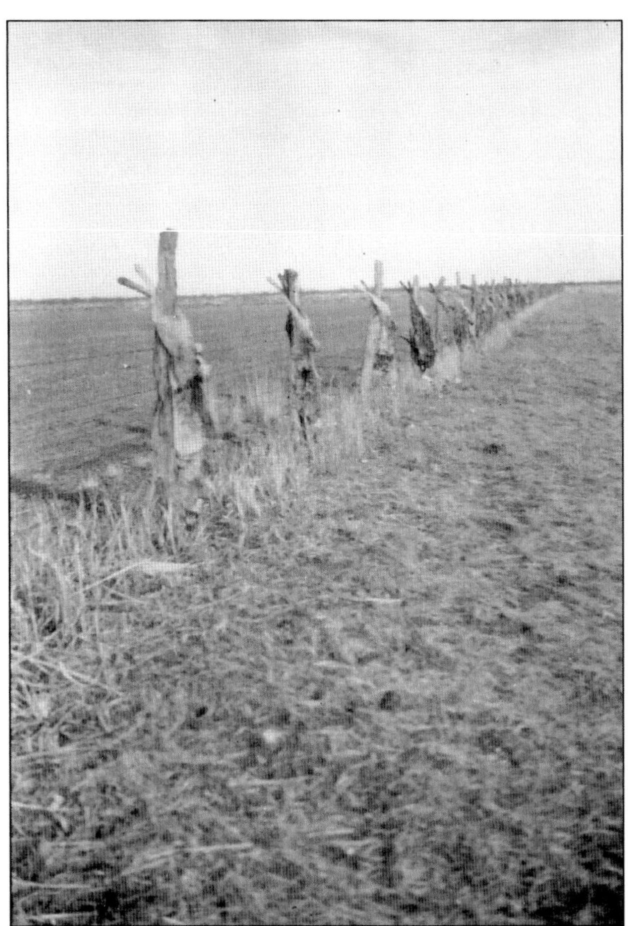

In 1916–1917, an effort was made to rid the county of a destructive element, the jackrabbit. Men would line up along the county's southern line and walk all the way to Red River, driving the rabbits in front of them. When the rabbits turned to come back they were shot. The jackrabbits hanging on the fence posts were part of that effort. (Author's collection.)

Pictured is an oil field on the Waggoner Ranch around 1918. As the story goes, W.T. Waggoner and his men were attempting to drill for water when they struck oil instead. Striking oil was a disappointment at this time, but five years later, the No. 1 Waggoner well was brought in. Waggoner later established the county's only oil refinery. It was operated from 1918 until 1958, when it was closed down. (Author's collection.)

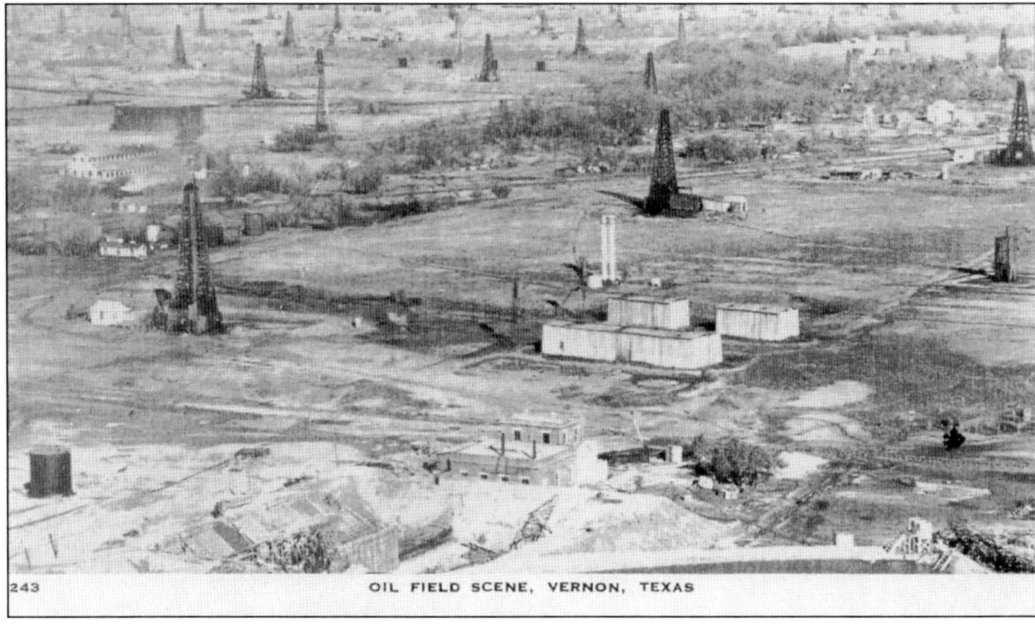

A child poses on top of a cotton sack, commonly referred to as the "long white train." Cotton was "picked" in the Northern states, but in the South and around Vernon, it was called "pulling boles." John M. Shelby, who came with his family from Alabama in 1891, was among the first farmers in Wilbarger County to successfully grow cotton. (Author's collection.)

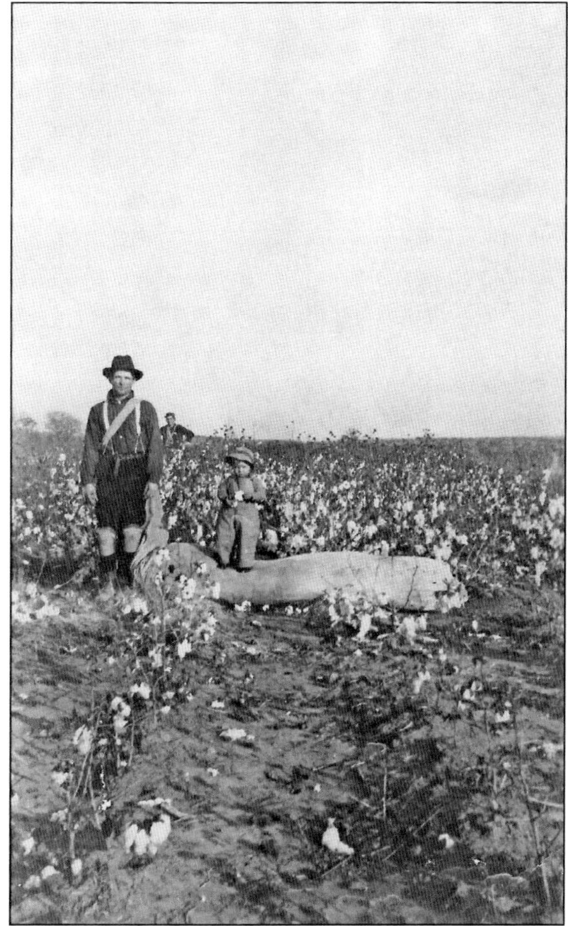

This team of mules was owned by Harry Skelton and was used on the farmland owned by Cy Long in Wilbarger County. For a sharecropper, a good team of mules was like owning a fine tractor. In all the early-day farming with horses and mules, every farmer had to keep back part of his land to grow feed for the work stock. (Author's collection.)

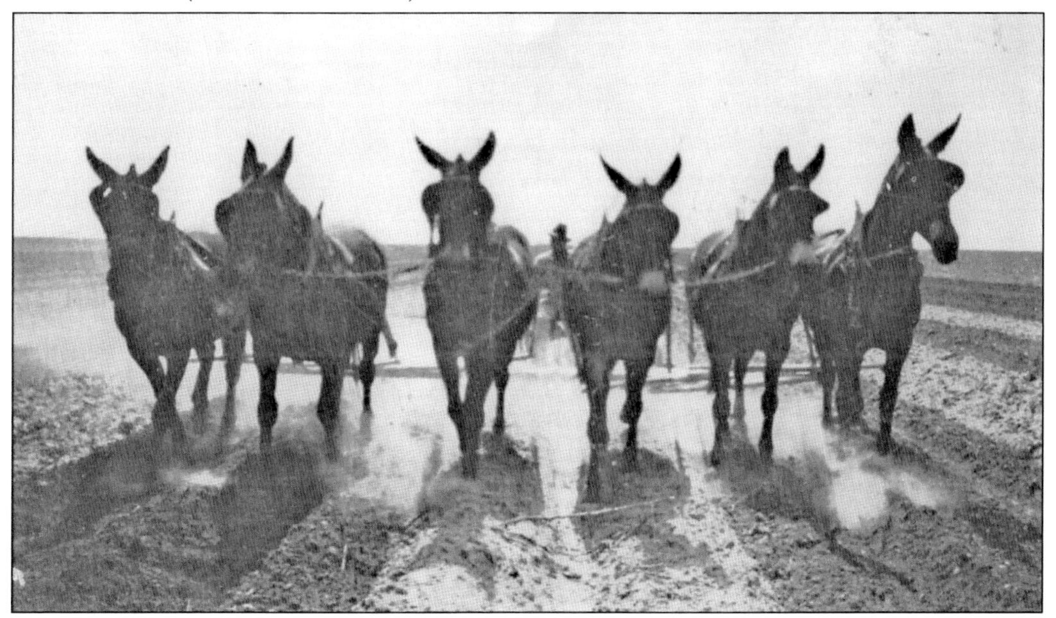

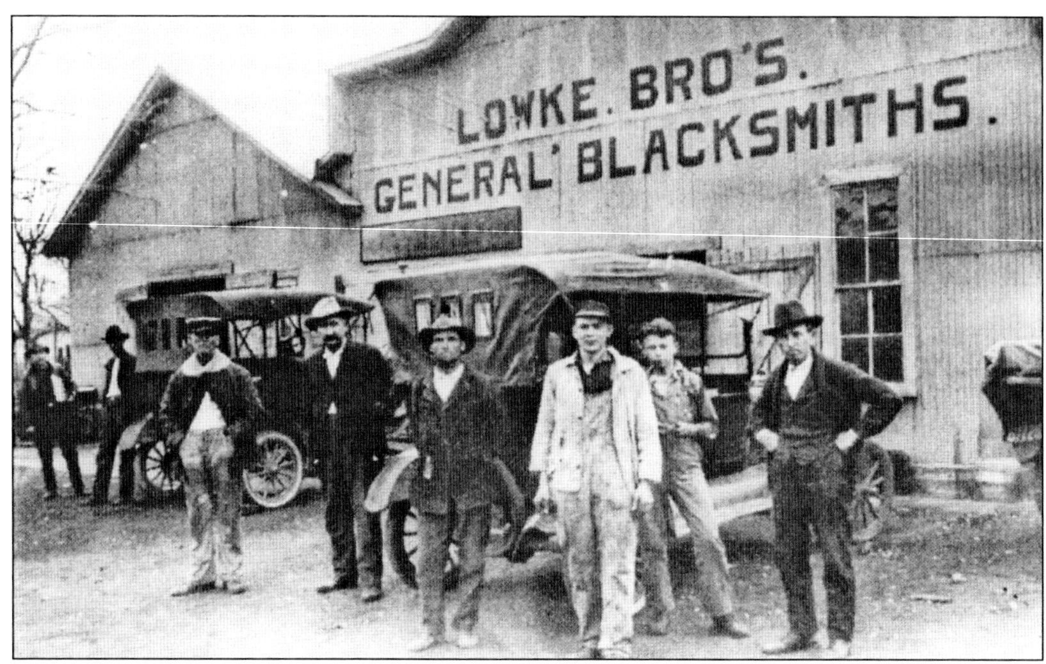

This original building on the southwest corner of Fannin and Pease Streets around 1918 was the location of the Lowke Brothers Hardware, founded in 1907. Patrons and proprietors in front are, from left to right, William Schur, F.E. Lowke, Carl Zoch, Gus Kahl, John Kretschmer, Martin Reidel, Walter Lowke, and Andrew Lowke. (Courtesy of Jo Jones.)

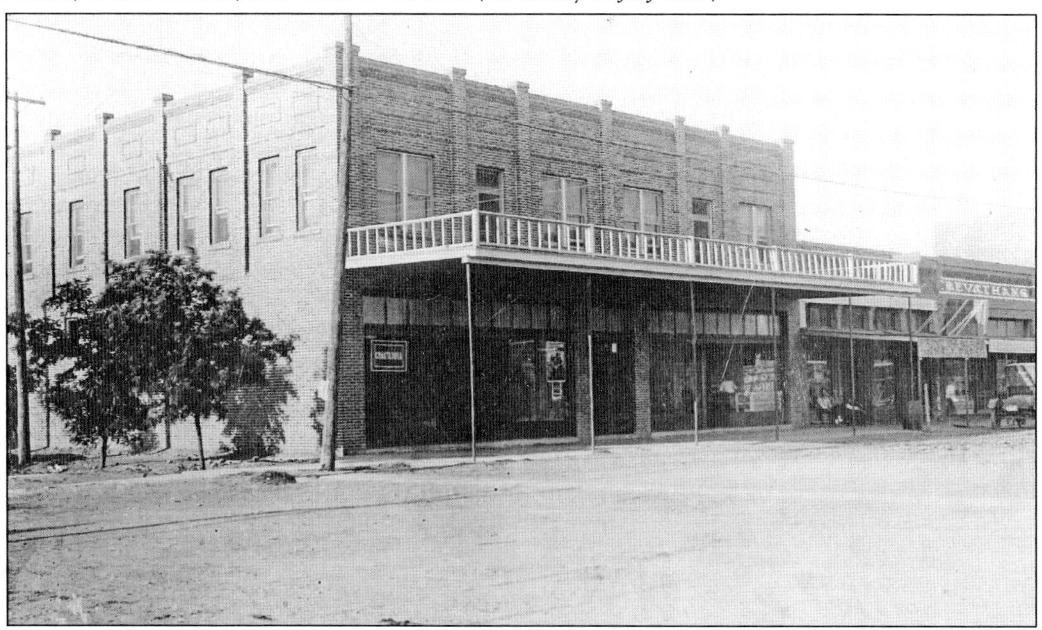

Herring Bennett Lumber Co., Inc., in 1918 was located on West Pease Street. The owners were C.T. Herring, president, and Wylie W. Bennett, secretary and treasurer. L.K. Johnson was vice president. They sold a line of hardware, lumber, and Domino-brand coal. The business next to the lumberyard was Stanley E. Trevethan's grocery store, which sold groceries and feed. (Author's collection.)

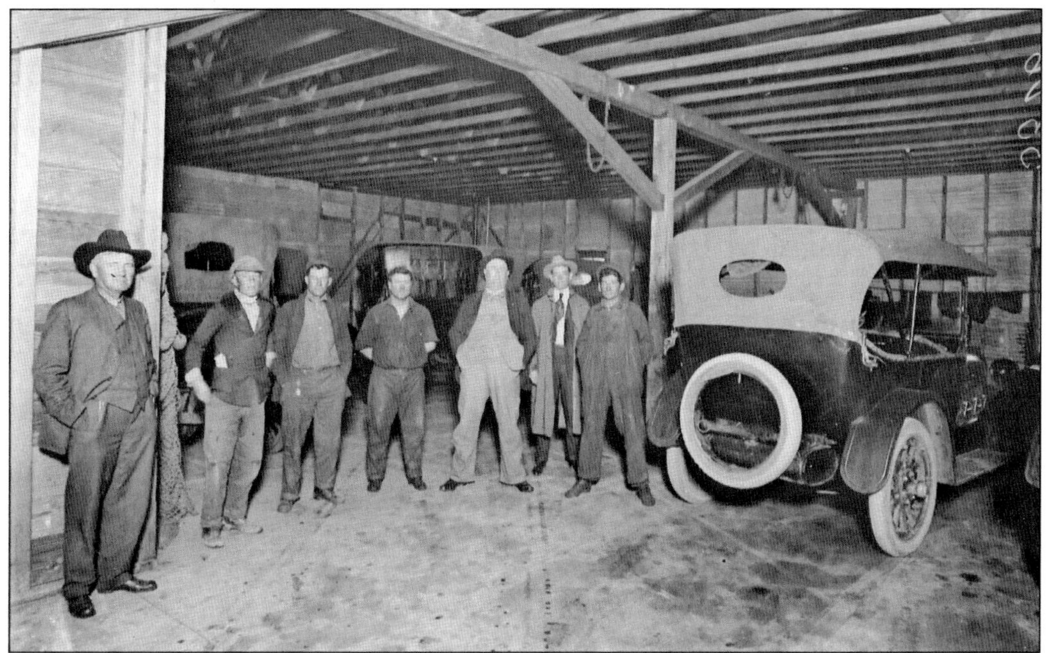

Pictured around 1919 is the interior of Napier Brothers Motor Company, located at 1419–1421 Main Street. This company advertised Lincoln, Ford, and Fordson sales and service and had the phone number 55. The owners of the company were Joseph A. Napier (standing at left) and S.M. Napier (at right. (Author's collection.)

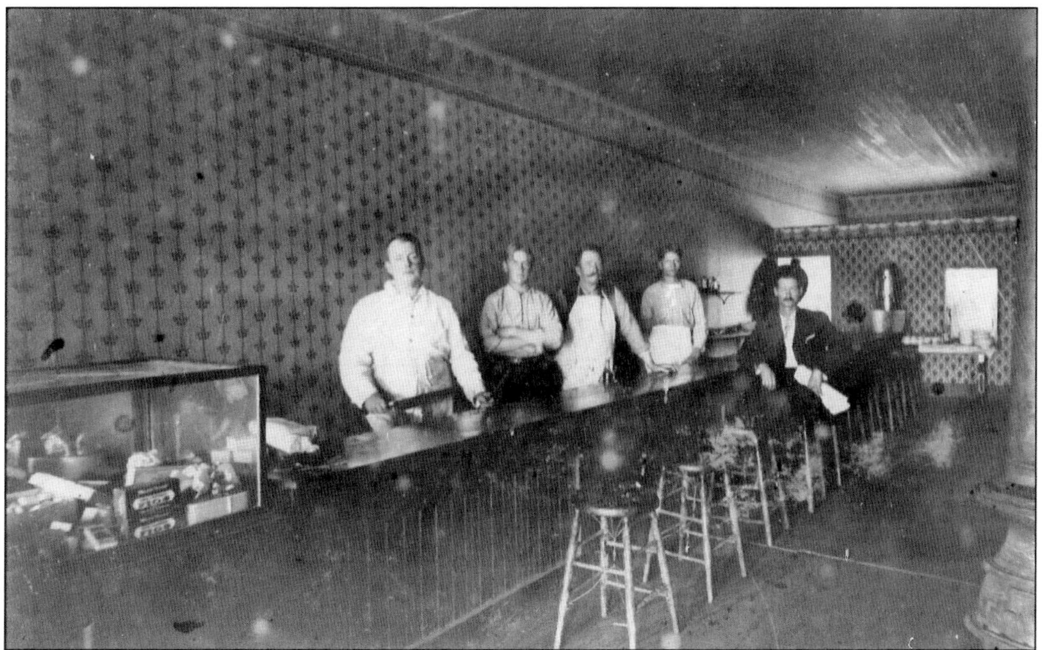

Pictured in 1919 is the interior of the Busy Bee Café, located on North Main Street. Jay Nathan, owner and operator, is standing on the left with his cooks, and one patron is seated. This type of café was referred to as "the greasy spoon" because of the good greasy hamburgers it sold off the grill. (Author's collection.)

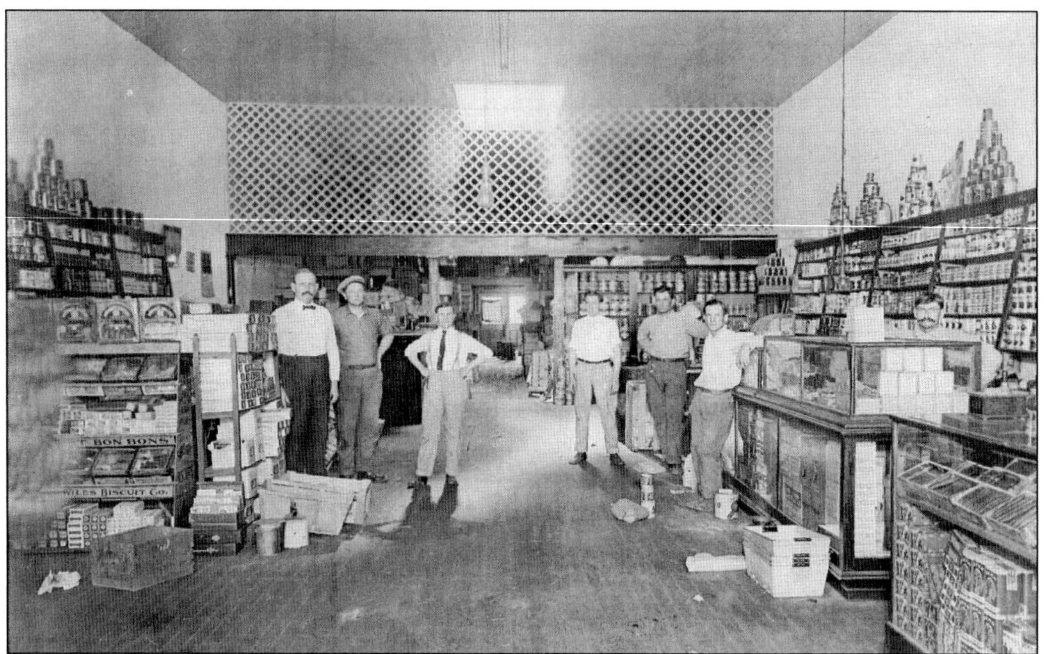

Pictured is the interior of Parker-Donges Grocery Store at 1524 Main Street in early 1920. B.J. Parker is seen standing on the left, and Adam Donges is in the center. It was advertised that it sold wholesale and retail groceries, choice meats, and vegetables and could be reached by phone at either 38 or 68. (Author's collection.)

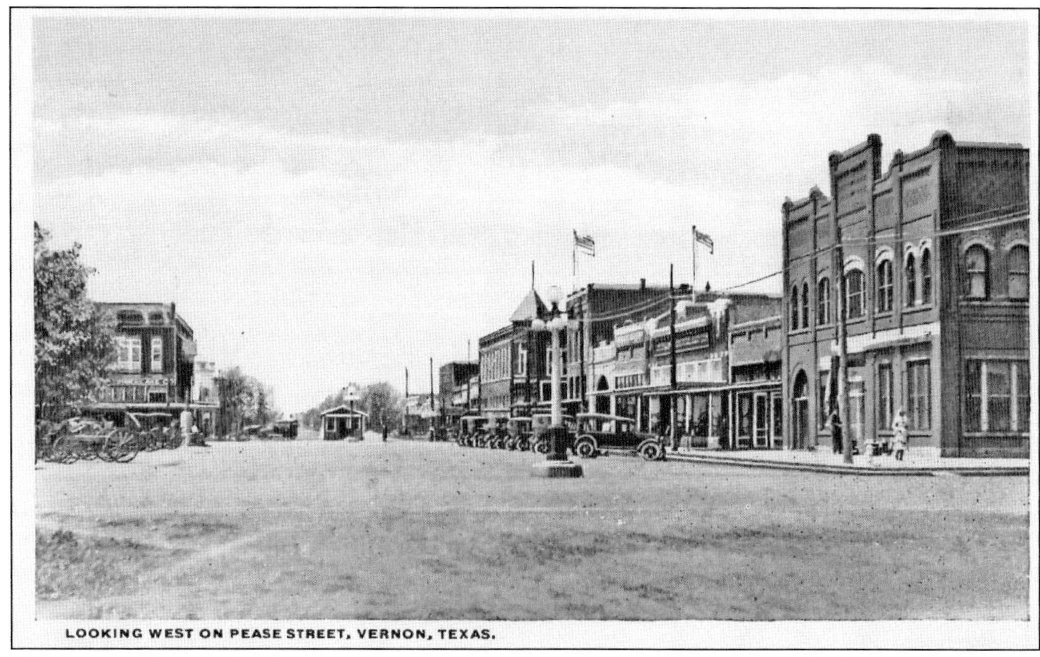

LOOKING WEST ON PEASE STREET, VERNON, TEXAS.

This postcard says, "Looking west on Pease Street, Vernon, Texas." On the left is the Perkins-Timberlake Building. On the right are the Bailey Hotel, with the newsstand and barbershop on the first floor; Liberty Café; Baker Drugstore; F.W. Woolworth; the Pictorium theater; and the Herring National Bank. (Author's collection.)

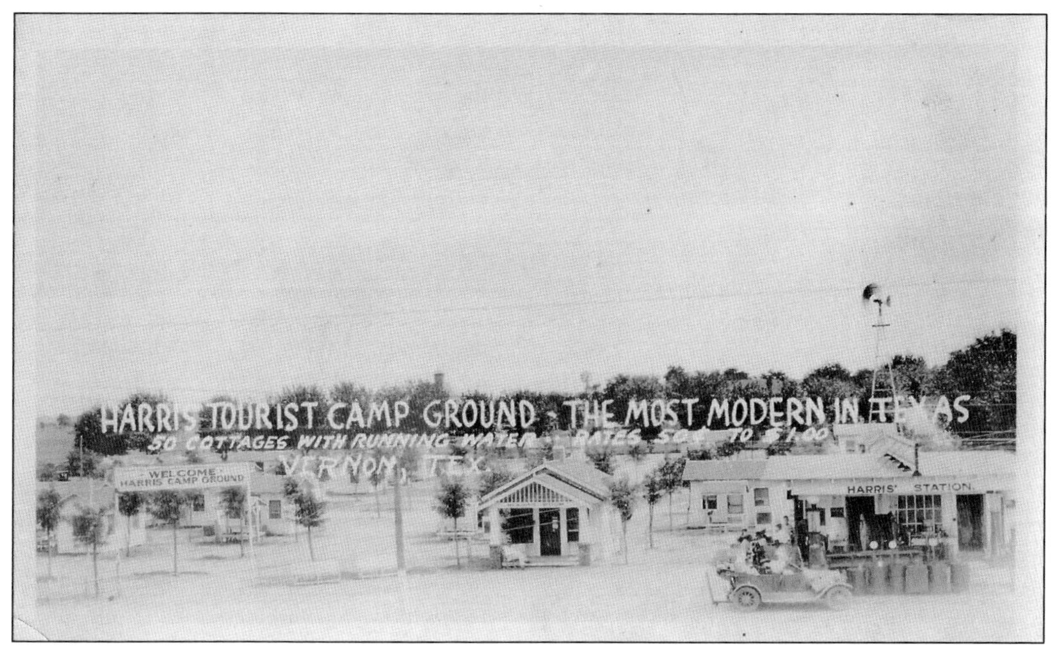

The Harris Tourist Courts was located at 619–628 Wilbarger Street in 1925. Along with the courts was the Harris Campgrounds, both owned by E.J. Harris. Cottages ranged from 50¢ to $1 per night. The Harris filling station was owned and operated by P.D. Chaney and sold Robert L. More's Water-White gas, oils, tires, and accessories. It located on the southeast corner of Pine and Wilbarger Streets. (Author's collection.)

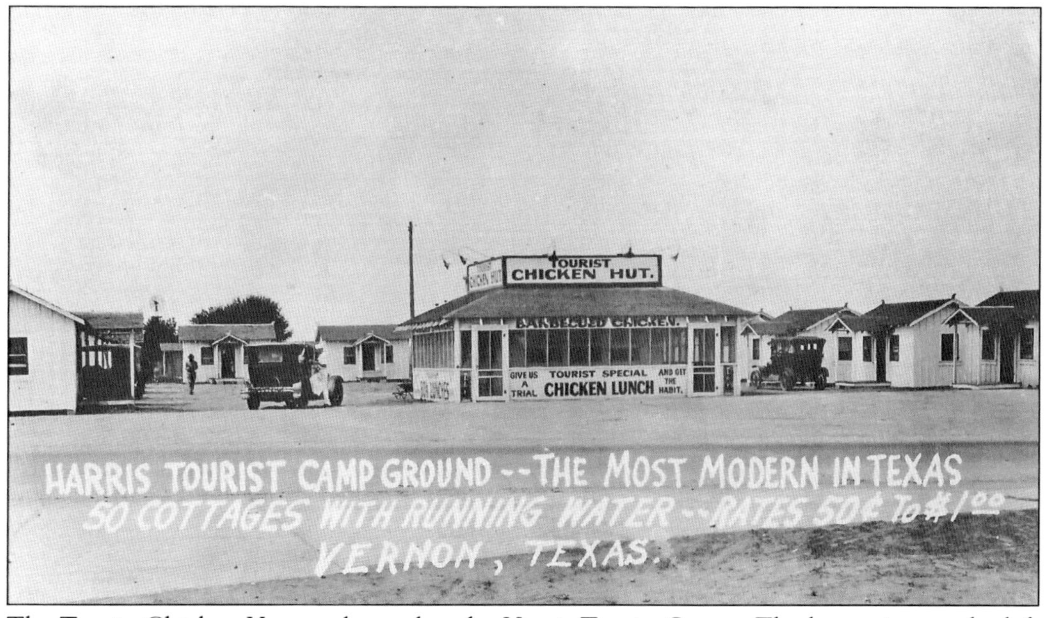

The Tourist Chicken Hut was located at the Harris Tourist Courts. The lower sign on the left side of the building says, "Tourist box lunches." The small signs on each side of the main sign say, "Give us a trial and get the habit." This is where the Wilbarger Park Apartments are located today at 631 Wilbarger Street. (Author's collection.)

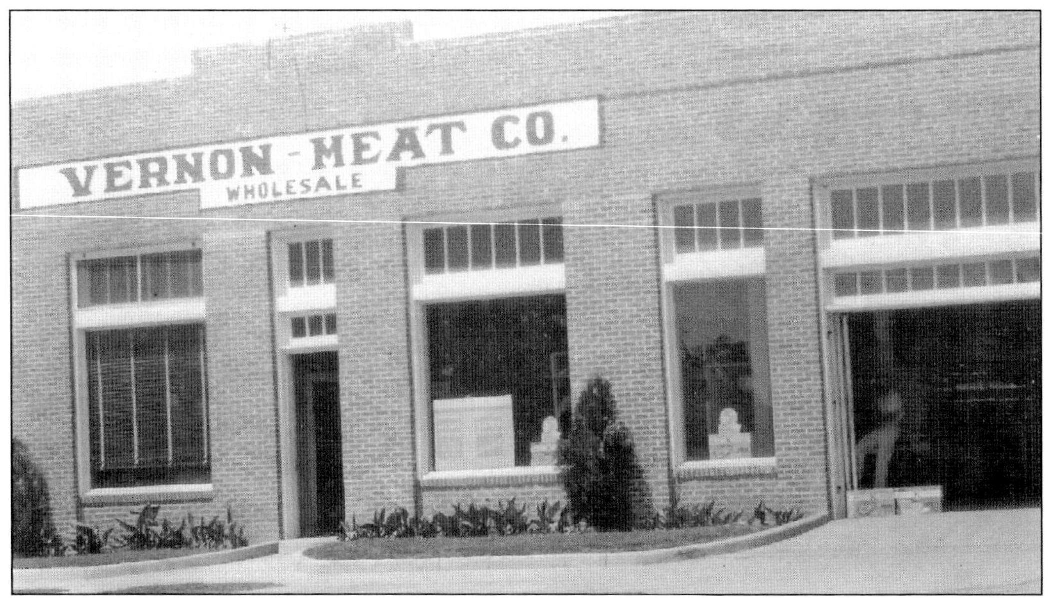

Egbert E. Eggleston, along with his sons J.L. and Fay and other members of his family, including Leroy Wright, established the Vernon Meat Company, located at 1314 Wanderer Street, in 1922. In 1939, the Vernon Packing Company was formed. Leroy Wright began construction of the Wright Packing Company, which opened November 1, 1946. William "Bill" Wright was associated from the beginning, and Robert L. Wright joined them the next year. (Courtesy of Bill Wright.)

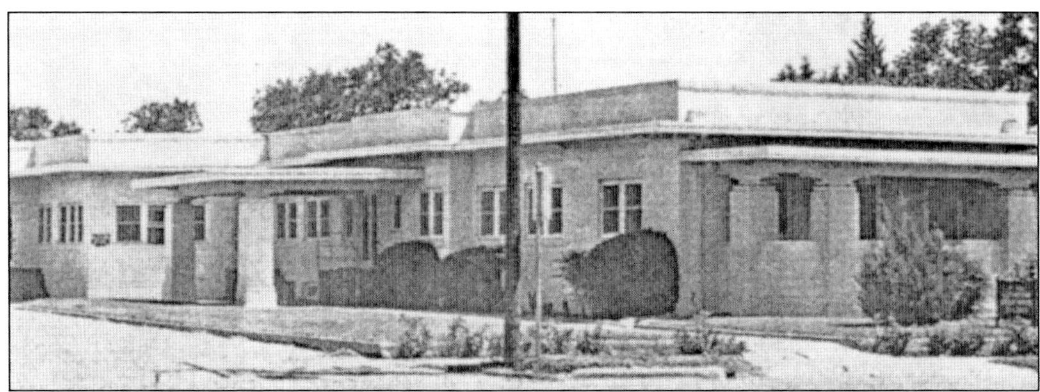

The first hospital was built in 1922 by Dr. T.E. Standifer. The 18-room hospital was sold in 1926 to Dr. E.J. Harris of the Harris Campground to be used as a public hospital, known as the Harris Sanitarium. Later, it was leased to Kramer Studio and was sold in 1955 to the St. Paul Lutheran Church for a Sunday school facility. The building, still standing on East Wilbarger Street, is now an apartment complex. (Author's collection.)

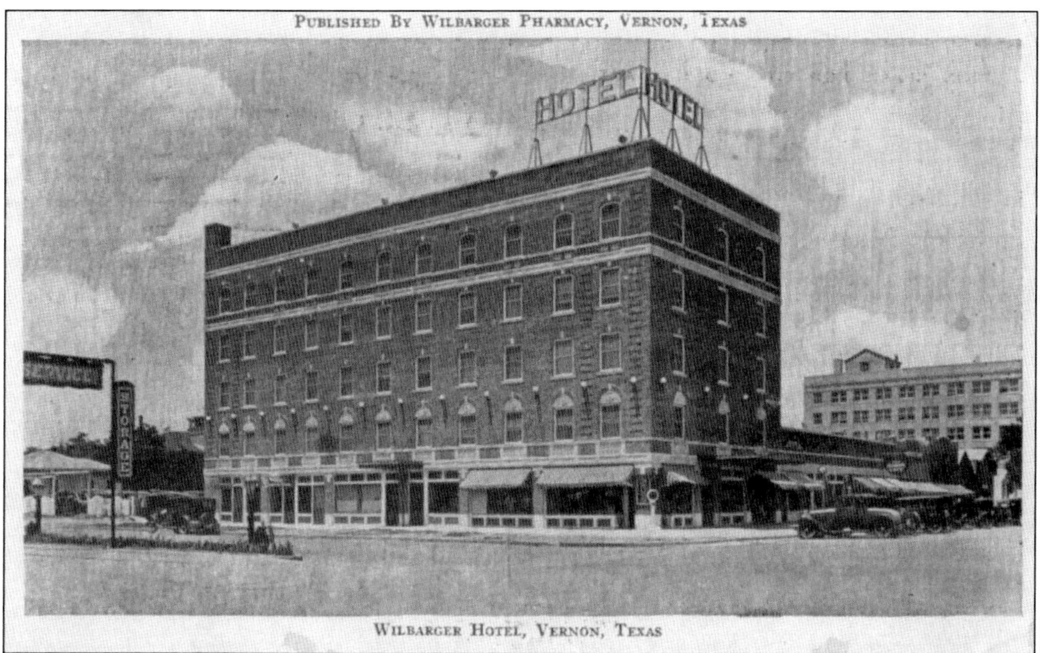

Around 1926, the Wilbarger Hotel on the corner of Wilbarger and Fannin Streets was a five-story building, with a barbershop and drugstore on the first floor. The hotel was owned by Mrs. B.A. Winter, and Charles C. Winter was the manager. Wilbarger Street was the main highway through Vernon, and this hotel was the best place to stay. (Author's collection.)

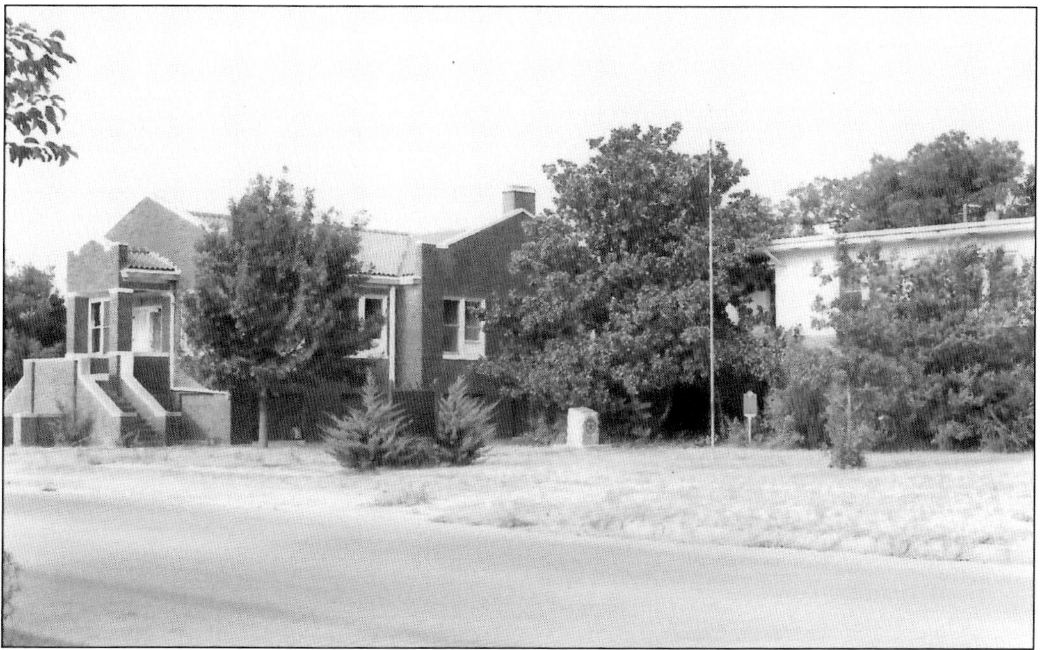

Dr. A.B. Garland, who came to Vernon in 1908, founded the Vernon Sanitarium in 1925. In 1937, it was reorganized as the Vernon Clinic-Hospital, with the addition of a 17-room annex. In 1950, the second floor was added. The old clinic at 2030 Cumberland Street was closed with the opening of the new Wilbarger General Hospital on June 11, 1969. (Author's collection.)

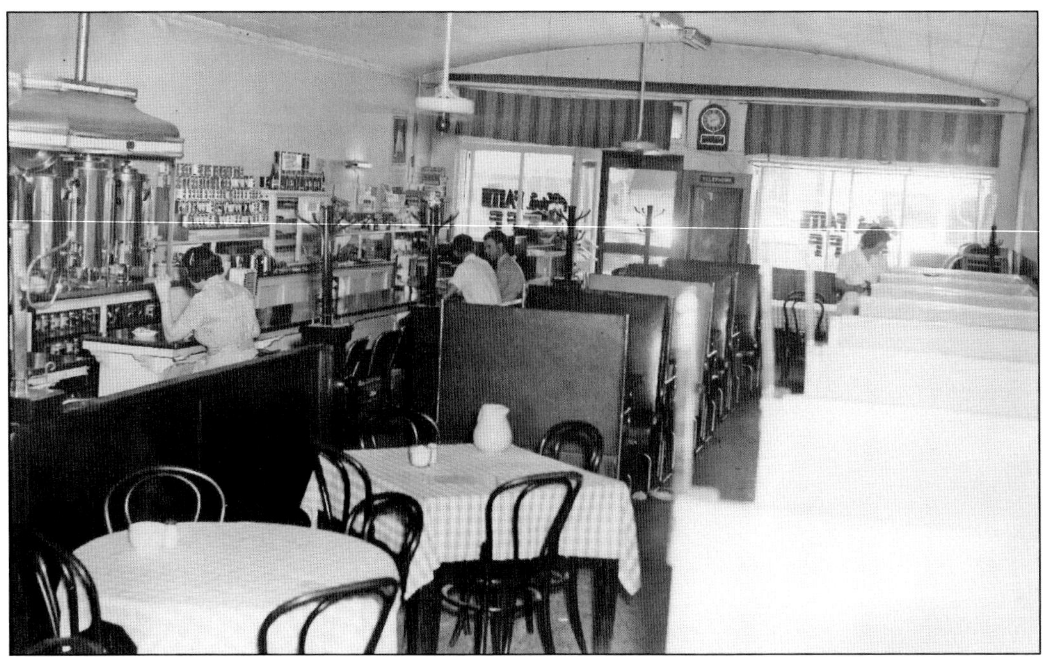

Pictured in 1926 is the interior of the Faith Café, located at 1607 Cumberland Street. Commonly known as Chris Faith Café, it was owned by Steve Marygol, and its phone number was 82. Looking across the street through the front window of the café, one can see Kirkland's Studio. (Author's collection.)

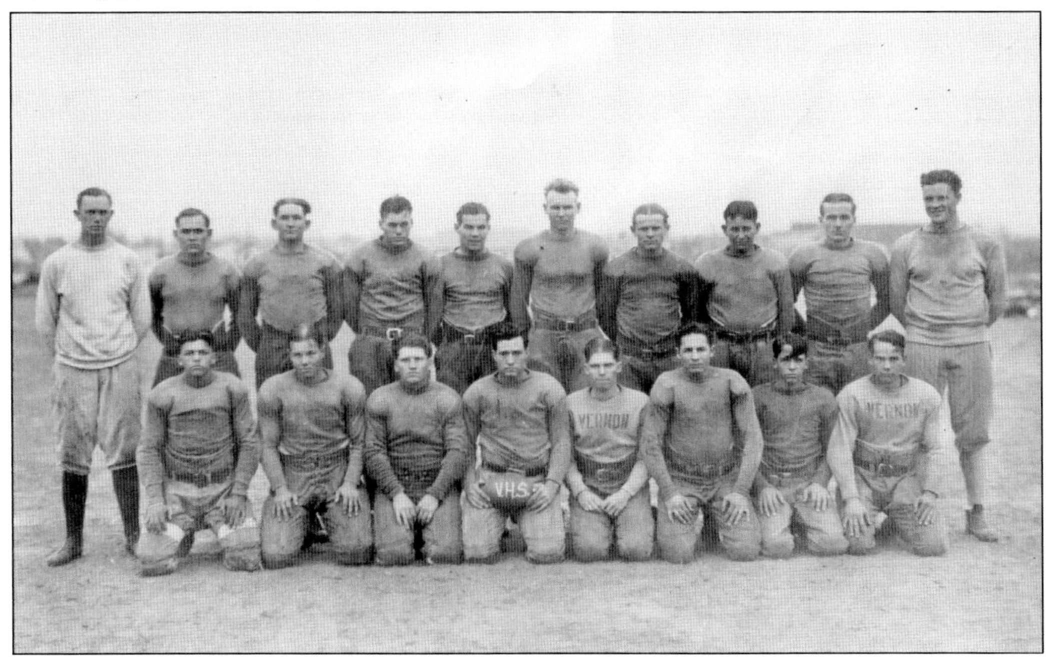

The 1926 football team includes, from left to right, (first row) Shorty Key, Red Black, Fat Parker, Bill Gelhausen, Chester Luttrell, I.D. Hollar, Jim Dodson, and Robert Nabors; (second row) coach E.A. Baggett, Delmas Johnson, Emil Hutto, Ted Key, F.A. Newth, Ben Hopkins, Lee Moore, Fat Norwood, Raymond Koontz, and coach Bob Vaughn. (Author's collection.)

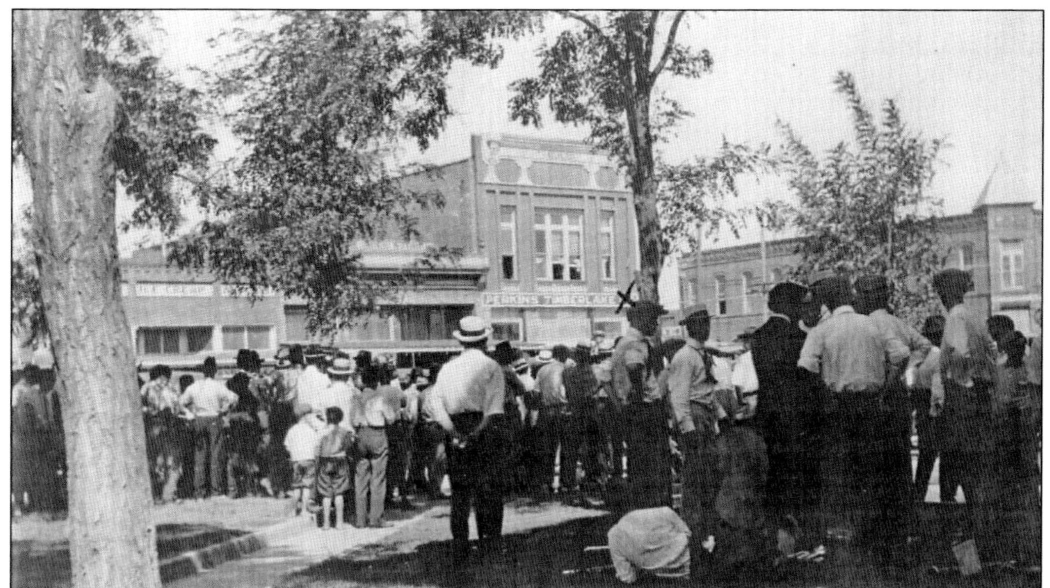

In the background of this gathering on the courthouse square is the Perkins-Timberlake Building on the corner of Main and Pease Streets at 1716–1718 Pease Street. It sold dry goods, clothing, ladies' ready-to-wear, shoes, and men's furnishings, and its phone number was 215. Cy Long was manager, and Dee Norwood was general manager. Later, Cy Long opened Cy Long's menswear at 1710 Pease Street and was manager from 1918 to 1929. (Author's collection.)

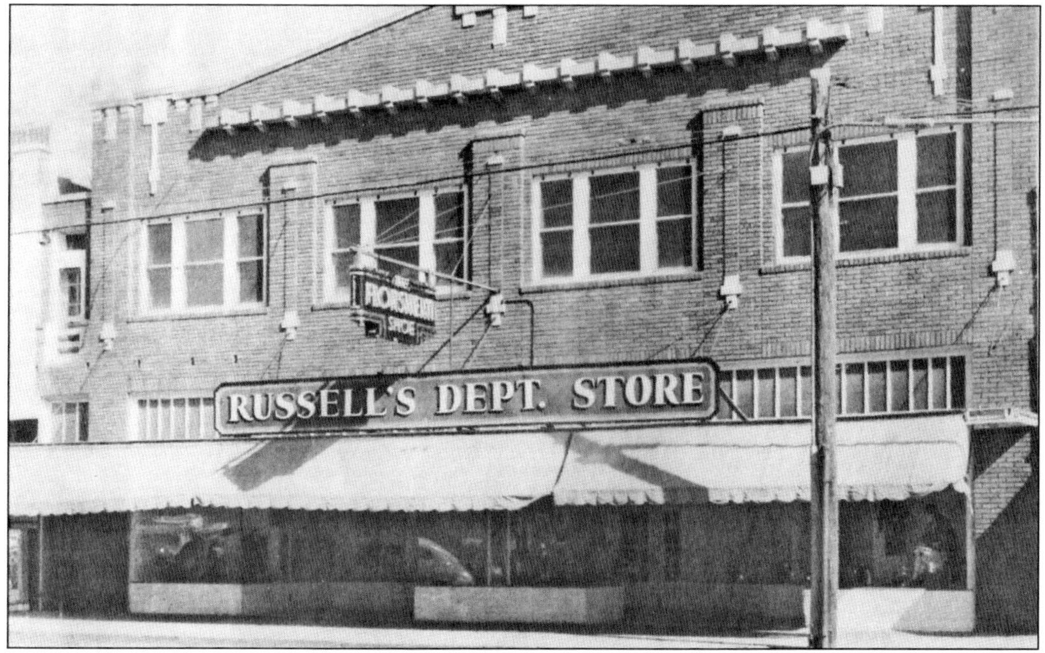

Russell's Department Store moved to this location at 1820 Pease Street in 1927 from the original location at 1628 Main Street, where it had been for 10 years. Started by H.C. Russell & Son, with C. Fred Russell as manager, it was advertised as Vernon's fastest growing dry goods store, selling ladies' ready-to-wear, men's furnishings, and Stetson hats. Pease Street was the location for the department store for over 30 years. (Author's collection.)

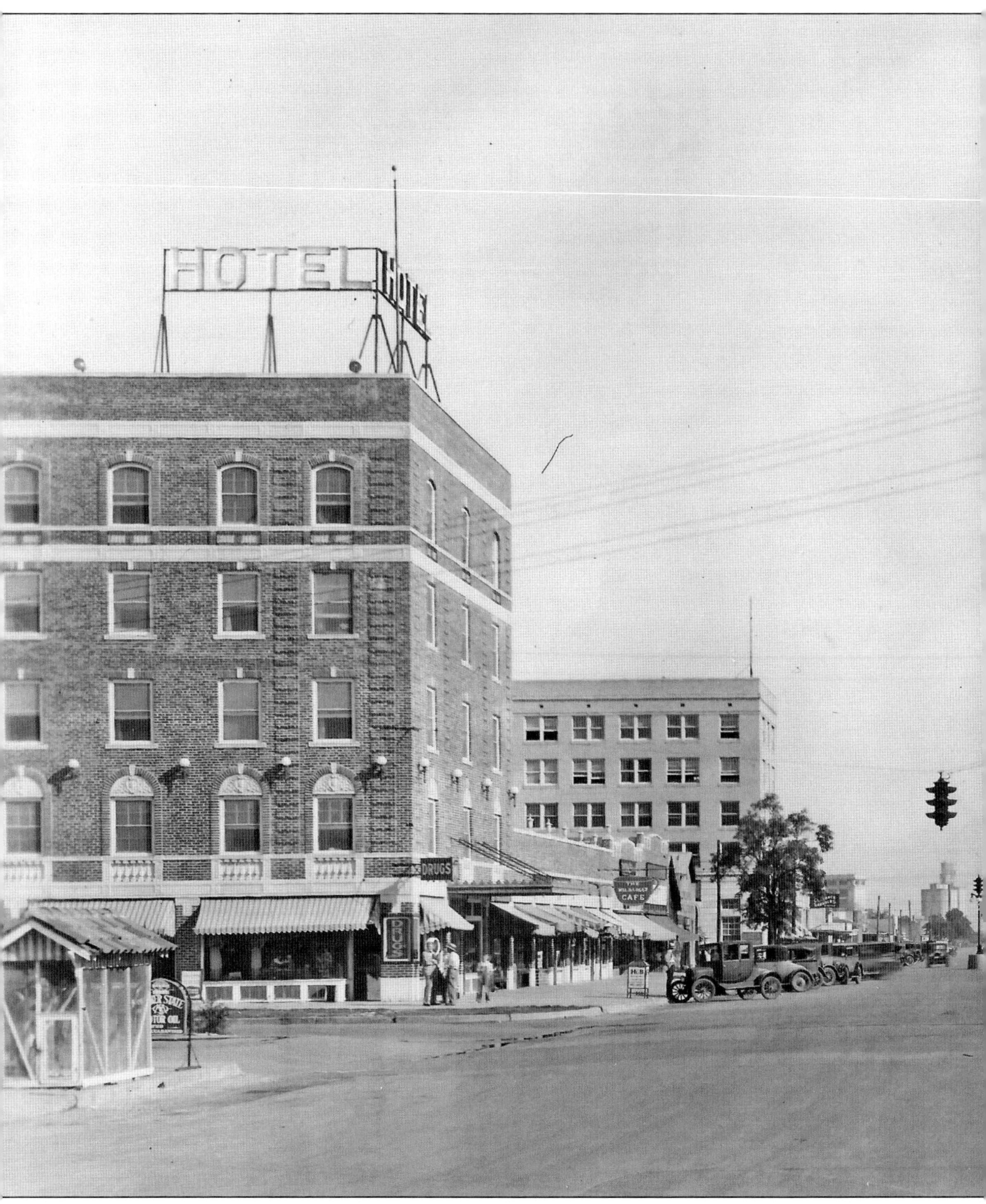

Looking north on Fannin Street in 1927 from Marshall Street, the businesses on the right are Hoffman's filling station and vulcanizing tire shop, located on the southeast corner of Fannin and Wilbarger Streets; and E.M. Leutwyler's jewelry store on the northeast corner of Wilbarger and Fannin Streets. Next to the jewelry store was an empty lot where the Montgomery Ward Building was constructed before

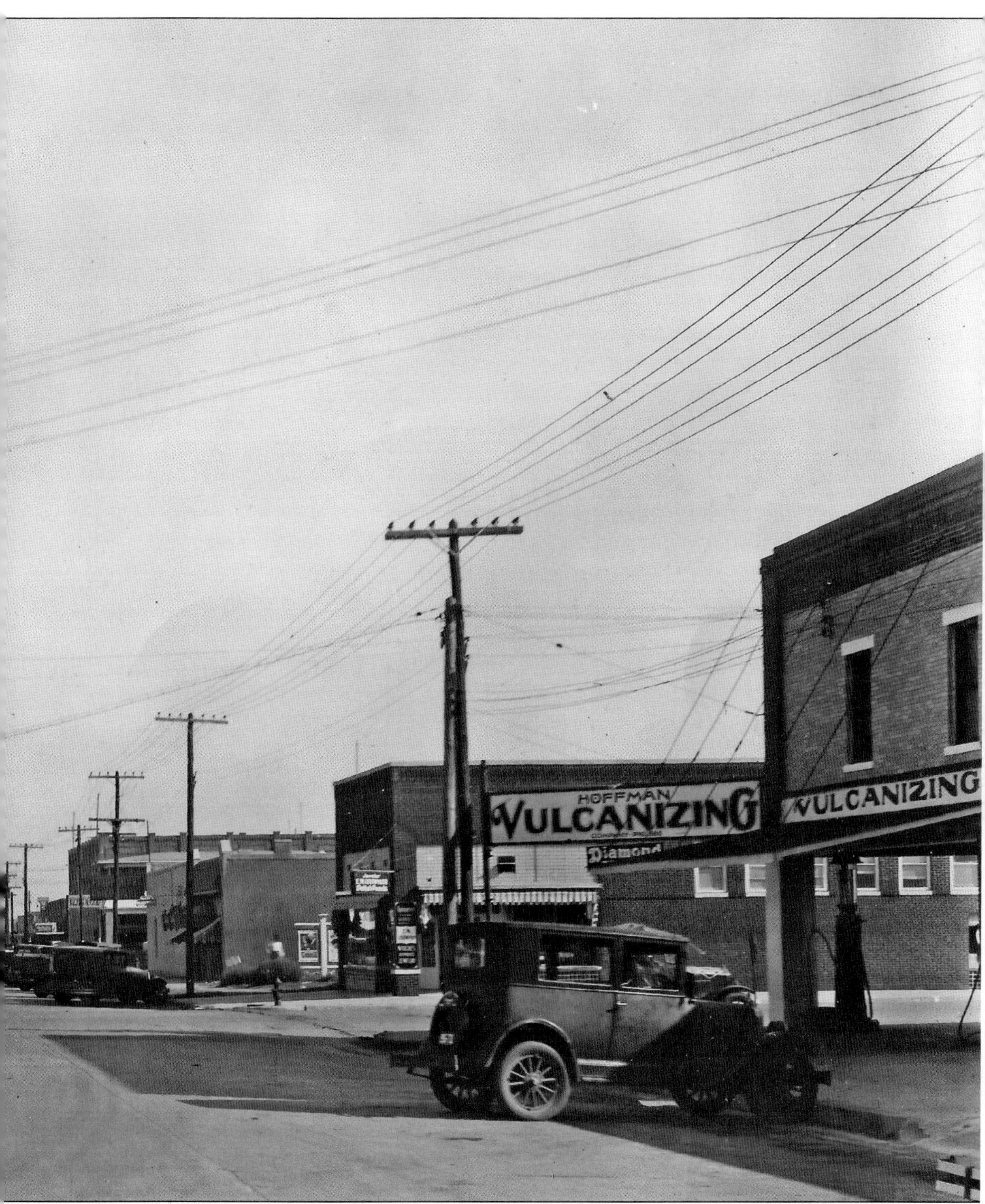

the end of the year. On the left side is the new Wilbarger Hotel, with Wilbarger Drug, a barbershop, J.D. Still Jewelry, and the Tic-Tock Shop on the first floor; the Darden Café; and Lowke Brothers Hardware. After crossing Pease Street is the new Herring National Bank. (Author's collection.)

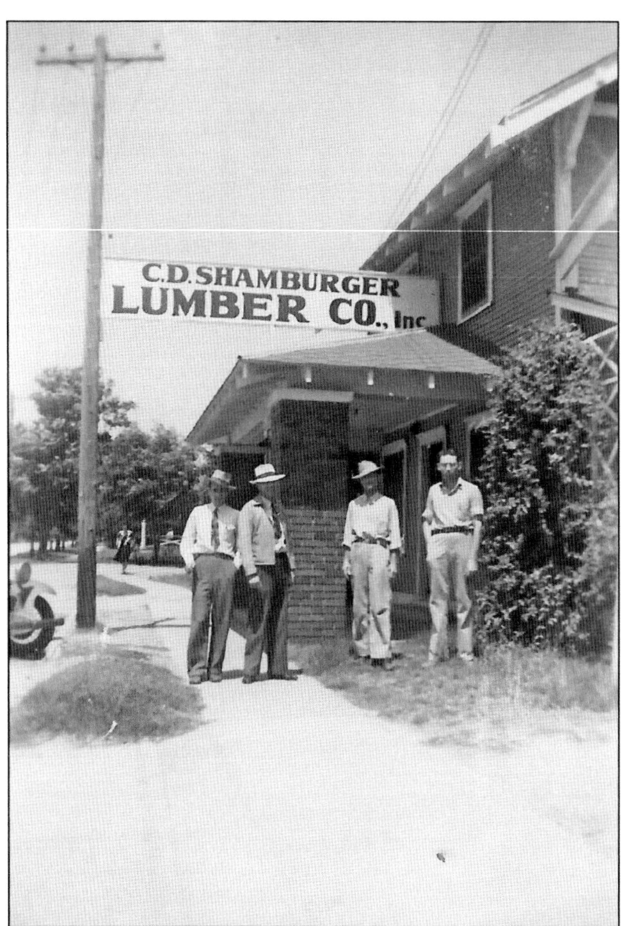

Pictured in 1928 is Joe Petty, third man from left, the manager of C.D. Shamburger Lumber Company, Inc. The Shamburger Lumber Co. was located at 1928 Texas Street. C.D. Shamburger went into business in the early 1920s, selling lumber, shingles, doors and windows, Bois d' Arc post, hardware, and window glass. The company's phone number was 130. (Author's collection.)

The J.C. Penney Company established its Vernon store in August 1924. With manager C.R. Buchanan and 15 sales people, it offered men's and women's clothing and was located at 1529 Main Street, with the phone number 543. J.C. Penney remained in this location until 1934, when it moved across the street to 1518–1520 Main Street, with J.R. Wright as manager. This location was used through the 1990s. (Author's collection.)

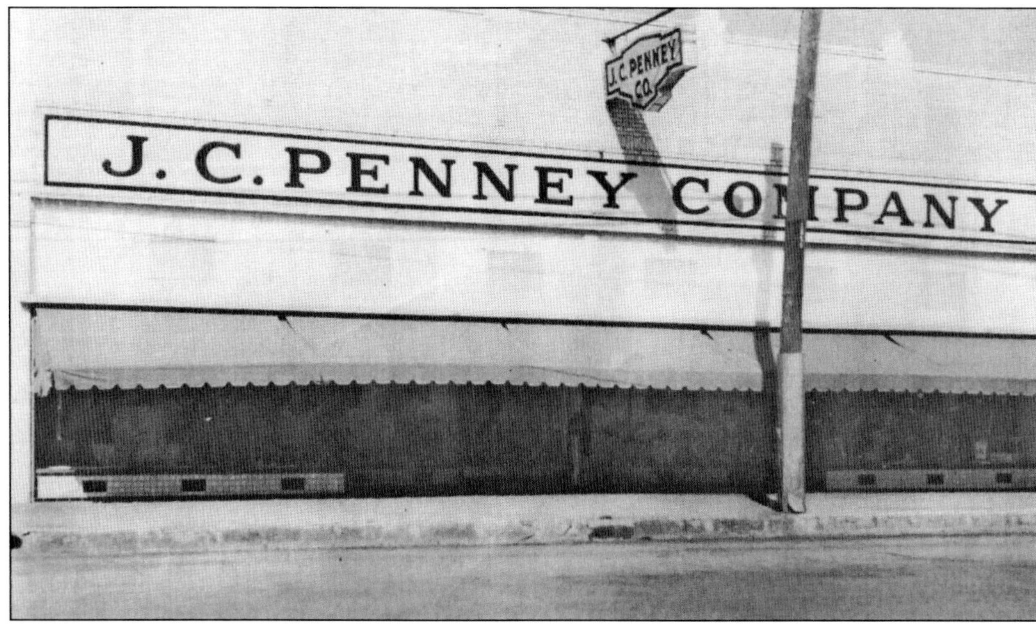

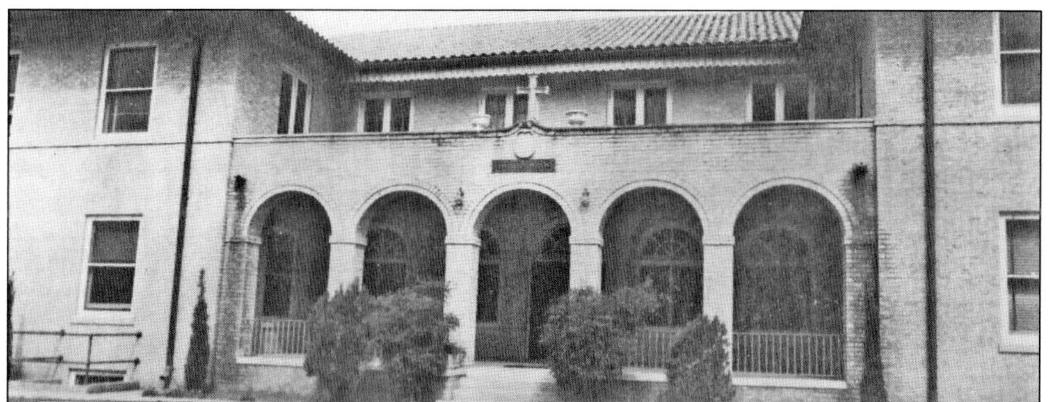

Dr. T.A. King established the King Hospital and Maternity Home in 1927 at 2006 Pease Street. In 1937, Sisters of the Holy Family of Nazerath came to Vernon to operate the 25-bed hospital. The Catholic group became owner of the hospital a short time after Dr. King retired in 1946, and the name officially became Christ the King Hospital. The building was demolished in the 1960s. (Author's collection.)

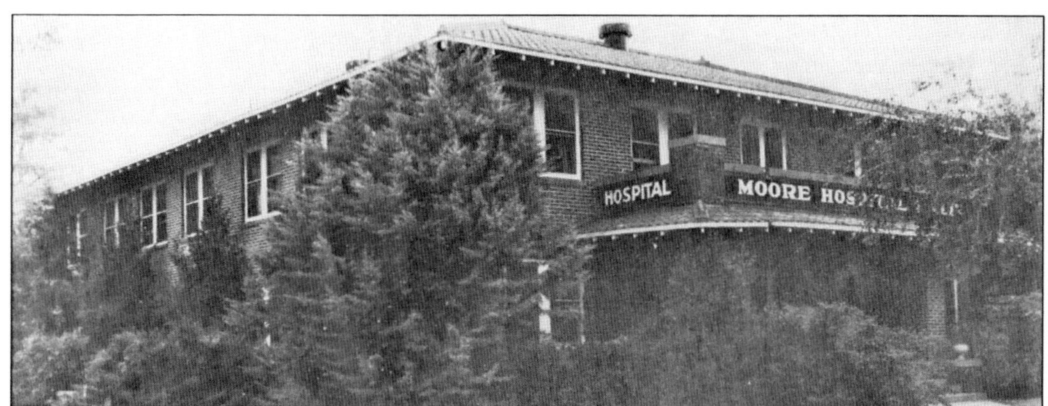

Moore Hospital, also known as the Moore Brothers Hospital, was established in 1923 by the Moore brothers William R. and Milton J. and was located at 2103 Marshall Street. In 1944, C.C. Prescott and Dr. Joe Shipman joined the brothers. In 1946, Q.L. Rutledge, Shipman, and J.J. Slaugenhop joined the medical doctors' association. In 1947, W.R. Moore moved his office to room 203 of the Herring National Bank. (Author's collection.)

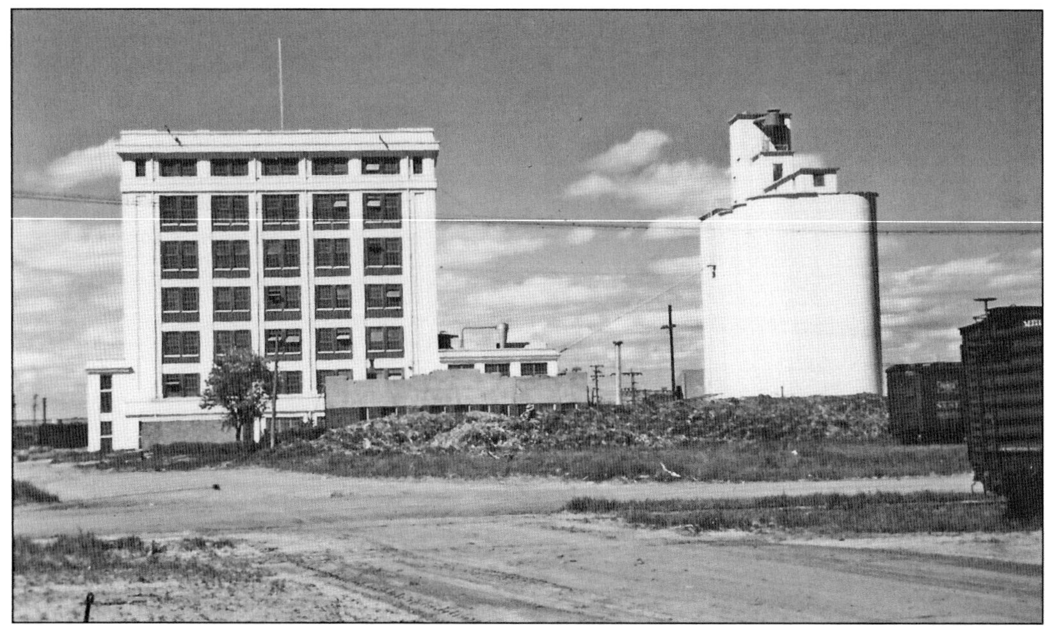

Pictured are the Marti-Lane Buildings. Originally the white building to the left was the Kell Milling Company, owned by Frank Kell of Wichita Falls, Texas. Kell was owner-president, W.O. Anderson was vice president, and J.A. Kell was secretary, treasurer, and gin manager. The mill was located on Fannin Street and on the southwest corner of the Fort Worth & Denver City Railroad. This was the home of Belle of Vernon Flour in the 1920s. (Author's collection.)

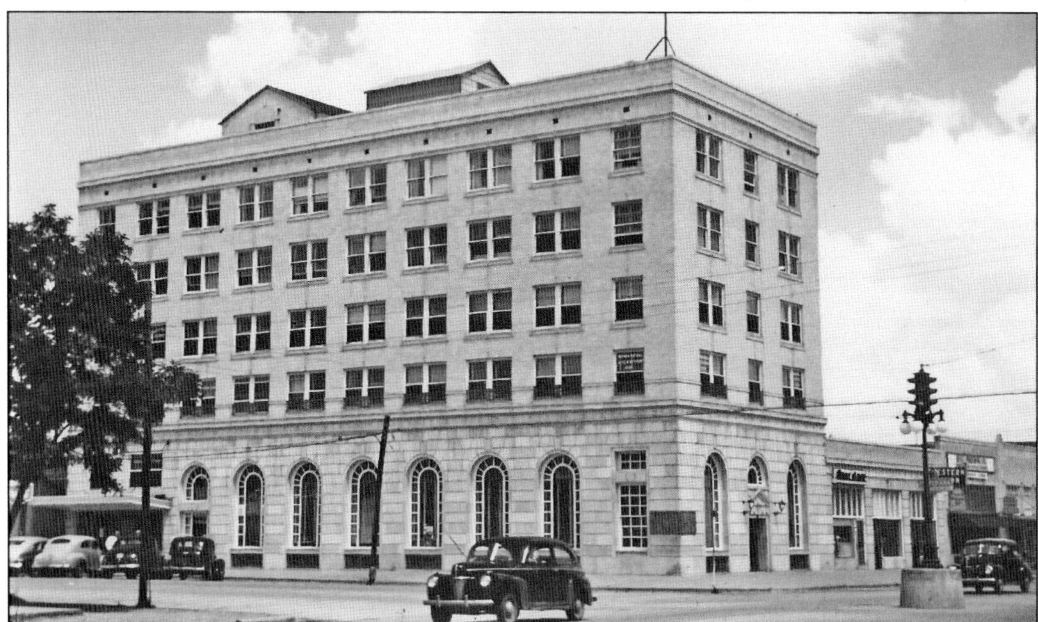

The Herring National Bank is shown in the 1940s. It was founded as the C.T. Herring Banking Company in 1899 and was moved from the northeast corner of Pease and Main Streets in 1927 to this location at the northwest corner of Pease and Fannin Streets. The entrance was changed from Fannin Street to Pease Street, and later an entrance was added on the north side to the parking lot. (Author's collection.)

Pictured in the late 1930s is the Montgomery Ward Building, constructed in 1928 as one of Vernon's leading department stores. The three-story building with a full-size basement was located at 1725–1727 Fannin Street, and R.L. Barrett was manager. This is now the location of Blessing's Antiques. (Author's collection.)

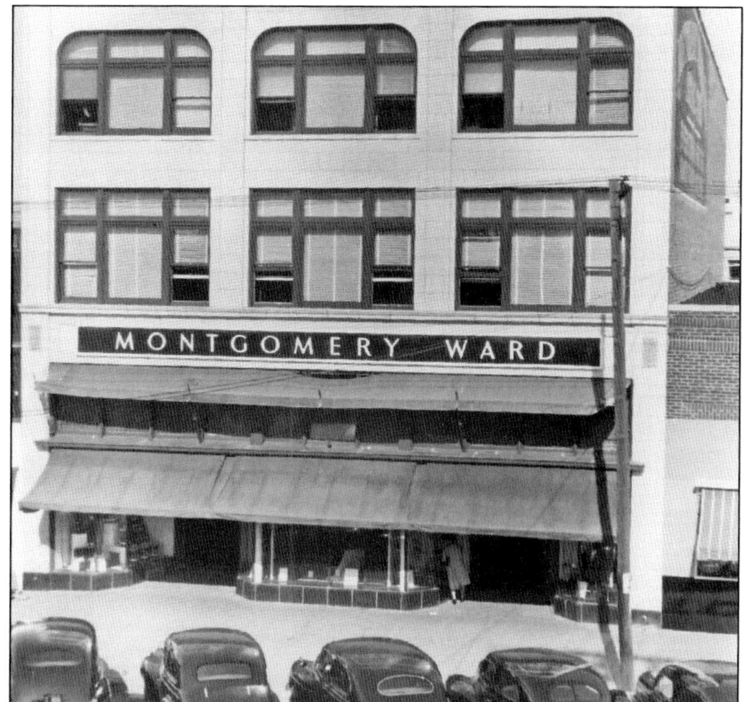

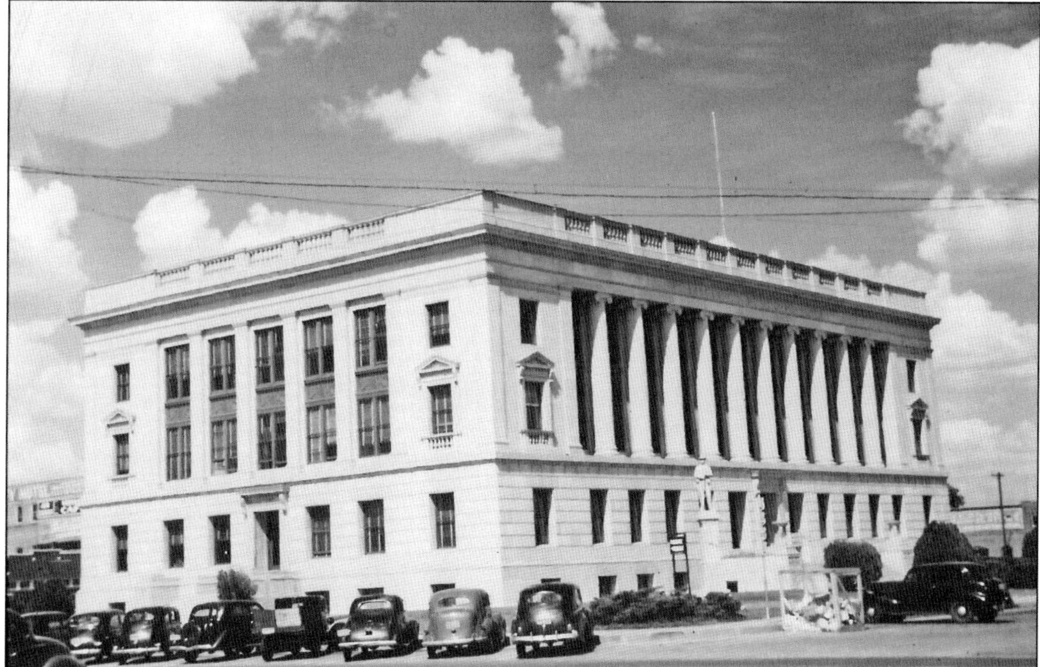

The Wilbarger County Courthouse, pictured in the late 1930s, was built in 1928–1929, replacing the first courthouse that was constructed in 1886. The cornerstone was laid at 2:30 p.m. on September 10, 1928, and the Bedford gray stone was chosen on May 17, 1929. The drawing by the architectural firm of Voelcker and Cixon stated that the design reflected ancient Greece and Rome in a look that was as "modern as tomorrow." (Author's collection.)

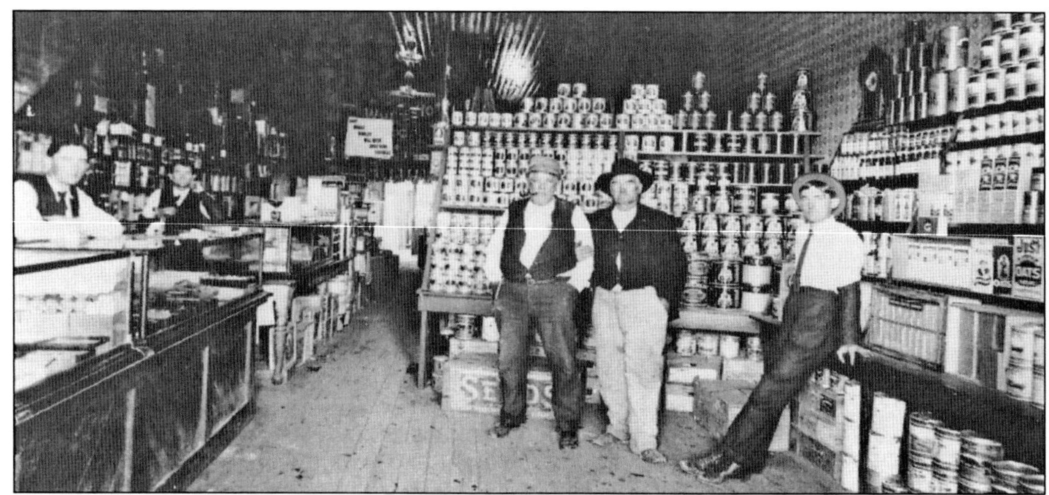

In 1928, the Massie-Sullivan store, along with Massie-Hogsett and Massie-Vernon, was part of the Massie chain of grocery stores until 1938, when the partnership was dissolved. This store was on the corner of Mesquite and Pease Streets and became the Sullivan Food Store. From left to right are A.P. McCelvey, Charles T. Sullivan, W.H. Evans, R.T. Britt, and Linton J. Sullivan. (Courtesy of Jo Jones.)

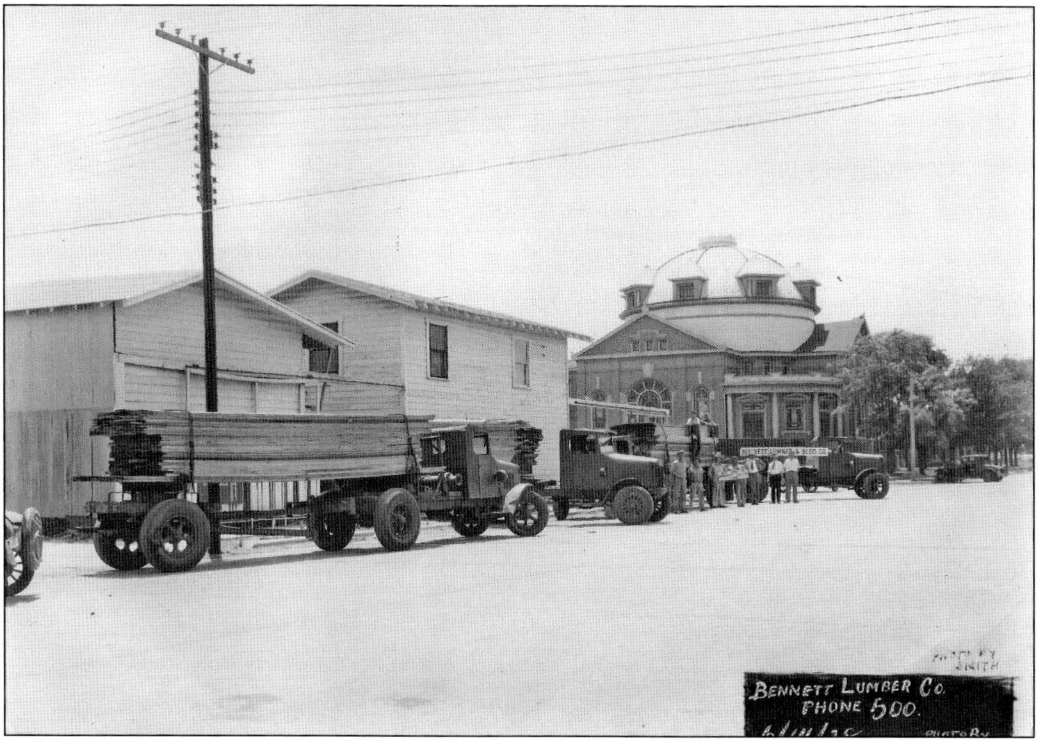

BENNETT LUMBER Co.
PHONE 500.

The Bennett Lumber Company, Inc., in 1928 was located on the corner of Wilbarger Street and Pease Street from 1925 to 1929. R.S. Allen was president, with W.W. Bennett as vice president, C.W. Showers as secretary, and Gordon T. West as treasurer. Today, the drive-through of the Herring National Bank is where the buildings on the left used to be, and the Methodist church on the right is the location of the Waggoner Estate Building. (Author's collection.)

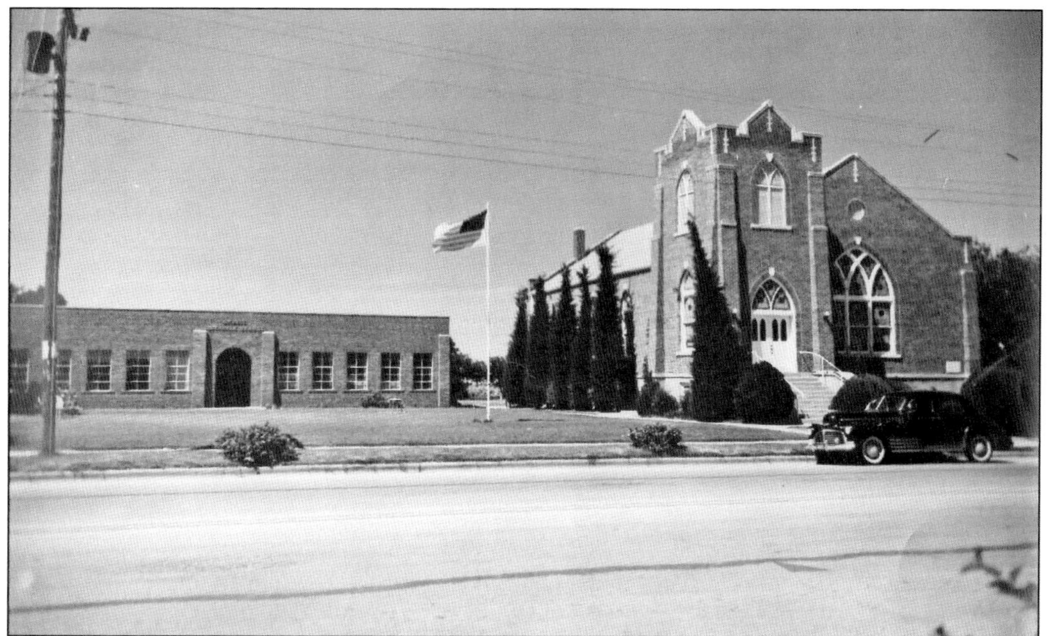

The St. Paul Lutheran Church, located at 70 East Wilbarger Street, was used from 1924 until 1977. The church was organized in 1912, and in 1916, J.A. Birnbaum was ordained as permanent pastor. The church-school classes met in the basement of the church from 1924 until 1949, when the congregation constructed the school building pictured at left. In 1955, a neighboring building was bought for a Sunday school. (Author's collection.)

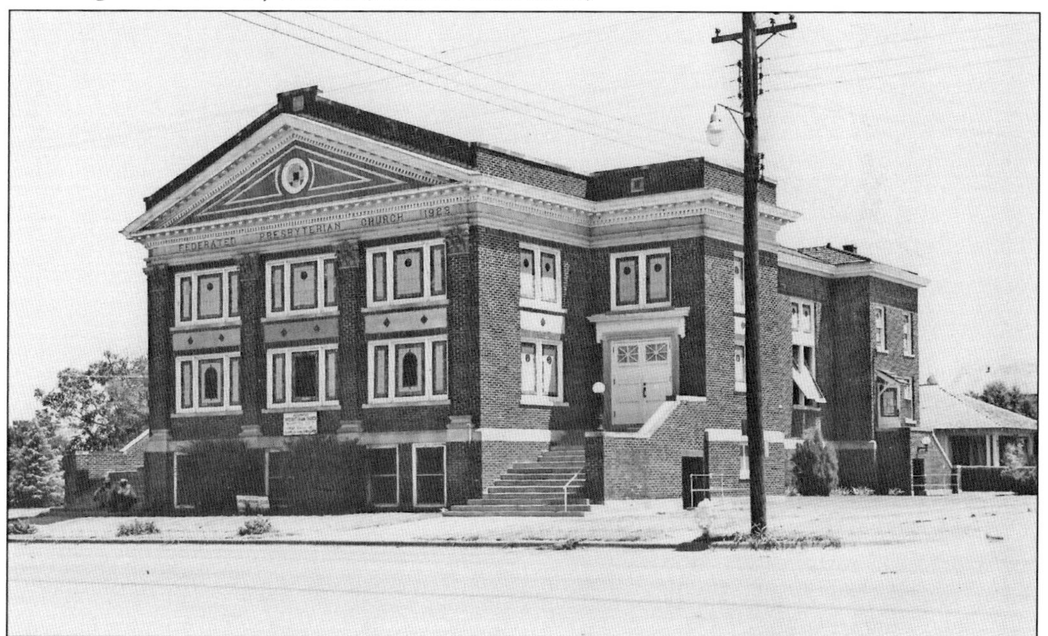

The First Federated Presbyterian Church in 1923 was located on the southeast corner of Houston and Wilbarger Streets, with Rev. E.L. Moore as pastor. This was the location of the church until 1968, when it moved to 201 Yucca Lane. It was from this building that the stained-glass windows were preserved and installed in the narthex of the present structure. (Author's collection.)

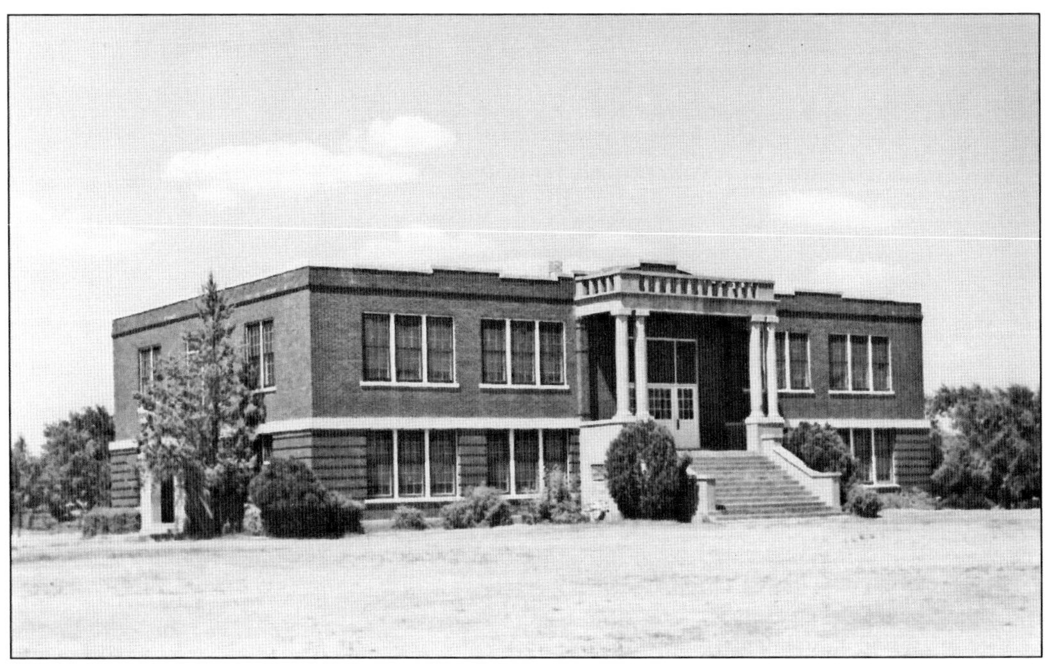

The high school at Fannin and Paradise Streets, built in 1909, was considered the first high school. It became the junior high in 1925. D.O. Fulton became the principal there in 1926. In September 1930, it was named Fannin School. It was closed in 1942 and sold to the First Baptist Church in 1949. This is now the location of the First Baptist Church Youth Center. (Author's collection.)

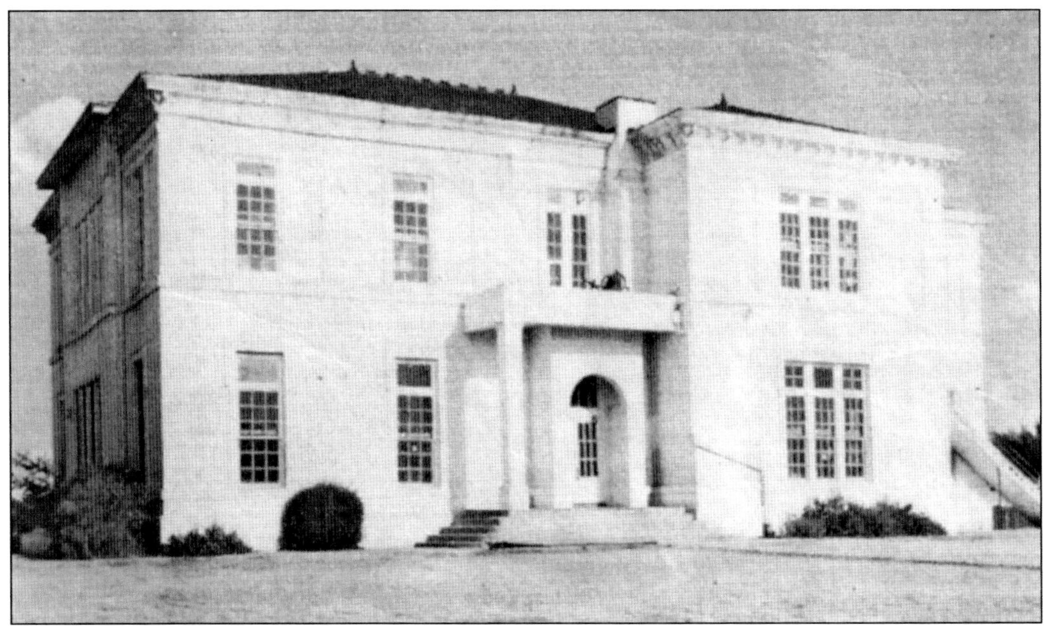

This, the second high school, located at 2203 Yamparika Street, was constructed in 1924. The plans were made for about 20 classrooms and an auditorium. This structure became the junior high, and the third high school building was constructed in 1929 and located at 2201 Yamparika Street on the east end of the two-block school campus. This high school was used until the fourth and present high school was built at 2102 Yucca Lane. (Author's collection.)

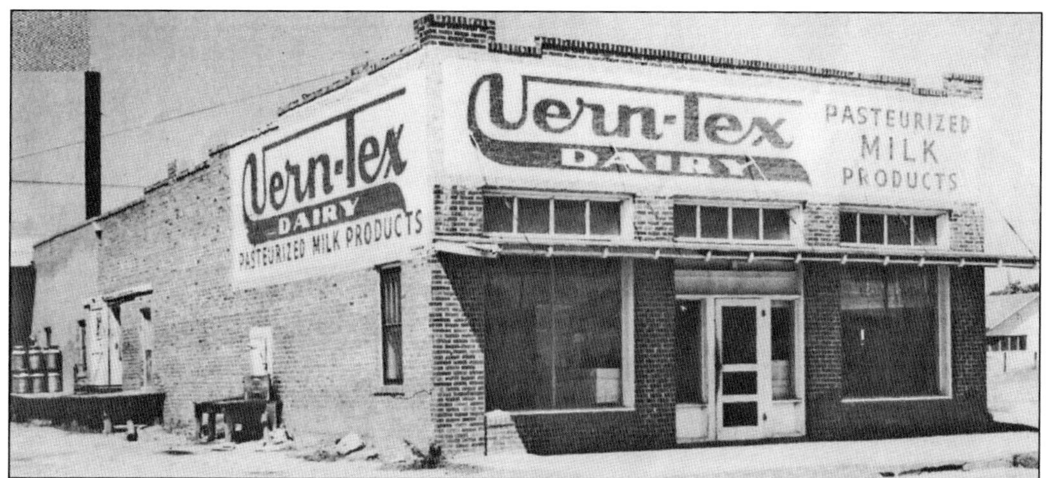

The Vern-Tex Dairy, located at 1310 Fannin Street, with the phone number 312, was established around 1929 by W.D. Curtis and W.I. Traxler. Products sold were creamery items, pasteurized milk, whipping cream, buttermilk, cottage cheese, and butter. These products were delivered to homes on request by a Vern-Tex delivery truck that would also pick up the empty milk bottles. (Author's collection.)

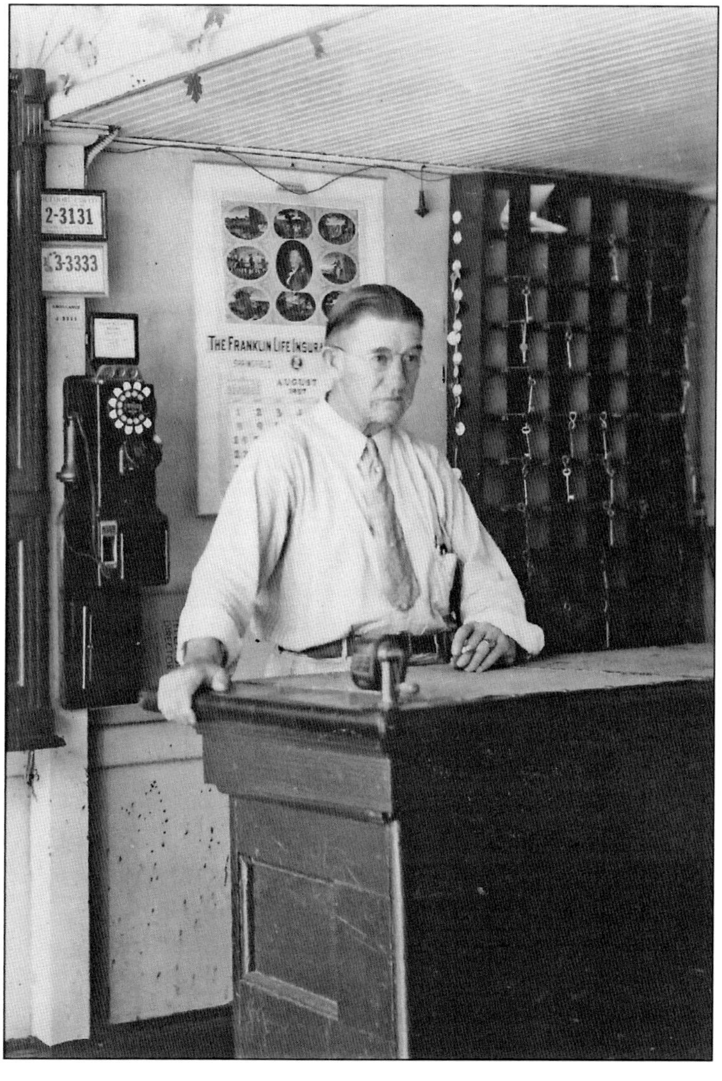

Here, in 1937, is an unidentified desk clerk at the Vernon Hotel, located at 1702 Texas Street. Originally, Mrs. A.F. Baughn owned it in the early 1930s, and its phone number was 36. In 1937, owner Ada E. Pierce, with the phone number 990, advertised the hotel as having steam heat as well as hot and cold water in each room. (Author's collection.)

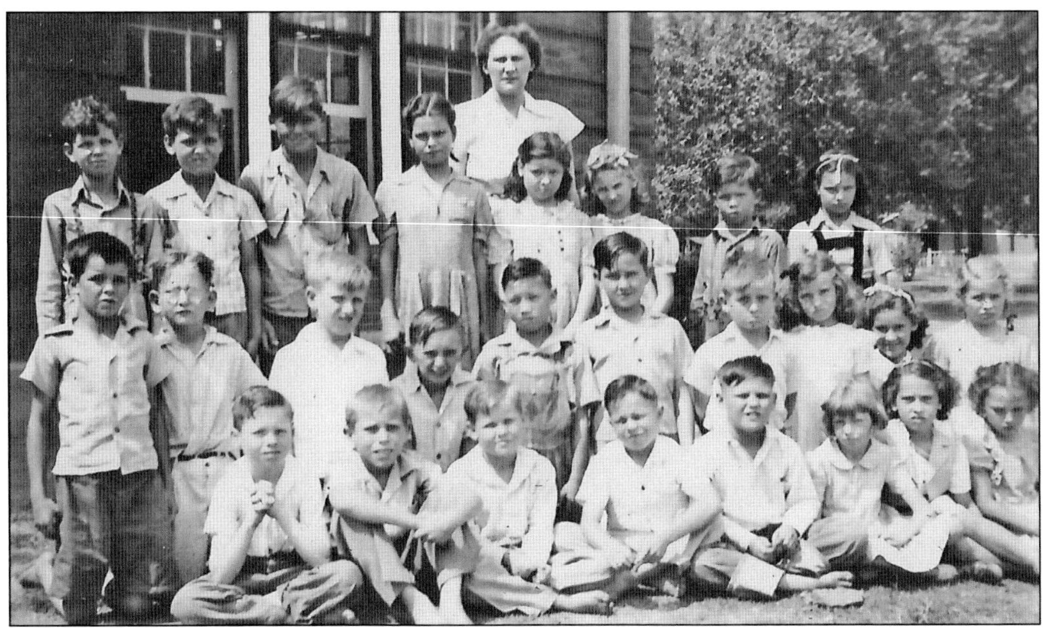

Taken for the 1944–1945 class picture at Parker Grade School in Vernon, this is one of the only known pictures of Roy Orbison at age nine. Those identified are, from left to right, (second row) Aubrey Barton, Roy Kelton Orbison, Lawrence Cox, Johnny Black, Richard Wood, Herbert Moerbe, Roy Sweeney, Joy Sweeney, and Roma Henry. The teacher-principal standing behind the students is Maggie Ruth McCaleb. (Author's collection.)

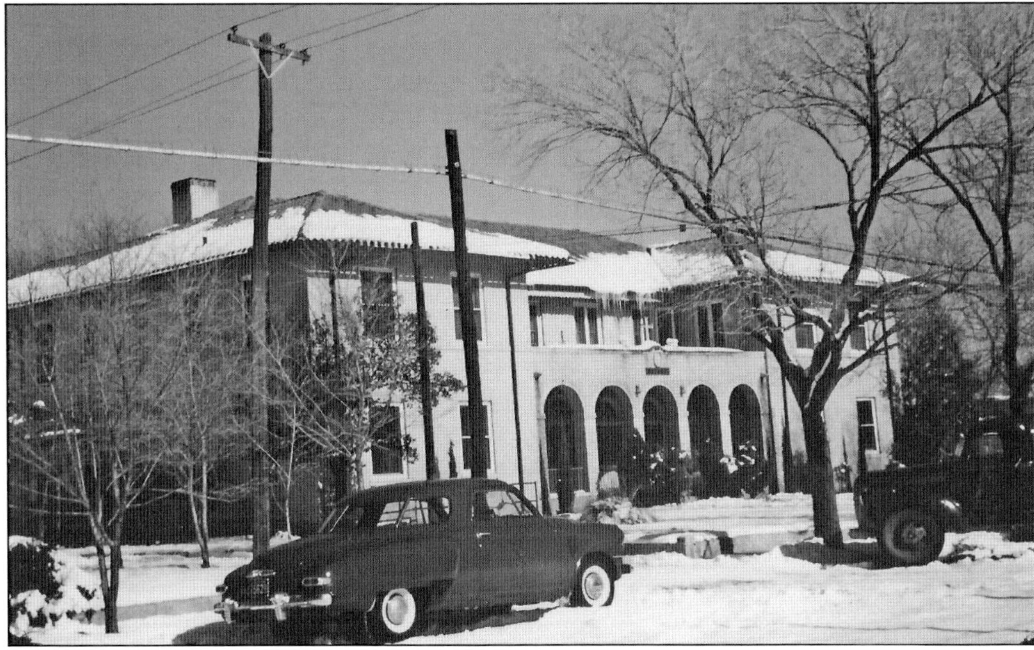

Pictured is the King Hospital and Maternity Home where Roy Orbison was born on April 23, 1936, to Orbie Lee and Nadine Orbison. This hospital would later become Christ the King Hospital. Roy Orbison's father worked for Vernon Storage and Battery Company at 1500 Cumberland Street, the location of present-day Buds Automotive and Machine Shop. (Author's collection.)

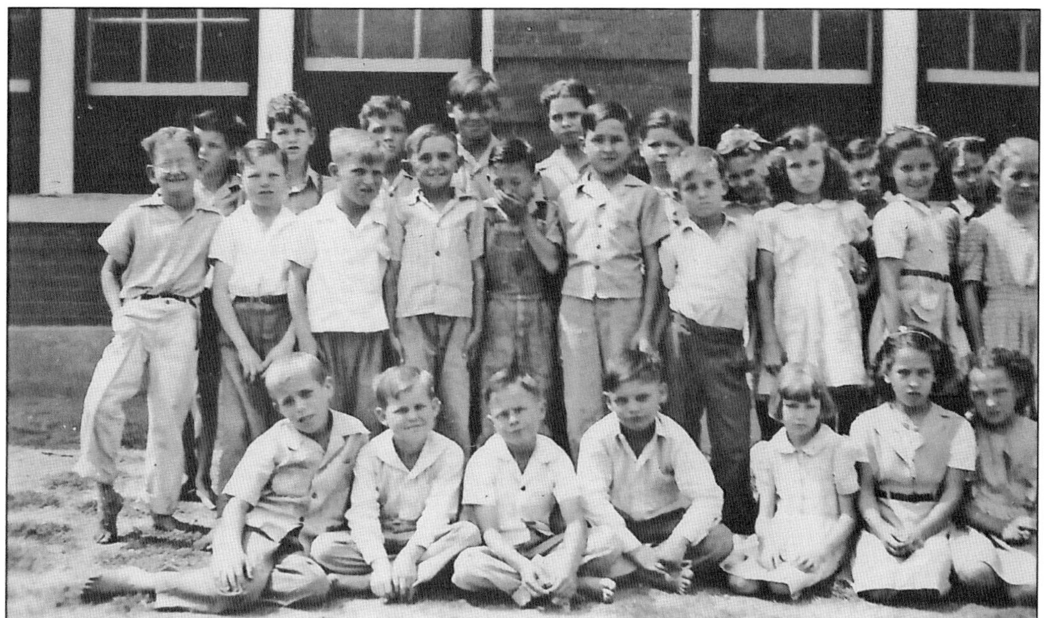

Nine-year-old Roy Orbison is shown standing at far left (second row) and barefoot on the Parker School playground. His father taught him to play guitar at age six in Vernon. His first chart hit, "Ooby Dooby," was with Sun Records in 1956. Later hits on Monument Records were "Oh, Pretty Woman," "Only the Lonely," "Running Scared," "Blue Angel," "Claudette," "Blue Bayou," "It's Over," and many, many more. (Author's collection.)

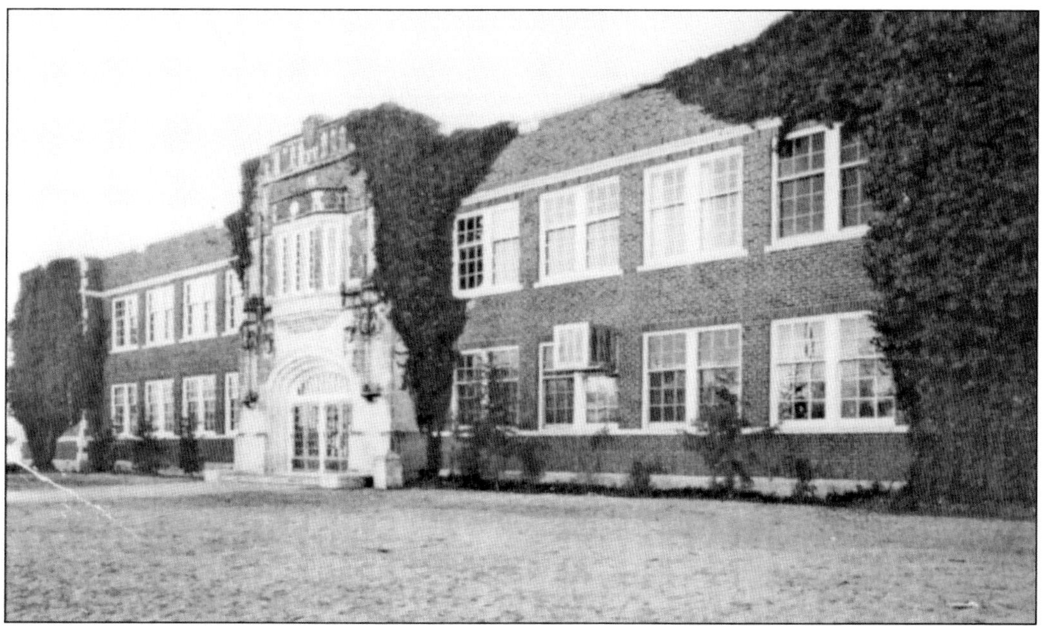

Pictured in 1939, Parker School, a two-story brick building located at 140 Violet Street, was purchased on October 16, 1916, and named in honor of school trustee B.J. Parker. Classes were held there for only the first four grades until 1966. Some of the principals were Rosa Coley, Maggie Ruth McCaleb, and Calvin Ashley, who was in that position when the school was closed. (Author's collection.)

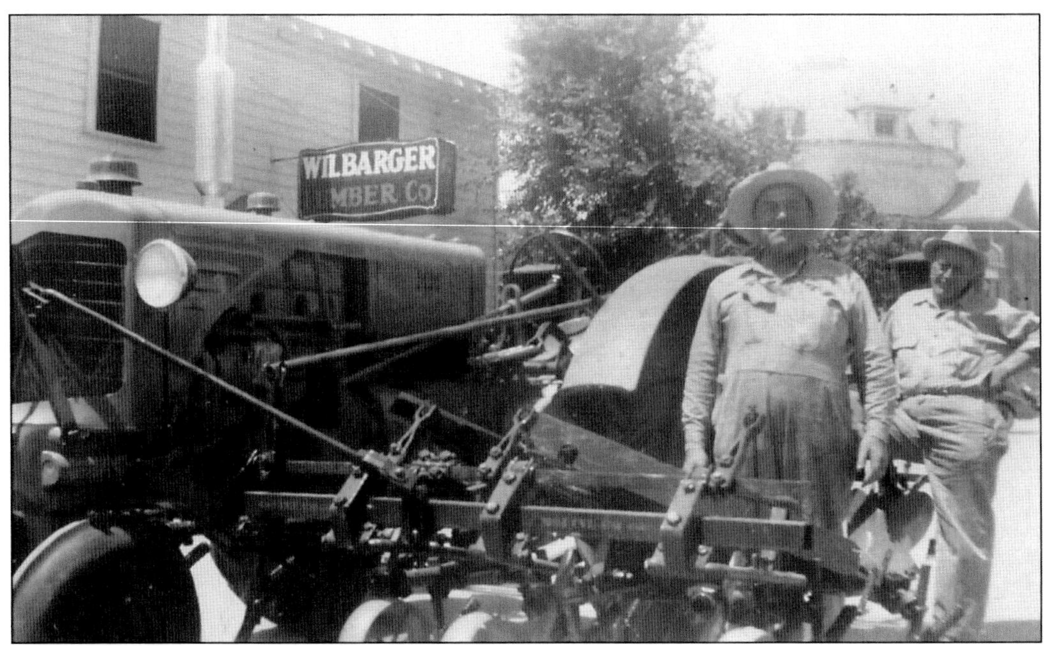

Two unidentified men are seen in front of the Wilbarger Lumber Company in 1938. The Wilbarger Lumber Company, Inc., opened in the late 1920s. R.S. Allen was the manager in 1931–1932. Located at 1925–1929 Wilbarger Street, G.T. West of Wichita Falls was president, Jenks Smith of Wichita Falls was treasurer, and C.W. Showers was vice president, secretary, and manager. (Author's collection.)

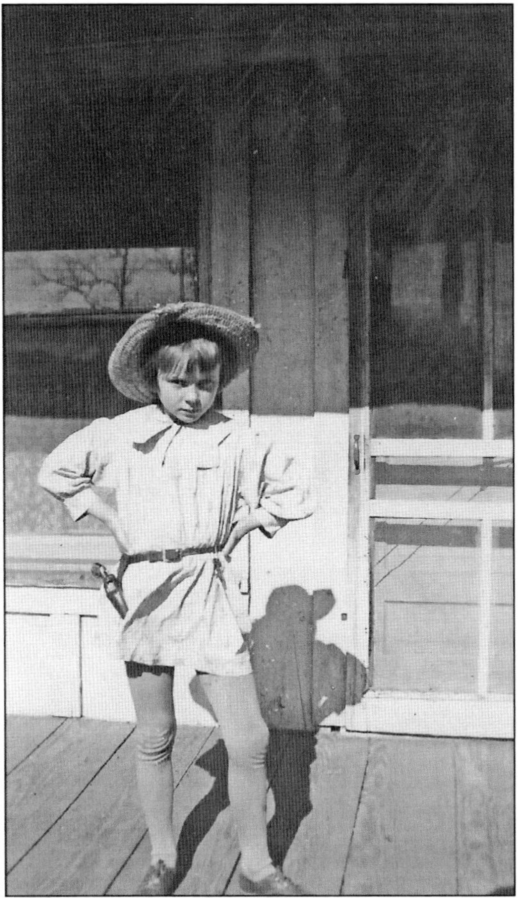

This photograph of a child dressed as a cowboy was taken by Clifton Studio, which closed in 1937. R.B. Clifton was the manager for Sink Studio until 1922, when he went into business for himself at 1728 Main Street. Being the photographer, he advertised high school portraits, Kodak finishing, and commercial photography. Other locations were 1815 Texas Street in 1929 and 3718 Wilbarger Street from 1931 to 1937. (Author's collection.)

Three

1940 to Present

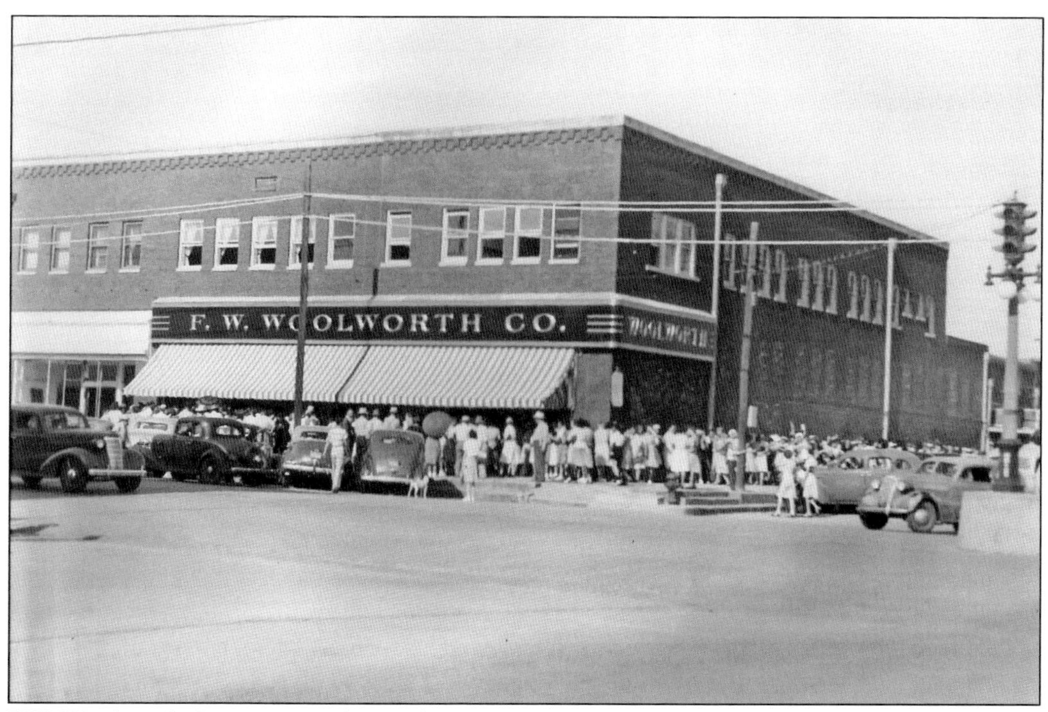

F.W. Woolworth Co. is pictured in early 1940. F.W. Woolworth, a five-and-dime store, went into business in Vernon at 1722 Pease Street in 1922, with manager J.H. Buzzell. In 1925, Leo N. Scull became manager until 1935, when R.H. Wilkerson took over that position. In 1937, R.L. Shaffer took over until this period, when C.L. Wheeler was the manager of the department store. (Author's collection.)

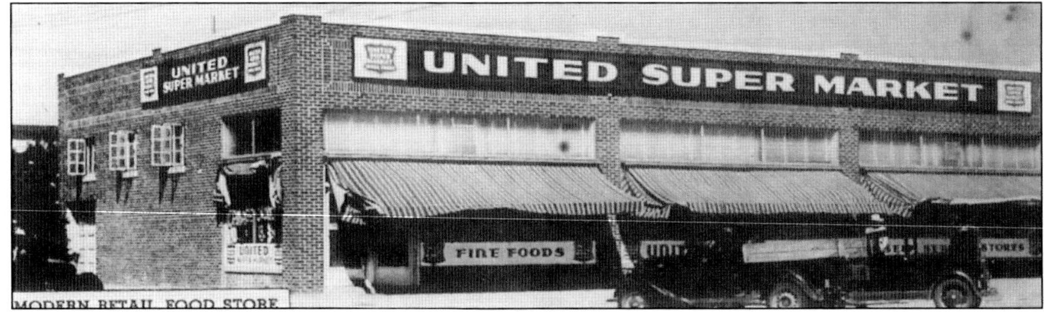

Located on the corner of Fannin and Texas Streets, this store was the second of six locations in Vernon for United Supermarket. This was a self-service store noted for its fine foods; George A. Snell was manager. In the early 1930s, Henry D. Snell established the first store in Vernon as the United Grocery Company at 1828 Pease Street. (Author's collection.)

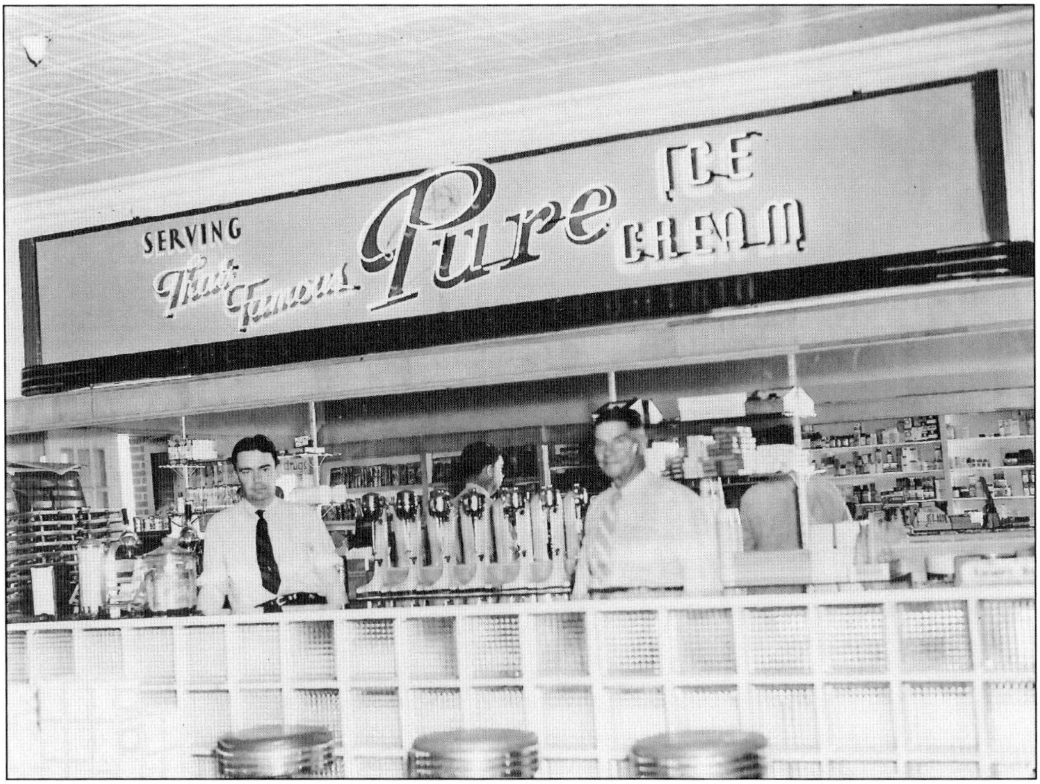

Paul Cargile, standing at left, was manager of the Pure Ice Cream Store, which was located at 1817 Texas Street in 1942. The man on the right is unidentified. The people that worked behind the counter were known as soda jerks and got the name from jerking on the handles that released the different kind of sodas or soda water. (Author's collection.)

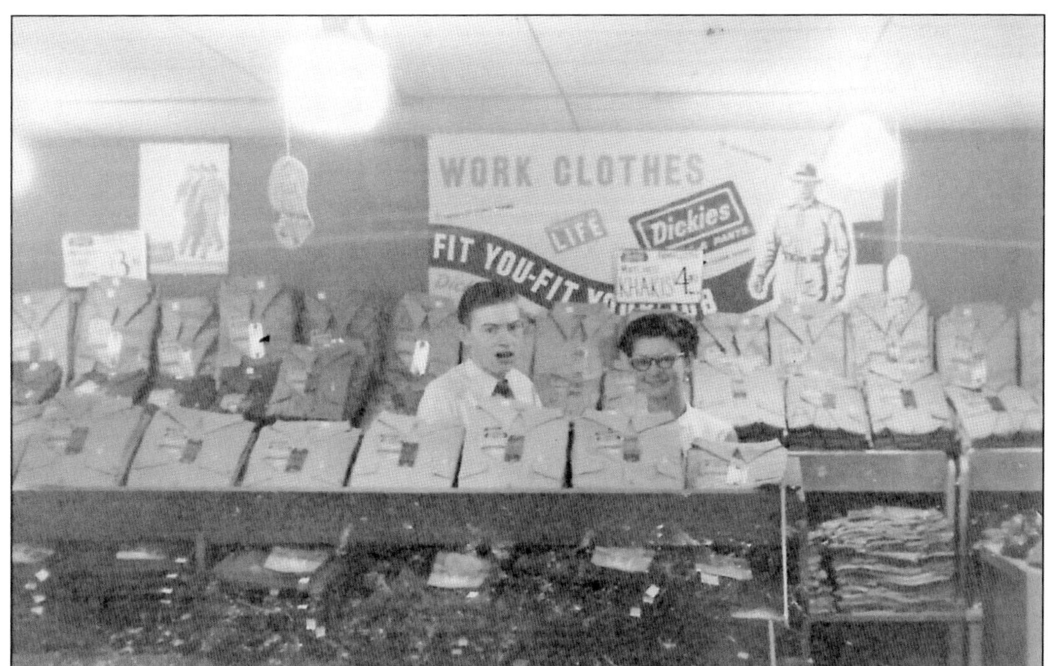

Here is the interior of Forman Department Store, located at 1526 Main Street. It sold dry goods and clothing for the whole family. Owned by Joseph and Rebecca Forman, it specialized in the sale of work clothes. Brands sold by Forman were Levi, Dickies, and Matched Khakis. (Author's collection.)

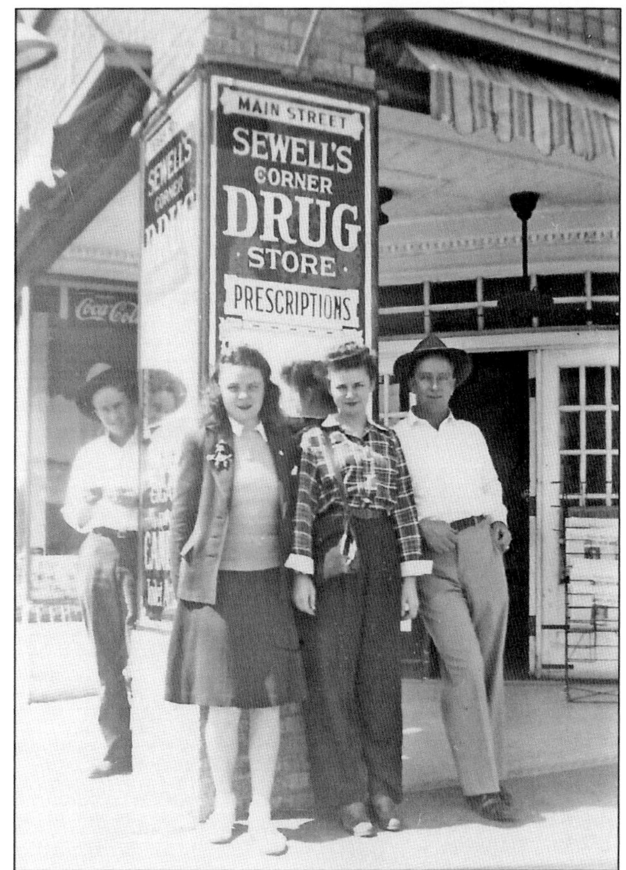

A group is seen posing for a picture on the northeast corner of Main and Texas Streets at Sewalls Corner Drug. The man on the right is Alton "Al" Skelton. Ira S. and M. Rupert Sewall were the owners of the drugstore and took pride in having A-1 prescription drug service, A-1 fountain and lunch service, and A-1 merchandise service at 1530 Main Street, with telephone number 402. (Author's collection.)

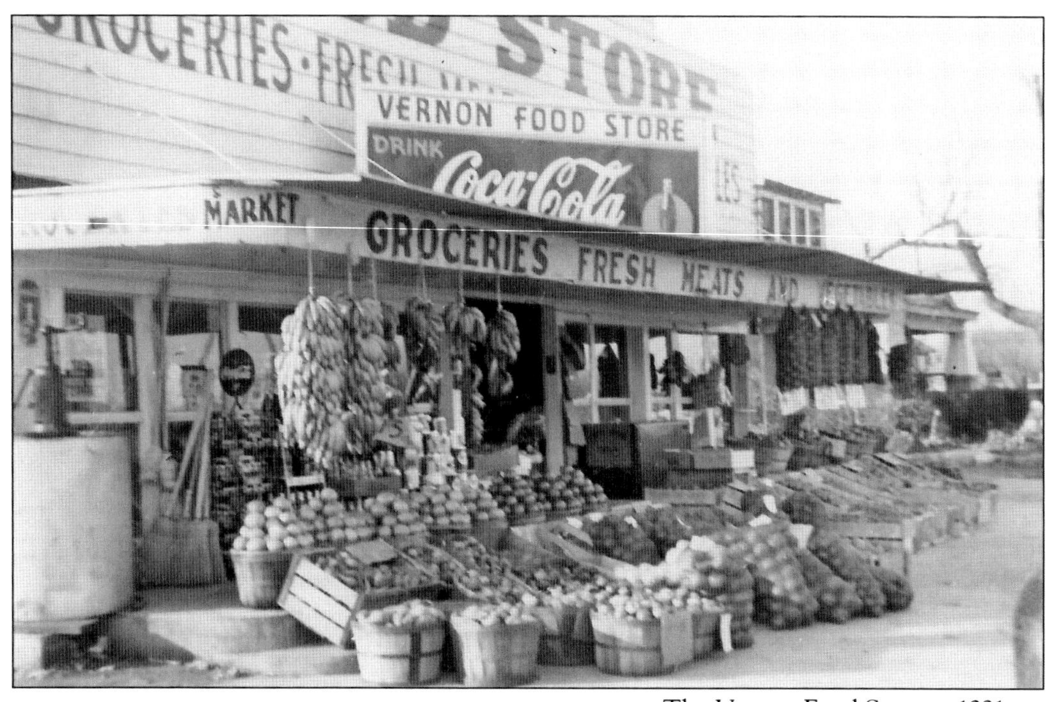

The Vernon Food Store at 1221 Wilbarger Street opened in 1939 and was managed by James R. Martin. John Caddell managed it from 1941 to 1949, when Earnest Lee Blevins took over. The Vernon Food Store carried a complete line of groceries, meats, fruits, and vegetables. Lee Blevins was manager until 1973, when Cecil Engram became manager until the store closed. (Author's collection.)

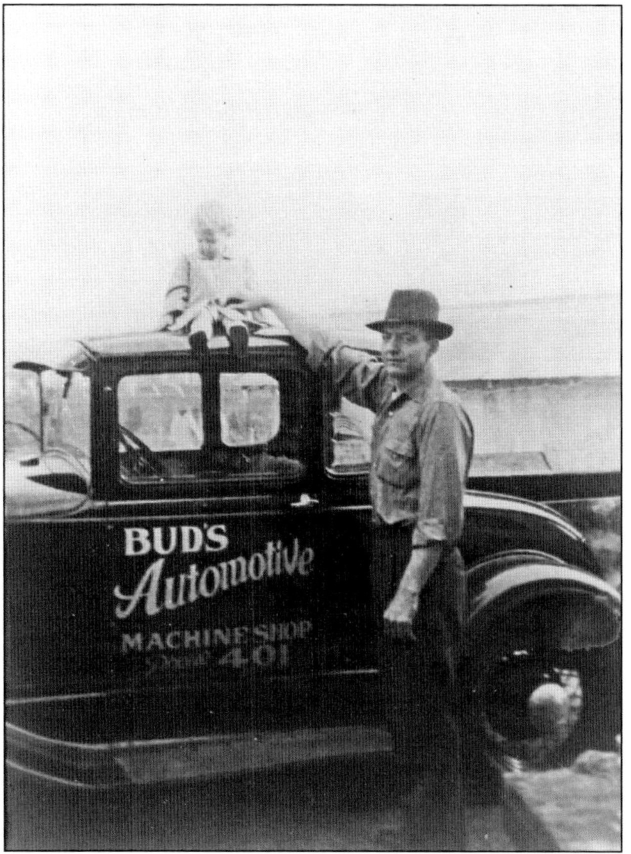

Bud's Automotive Machine Shop's delivery truck is pictured here with Bud and George Glendale McKenney, his daughter, on top. In 1939, Charles Millard "Bud" McKenney started Bud's Automotive Machine Shop at 1817 Cumberland Street. From there, he moved to a couple of different locations and in 1944 to its present location at 1500 Cumberland Street. Travis Farrar, his son-in-law, started working in the shop in July 1958. (Courtesy of Travis Farrar.)

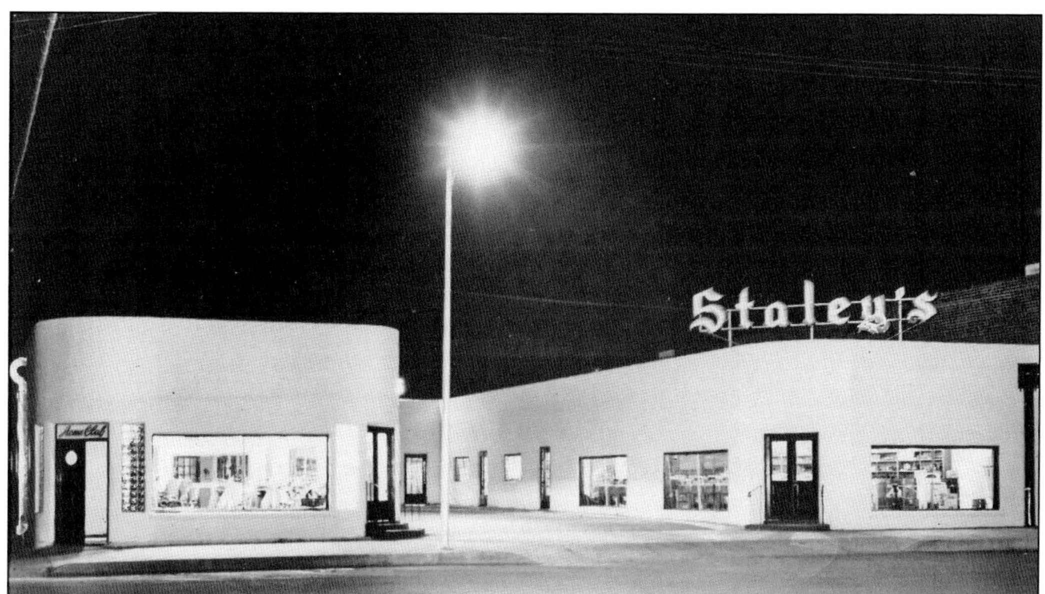

Staley Electric, pictured in 1940, was established in 1929 at corner of Marshall Street and Main Street. Owners Theron C. and C.R. Staley were builders of neon signs and sold quality outdoor signs, motors, appliances, fixtures, and lighting. They were also authorized Maytag dealers and offered repair service on all makes as well as repaired gas engines. (Author's collection.)

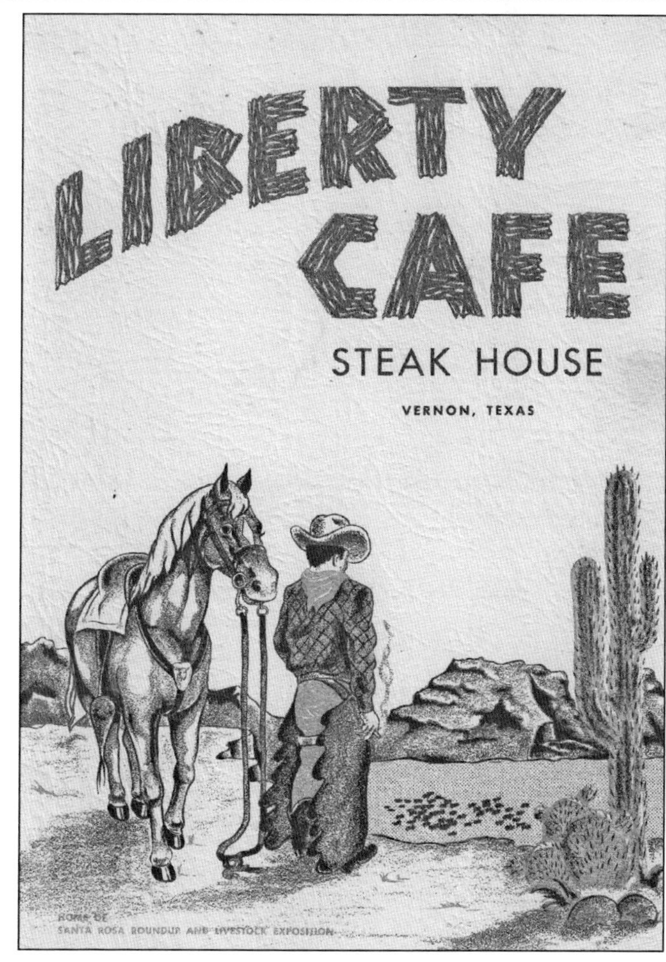

This is the breakfast menu from the Liberty Café in 1952. George Zelios began as the manager of the Liberty Café in 1929. In the early 1930s, George and his brother Jesse became the owners of the café, located at 1706 Pease Street. In 1940, George and Myrtel Zelios became the owners of an air-conditioned dining room for clubs and dinner parties at 1819 Wilbarger Street. (Author's collection.)

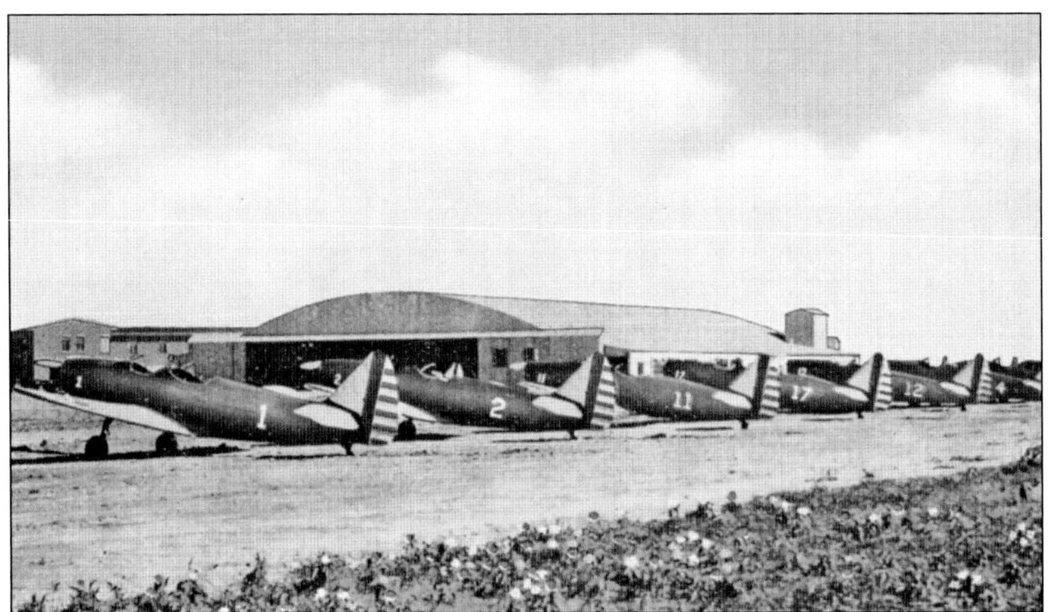

Trainer planes are lined up on the flight line at Victory Field, which was a primary training base for Army Air Force pilots. The field's beginning goes back to June 1941 when 10 commercial flight instructors began their training as primary instructors near Fort Worth. They finished their special training and came to Vernon in August 1941. (Author's collection.)

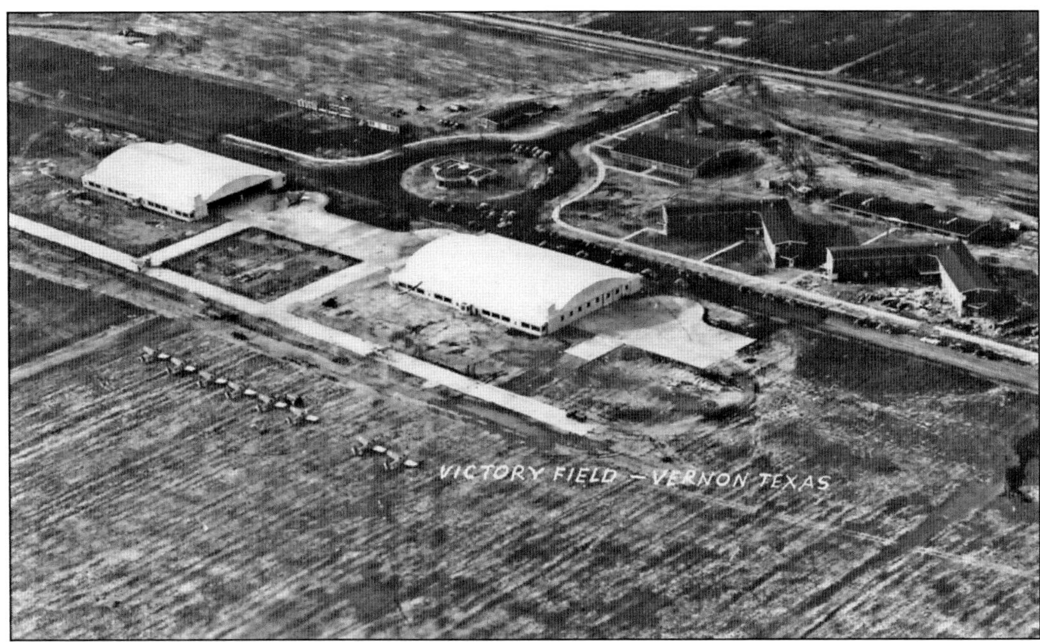

This aerial view of Victory Field shows two white airplane hangars and the Administration Building in the circle at the top. The buildings at top right in a V-shape are the barracks. The base began with one hangar, no barracks, 35 instructors, 48 cadets, and 25 aircraft (PT-Fairchilds with 175-horsepower Ranger engines). It grew to 122 instructors, 175 aircraft, and about 40 cadets for each class. (Author's collection.)

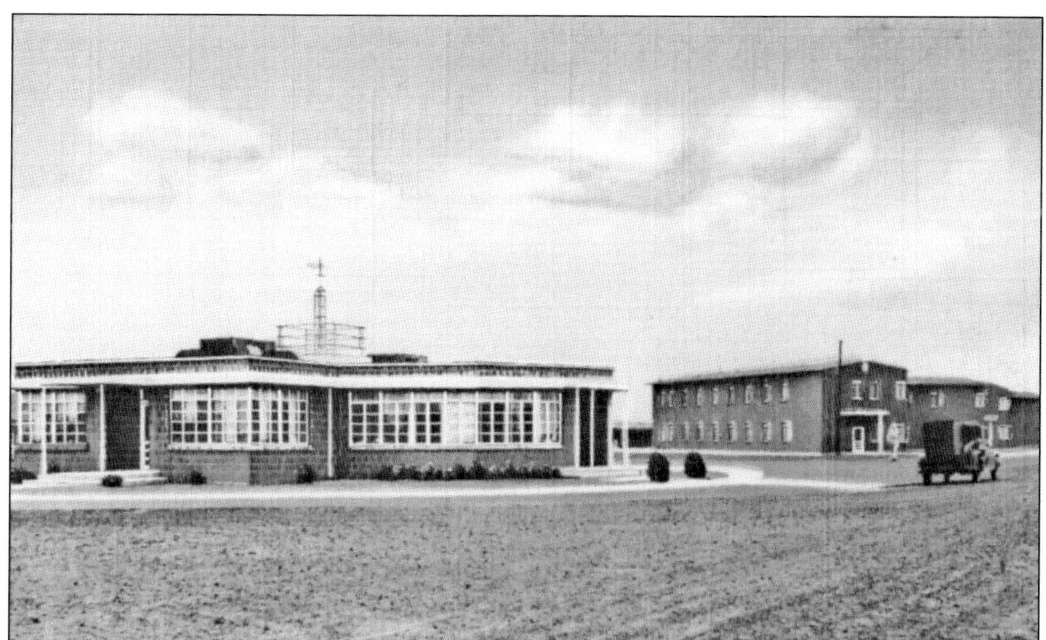

The Victory Field Administration Building is at left in the picture above, and the barracks are to the right. The first 47 cadets arrived and began training on October 4, 1941. They were housed at the Wilbarger Hotel until the barracks were completed. The hotel was also home of the Cadet Club, formed by Vernon citizens. The base was closed in October 1944 because of the excessive number of Air Force pilots. (Author's collection.)

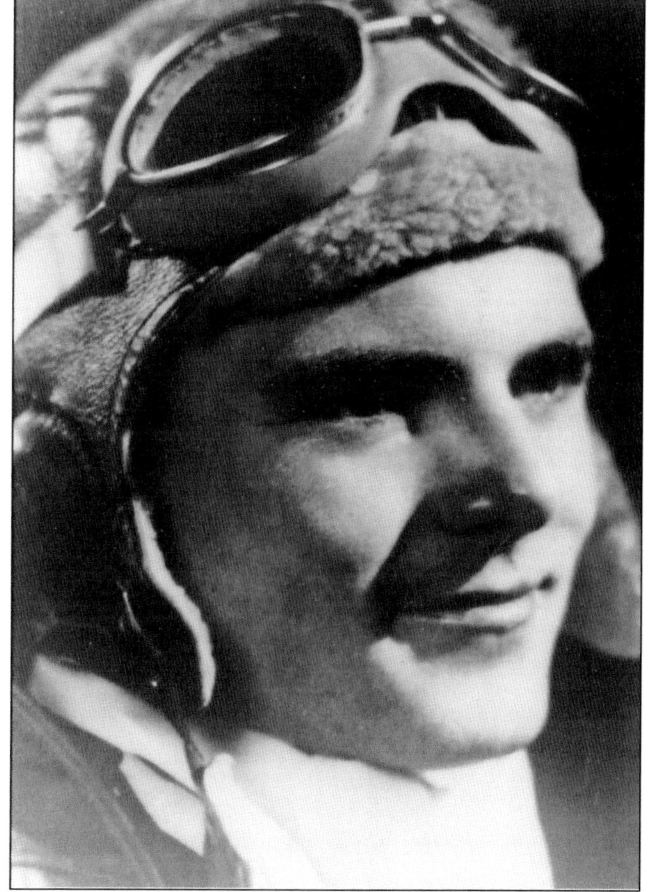

H.D.W. "Hamp" Naylor is seen in his flight gear while serving in the US Navy during World War II. In 1969, Hamp succeeded his father as mayor and equaled the record for the longest tenure of a Vernon mayor. Hamp was instrumental in having the hangar moved from Victory Field to the Wilbarger County Airport. Another hangar from Victory Field was moved to the high school on Yamparika Street for a gymnasium. (Courtesy of Karen Gfeller.)

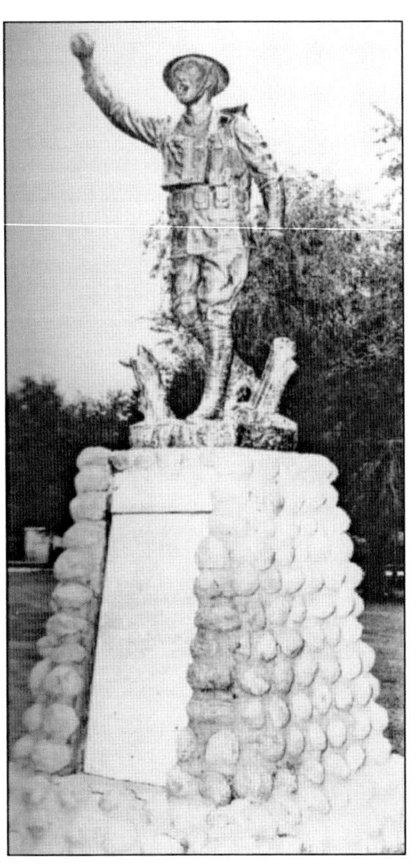

A memorial doughboy statue was unveiled December 14, 1926, on the courthouse square but was later moved to Allingham Park. The statue was later moved back to the courthouse where it stands today. The bronze soldier holds a grenade in his right hand; his left hand holding a rifle was missing until 2012, when it was replaced. (Author's collection.)

Alvey Conoco was located at 1528 Wilbarger Street. Walter Vance Alvey Sr., owner and operator, is pictured standing on the right. This was a full-service gas station. In the background is the Dabney and Harvey Chevrolet auto dealership. The last known business in this location was a tire shop, owned by Earnest Bledsoe in the 1970s. (Author's collection.)

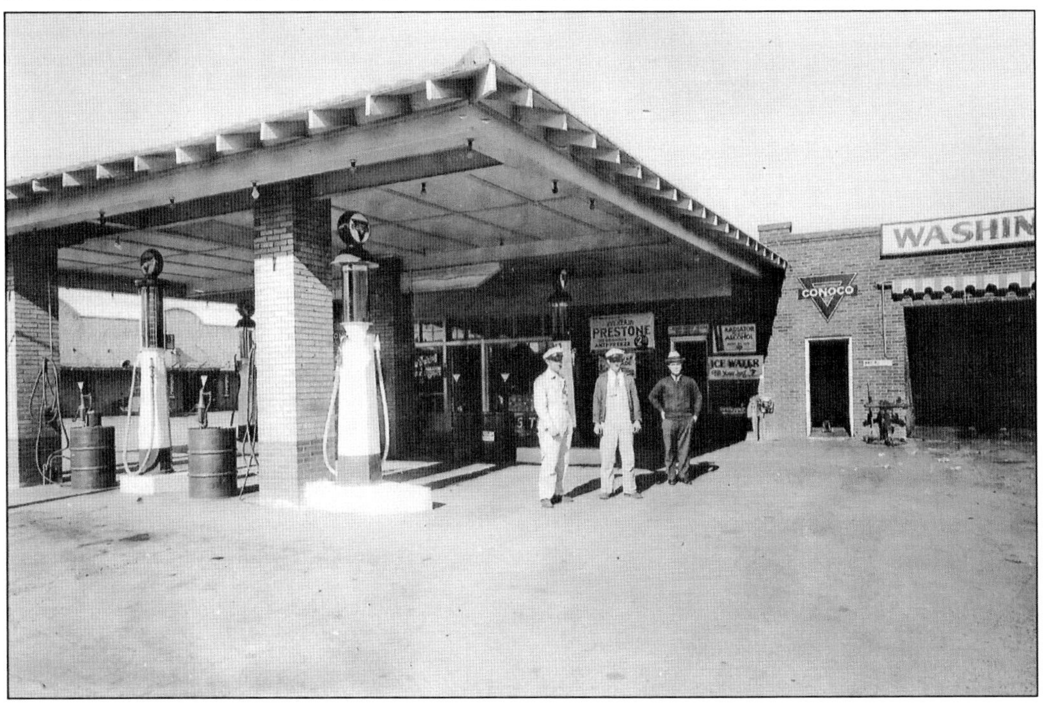

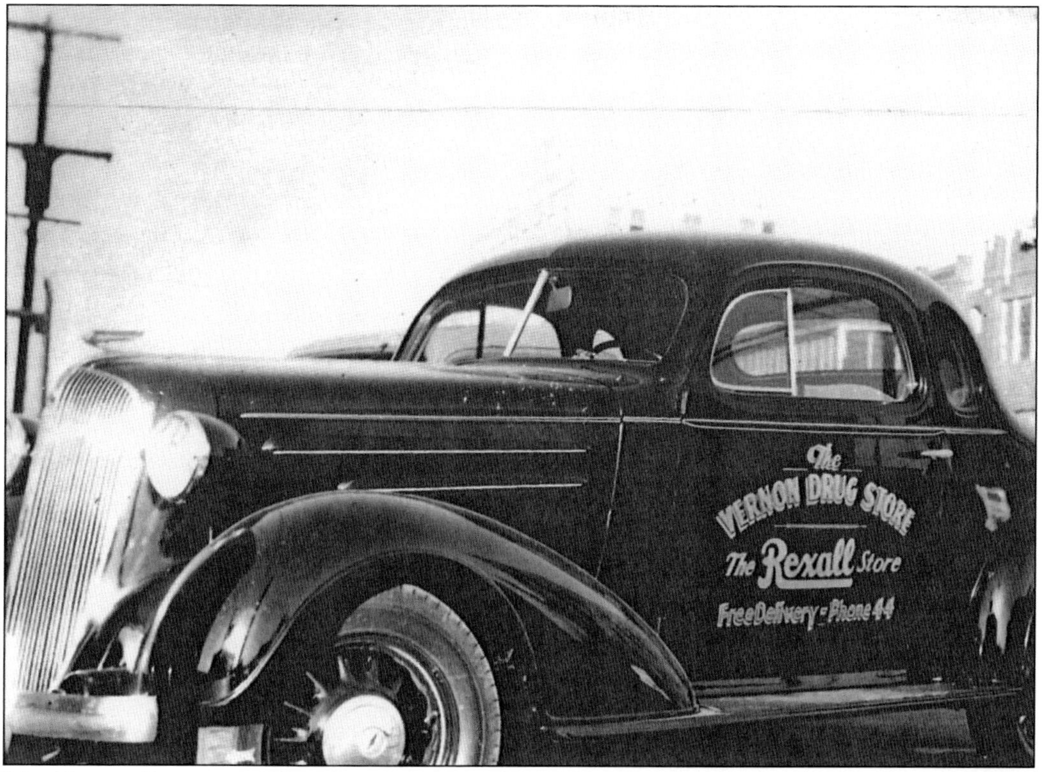

The Vernon Drugstore delivery car sitting in front of the drugstore, located at 1704 Main Street around 1938, advertises, "Free Delivery Phone 44." T.M. Fergeson and J.H. Pendleton established the Vernon Drugstore; the partnership dissolved in 1897. By early 1902, the Vernon Drugstore was owned by Georg S. Hardin, R.O. Brown, and J.J. McGaughy. (Courtesy of Jo Jones.)

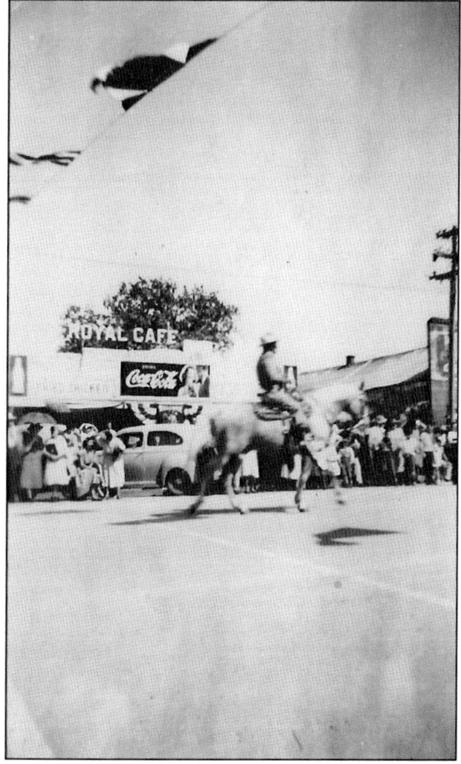

This picture taken at the first rodeo parade in 1946 shows the Royal Café in the background, owned by Clyde Rich. Located at 1703 Cumberland Street, the café was originally established by G.Z. Riedel in 1937. The rider on the Palomino horse is E. Paul Waggoner, the owner of the rodeo grounds. (Author's collection.)

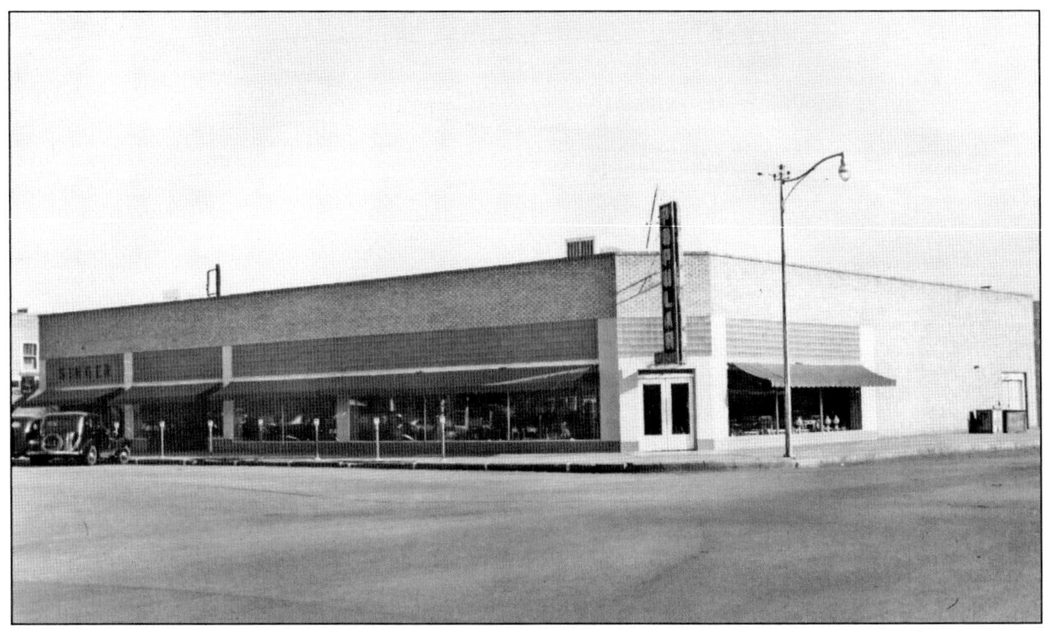

Popular Furniture was established around 1946 by William B. Marks, with J. Leslie Swim as manager. Located at the corner of Cumberland and Texas Streets, Popular Furniture sold furniture, household appliances, and carpet. This furniture store was in this location through the 1980s but is now vacant. The Singer Sewing Machine Company to the left of Popular Furniture was located at 1714 Texas Street, with M.G. Walker as manager. (Author's collection.)

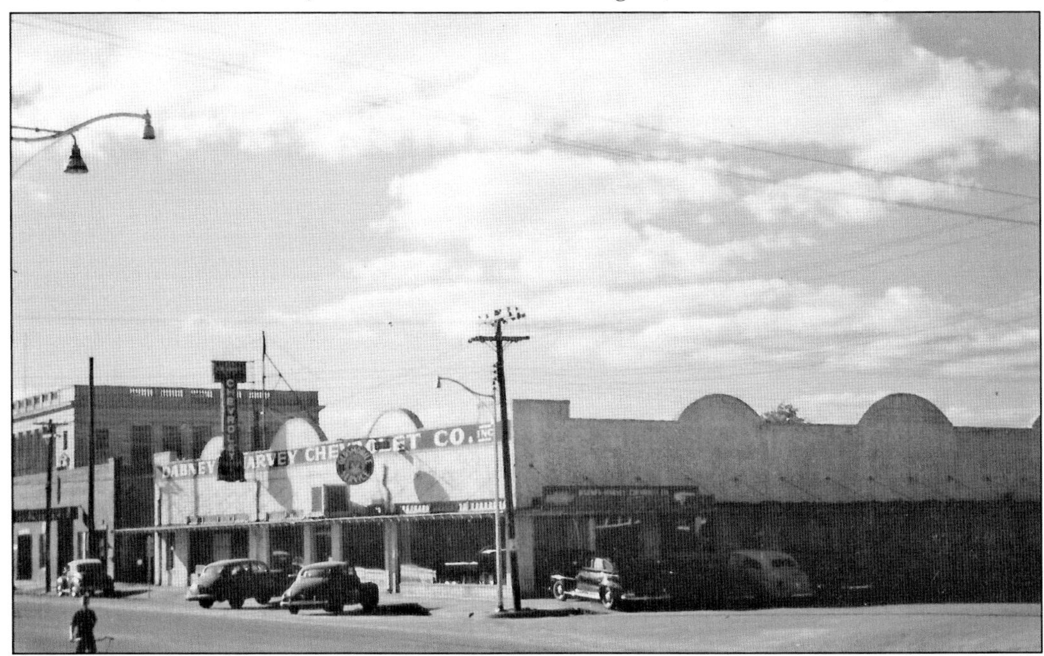

Dabney-Harvey Chevrolet Company, Inc., in 1941 was located at 1608 Wilbarger Street and established by Fred T. Dabney, president, and Otis E. Harvey, secretary and treasurer. This was the location for the sale and service of Oldsmobile and Chevrolet and also for the storage, repairing, washing, and lubricating of automobiles. (Author's collection.)

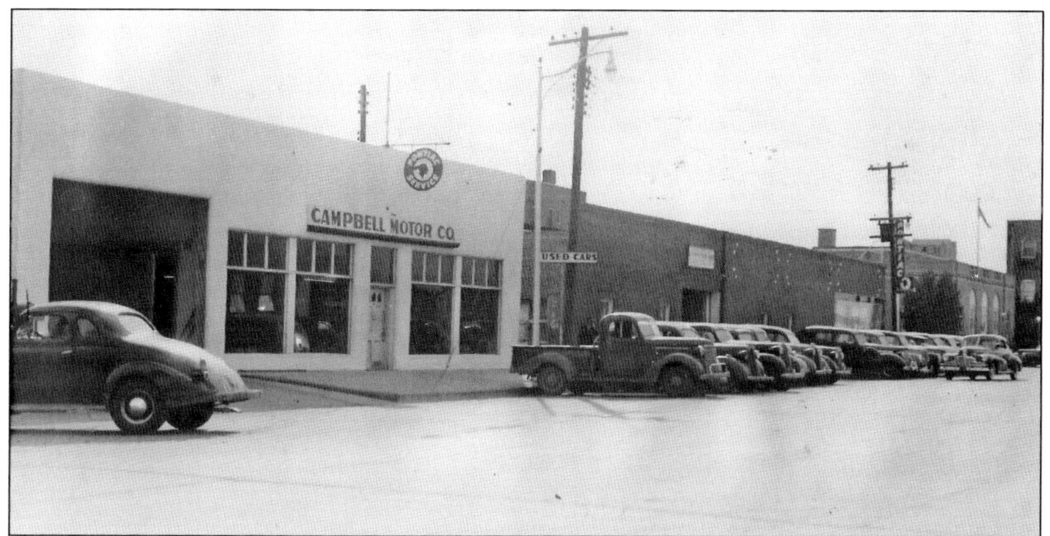

In 1946, Campbell Motor Company at 1613 Cumberland Street was owned by Clarence L. Campbell and sold Packard cars and White trucks. By 1948, Campbell Motor Company had become a Pontiac automobile dealership with the service department in the rear. Looking south is the post office on the corner of Cumberland and Texas Streets. (Author's collection.)

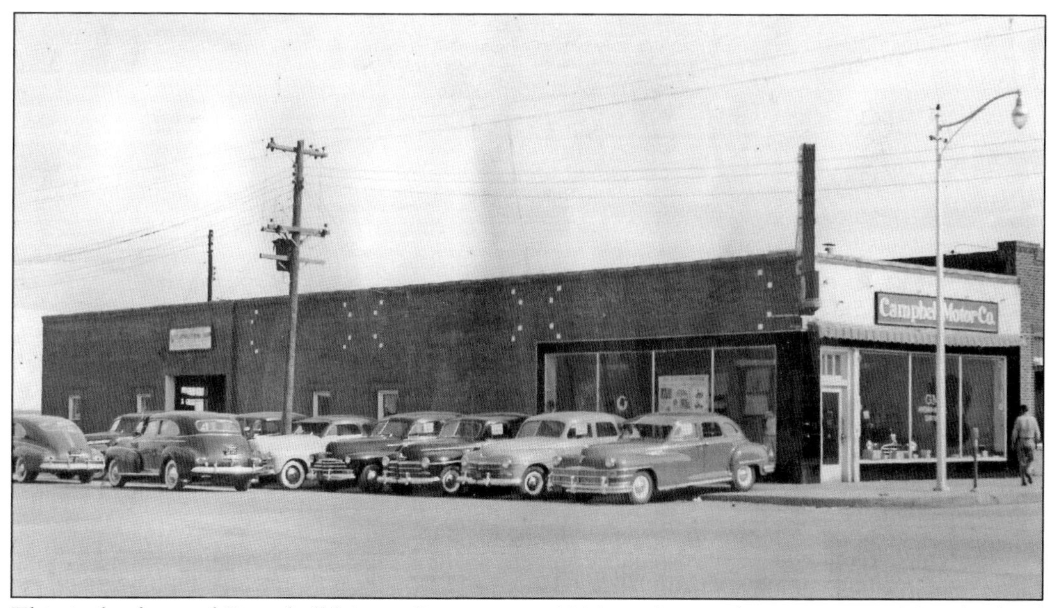

This is the front of Campbell Motor Company in 1946 on the northwest corner of Cumberland and Texas Streets, with the window of the showroom facing Cumberland Street. The mechanic shop and an upholstery shop were at the back entrance. In the early 1950s, Campbell Motor Company moved to 1608 Wilbarger Street. (Author's collection.)

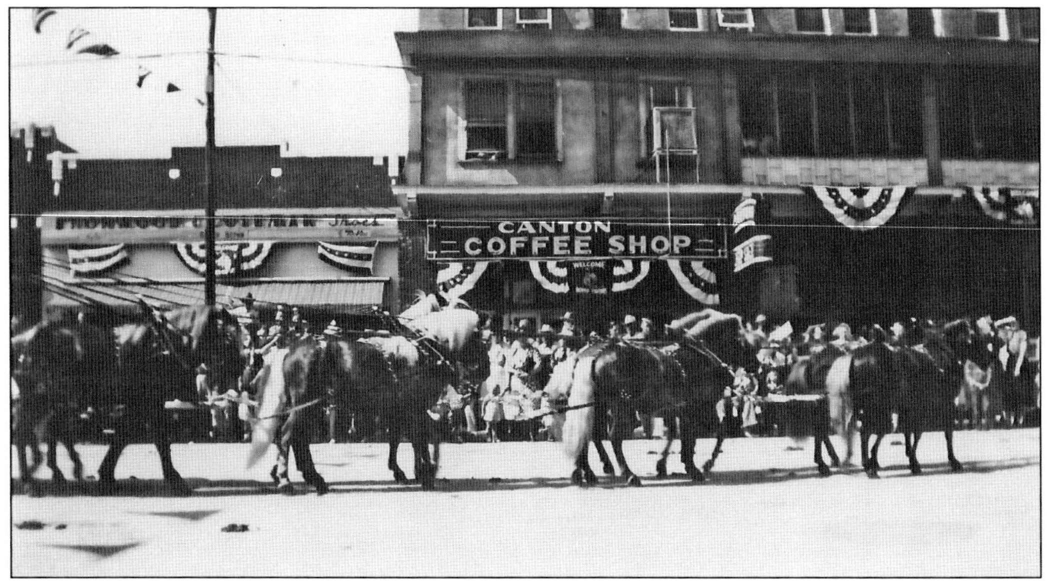

In one of the first rodeo parades, a team of miniature ponies is seen pulling a coach in front of Norwood & Colman's Shoe Store, located on the left at 1710 Pease Street. Ray Colman was the manager and sold Buster Brown shoes. To the right is the Canton Coffee Shop, which later became the Canton Café. Henry Huie established the Canton in 1944 at 1706 Pease Street. (Author's collection.)

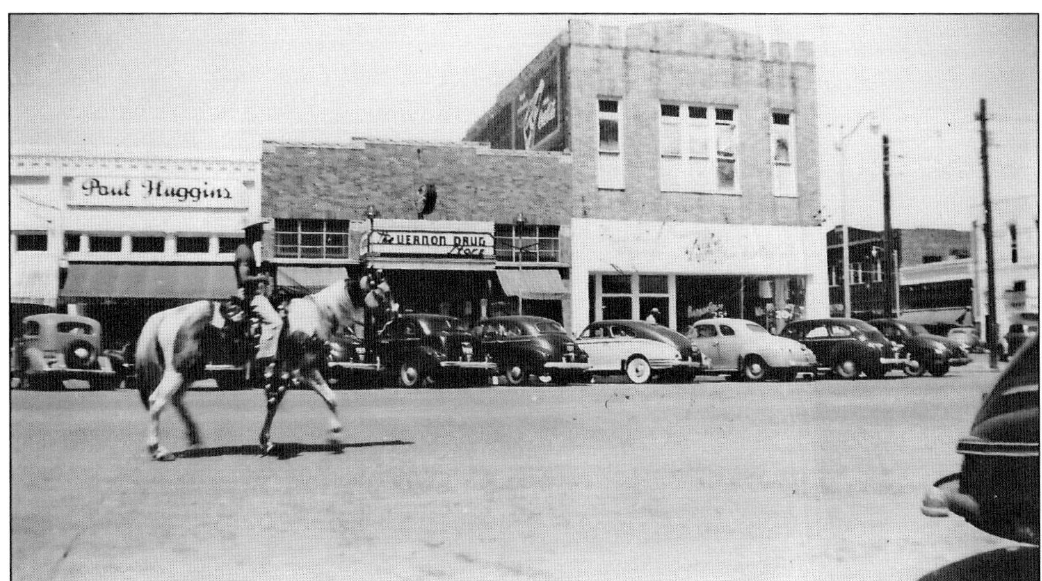

Bobby Hershman is riding a horse named Tarzan in front of Paul Huggins, a men's clothing store, located at 1708 Main Street. Also pictured are the Vernon Drugstore, a Rexall drugstore at 1704 Main Street, owned by R.O. Brown and Ed S. Malone and the Pure Ice Cream Store at 1817 Texas Street, managed by Paul Cargile. (Author's collection.)

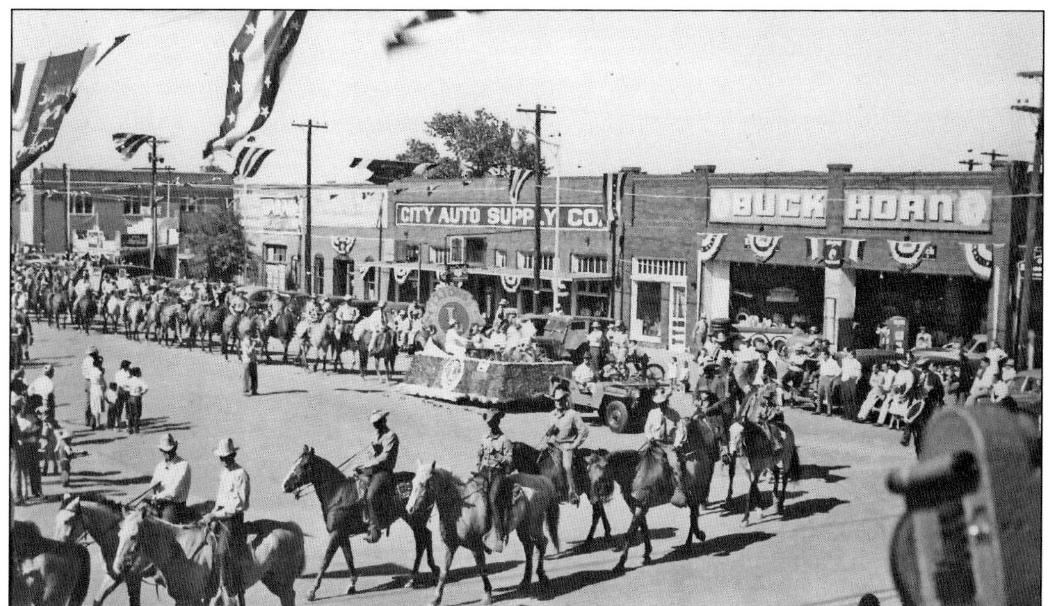

This picture of the first rodeo parade in 1946 gives a great view of the Buck Horn station on the corner of Wilbarger and Cumberland Streets. It was established in 1937 by T.W. Danial as the Buck Horn super service station. In 1946, owned by Coen C. Neff, it was called the Buck Horn service station and garage. To the left is the City Auto Supply Co., and the last large building to the left is the Carnegie City Library. (Author's collection.)

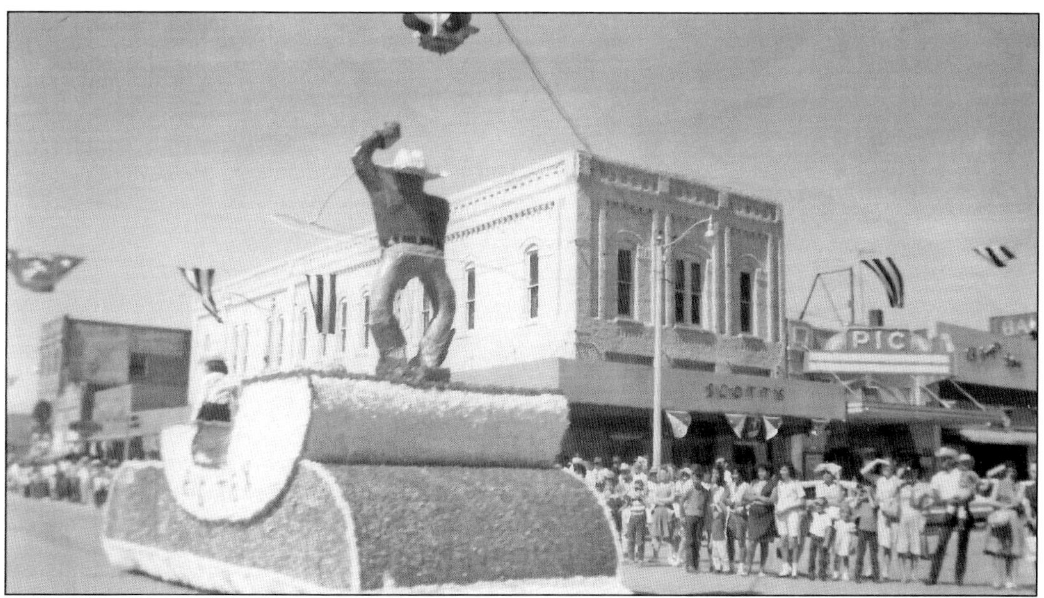

The float "Big Tex" barely clears the traffic light as it heads up Wilbarger Street in an early parade. The old Herring National Bank Building is to the right, with Scotty's Studio on the first floor. Claude H. Wainscott owned the studio located at 1820 Wilbarger Street that featured photographs of distinction and commercial photography. (Author's collection.)

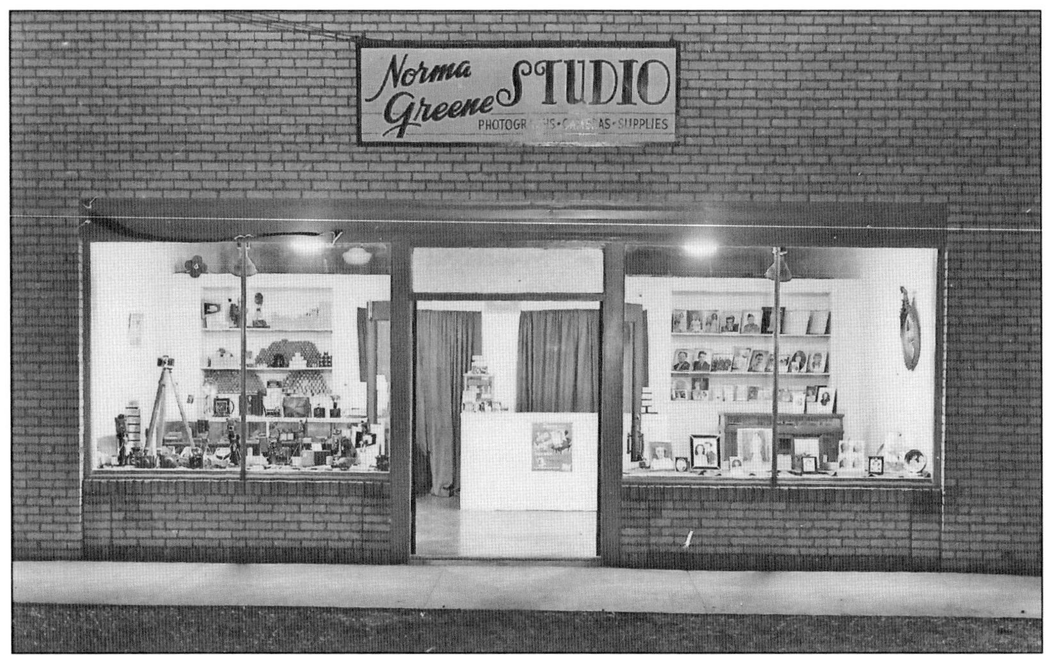

In 1944, Norma Greene was employed at Whit's Camera Shop, located at 1711 Wilbarger Street. In late 1945, Norma Greene established this store at 1826 Pease Street, specializing in developing, printing, enlarging, portraits, and all camera supplies. In 1947, she moved the business to its last location at 2427 Main Street. (Author's collection.)

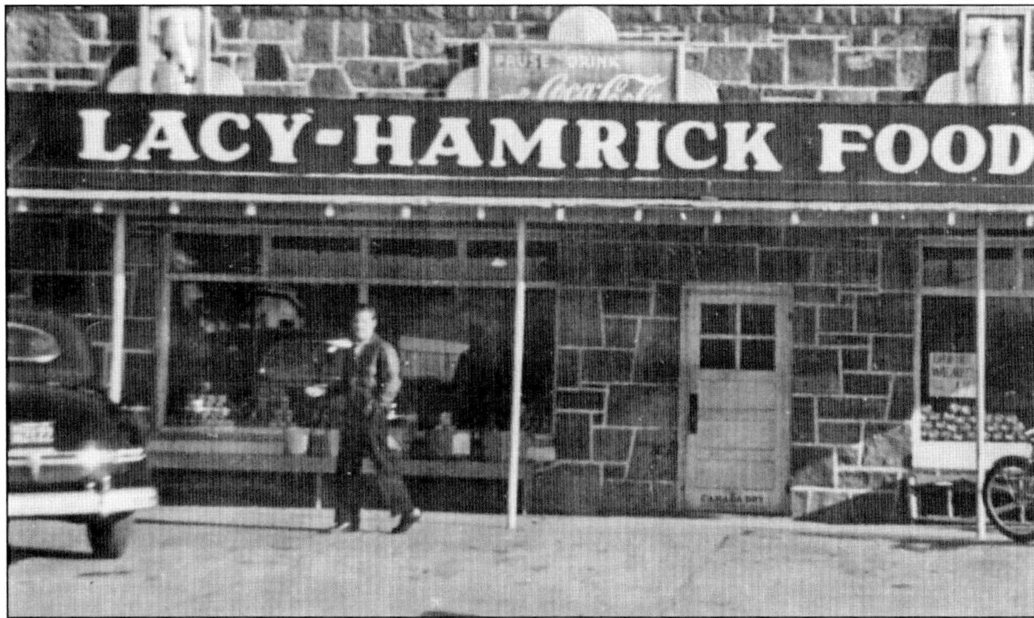

By 1944, William Hamrick was already in the grocery business, and Edward Lacy was a salesman for White Swan. In 1946, Edward Sterling Lacy and William D. Hamrick established the Lacy-Hamrick Grocery & Market, located at 3100 Wilbarger Street, in this old rock building, erected by Fred Schmoker in 1938. In 1961, this grocery business became Cashway Foods, owned by Edward S. Lacy. In 1963, it became Joe's Food Store. (Courtesy of Joe and Betty Ermis.)

Pictured is an unidentified girl in front of the Hill Hotel, located at 1603 Mesquite Street in 1946. Mrs. Narsie Hill was the owner of two hotels, the Hill Hotel on Mesquite Street and the Crystal Hotel at 1612 Texas Street. From 1959 to its closing in the late 1960s, the Hill Hotel's manager was Cora Reese. (Author's collection.)

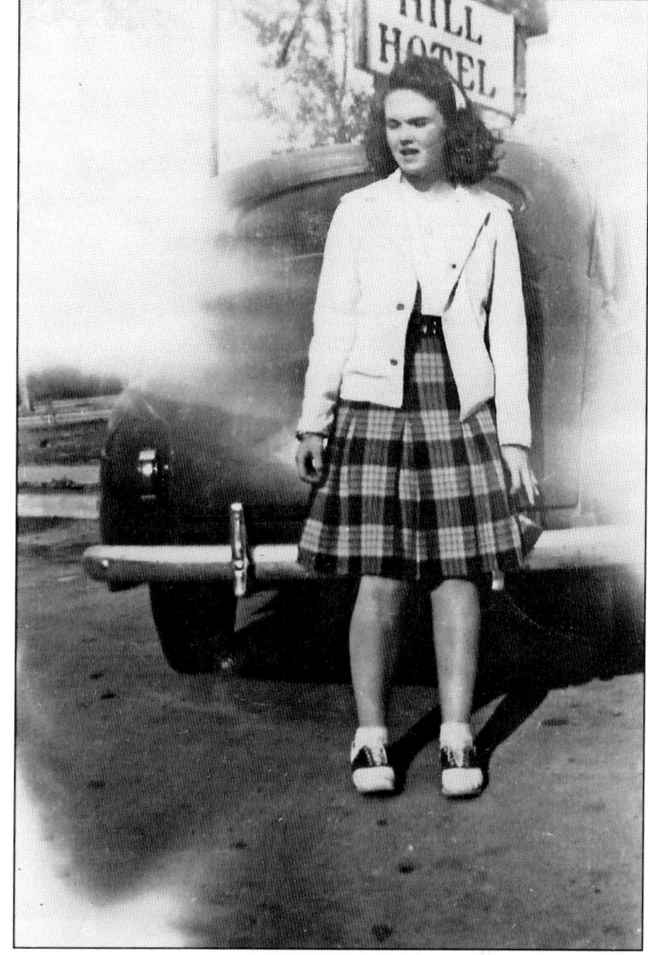

The Pure Ice Cream Store is pictured as it looked in 1946 at 1700 Main Street, its new location on the northwest corner of Main and Pease Streets. It was originally located at 1817 Texas Street in 1942. Paul Cargile was manager at both locations. On the store window, it says a banana split is 25¢. (Author's collection.)

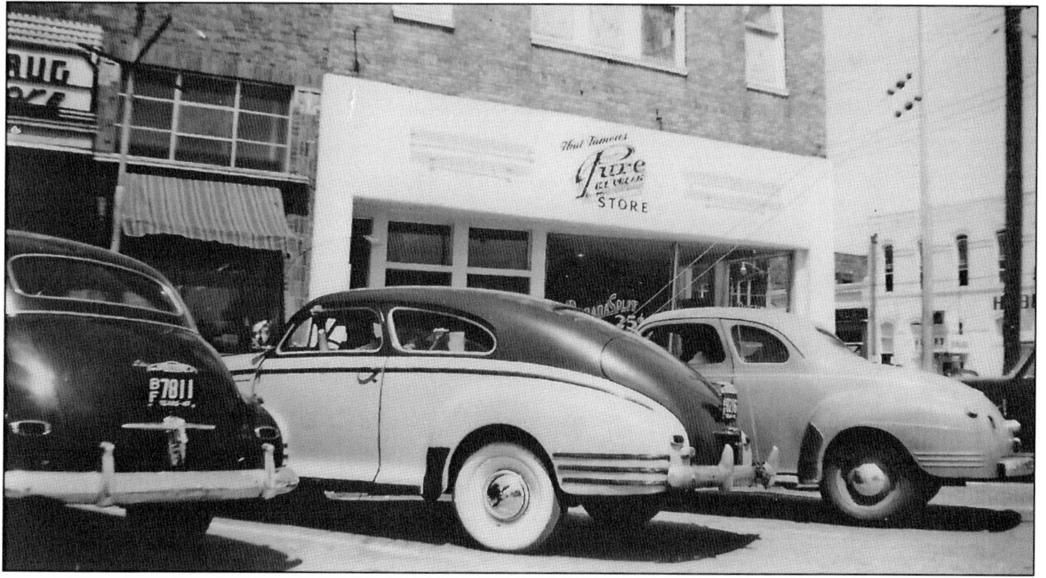

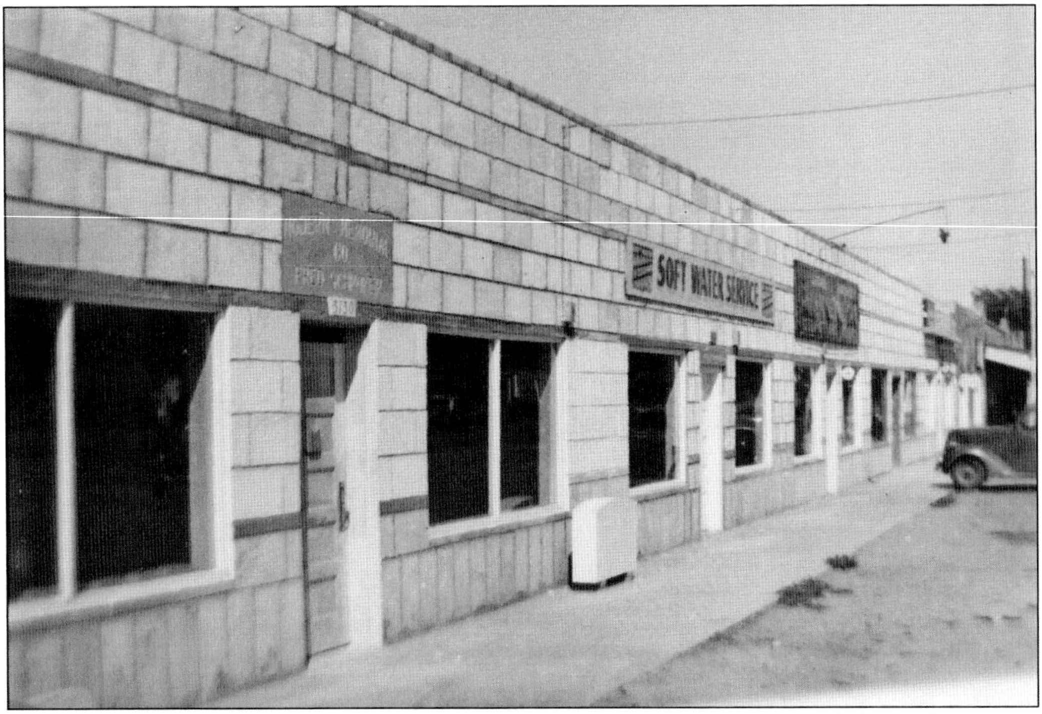

This row of block buildings, constructed by Fred Schmoker, housed many different businesses in 1946. The first one is the office of Modern Memorial at 3130 Wilbarger Street. It made headstones and monuments and was owned by Fred Schmoker, with Earnest Schmoker as the art designer. Culligan Soft Water, owned by A.E. Shipley, was located at 3122 Wilbarger Street. (Author's collection.)

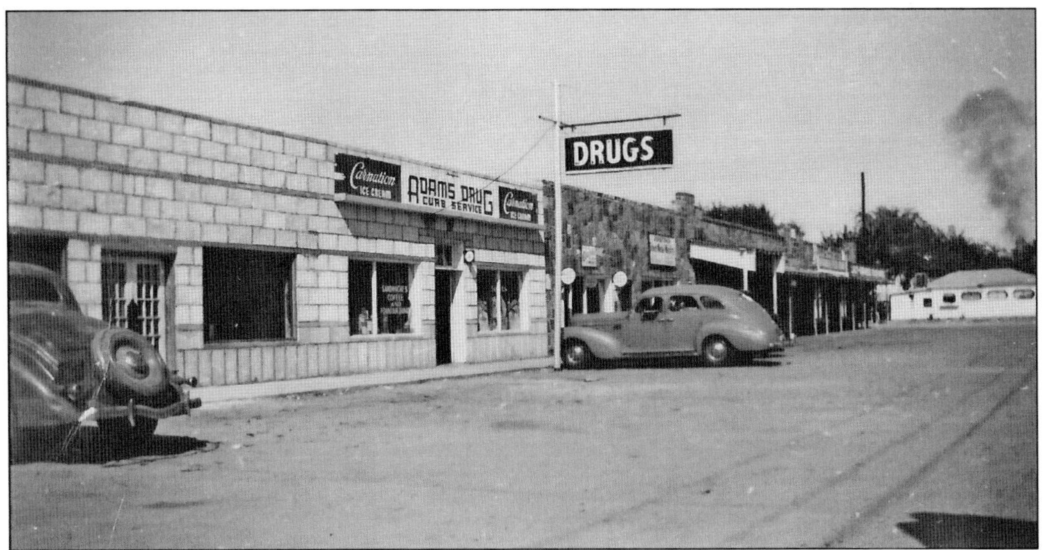

In 1946, Adams Drugstore was located in the Schmoker buildings at 3116 Wilbarger Street, with a fountain service that served sandwiches, coffee, and fountain drinks. It also offered curb service. To the right is Justin Sheet Metal Works at 3112 Wilbarger Street, and to the far right is the Hamrick Feed Store and the Lacy Hamrick Food Store. (Author's collection.)

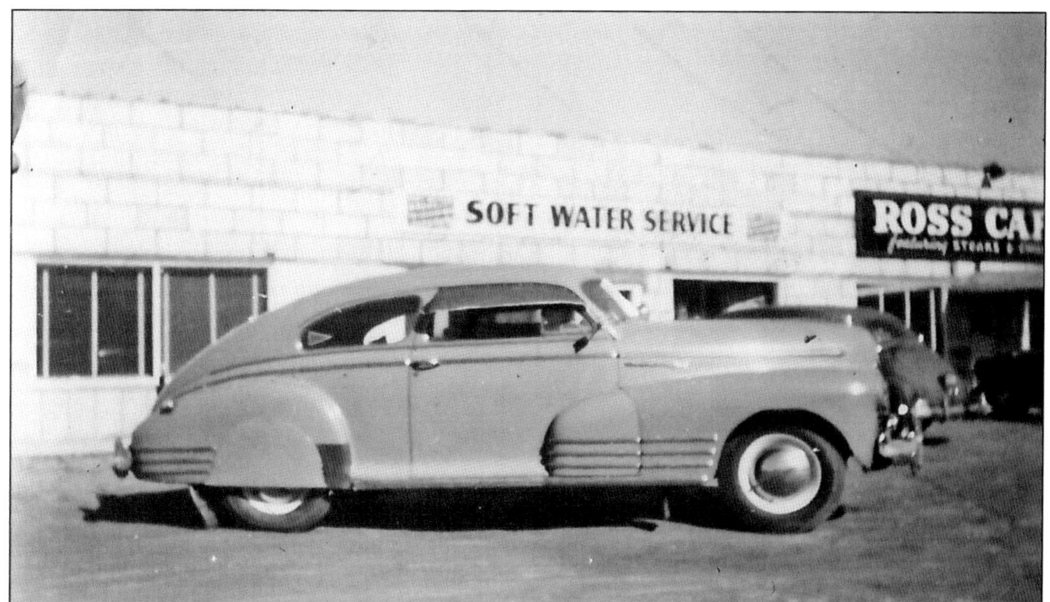

In 1947, Lewis Ross established the Ross Café, located at 3120 Wilbarger Street in the buildings erected by Fred Schmoker. Fred Schmoker and Ballard Ramsey had the Stonewall Grocery and the Stonewall Feed Store in this line of buildings at 3104–3106 Wilbarger Street in 1941 and 1942. (Author's collection.)

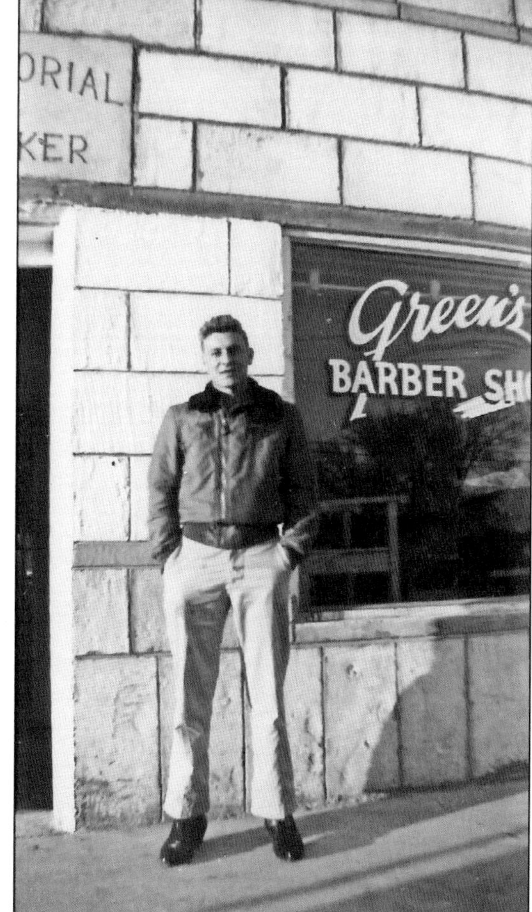

An airman is seen standing in front of Green's Barbershop, located in the Schmoker buildings at 3130 Wilbarger Street, which was the old office of Modern Memorial. Paul Green was the owner and the main barber. In this type of barbershop, one could get a haircut and shoe shine. (Author's collection.)

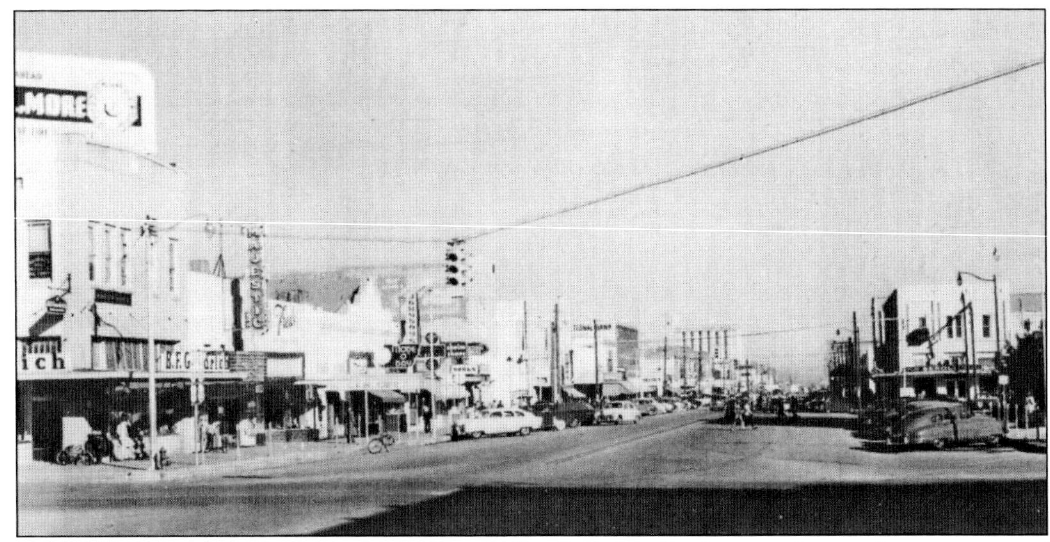

Looking north on Main Street in the late 1940s, B.F. Goodrich is on the northwest corner of Main and Wilbarger Streets, followed by the Majestic Theater, Fred's clothing store, C-H Café, Mod-O-Day woman's wear, Johnson's Jewelry, Paul Huggins men's wear, and the Vernon Drugstore. On the right is the Hoffman & Serold Firestone tire shop, located in the old Herring National Bank Building, with the telephone company upstairs. (Author's collection.)

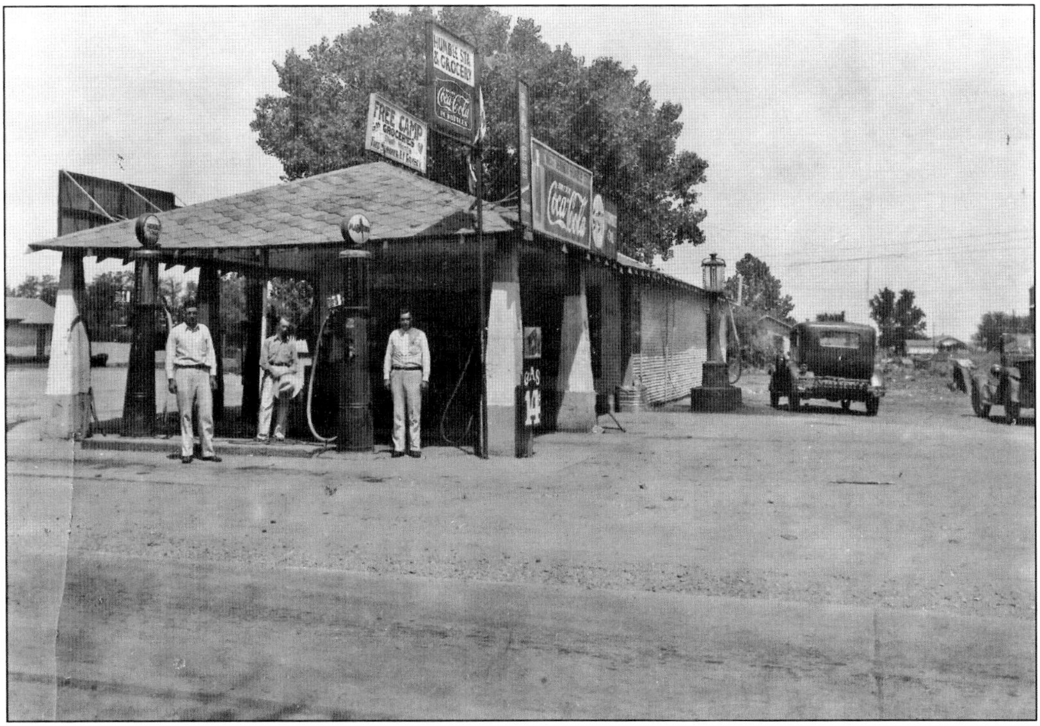

West Vernon Humble-Ramsey & Ray Grocery and Market, located at 3630 Wilbarger Street, was owned and operated by Ballard F. Ramsey and Charles E. Ray with a complete line of groceries and a meat market. Ballard Ramsey made his own homemade block chili that he sold in the store. The price of gas was 14¢ a gallon. This is the location today of West Allsup's. (Author's collection.)

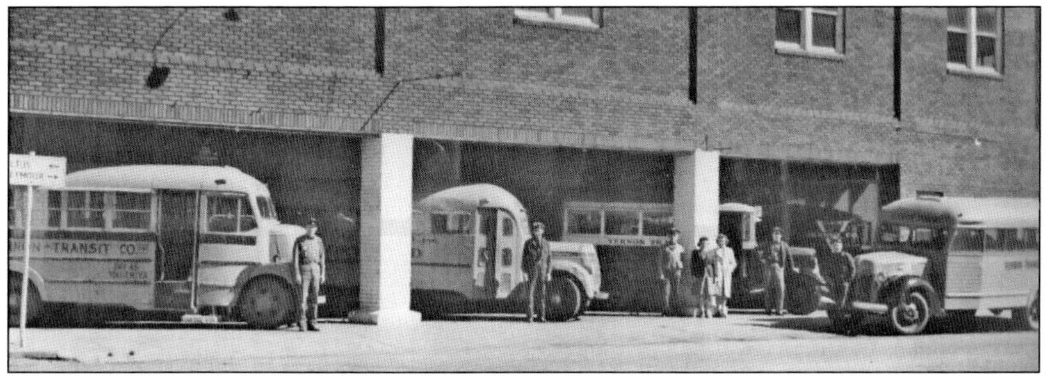

The Vernon Transit Company, located on the corner of Main and Wilbarger Streets, was managed by O.L. Bridges and advertised as "Vernon's Center of Transportation." The Vernon Transit Company had a bus line and the Yellow Cab Service and could be reached at phone number 13. Employees are, from left to right, Henry McNabb, Harry Shannon, owner Wilson Hollars, Ruth Garrett, Dessie Fowler, Dub, and Shelie Cox. (Author's collection.)

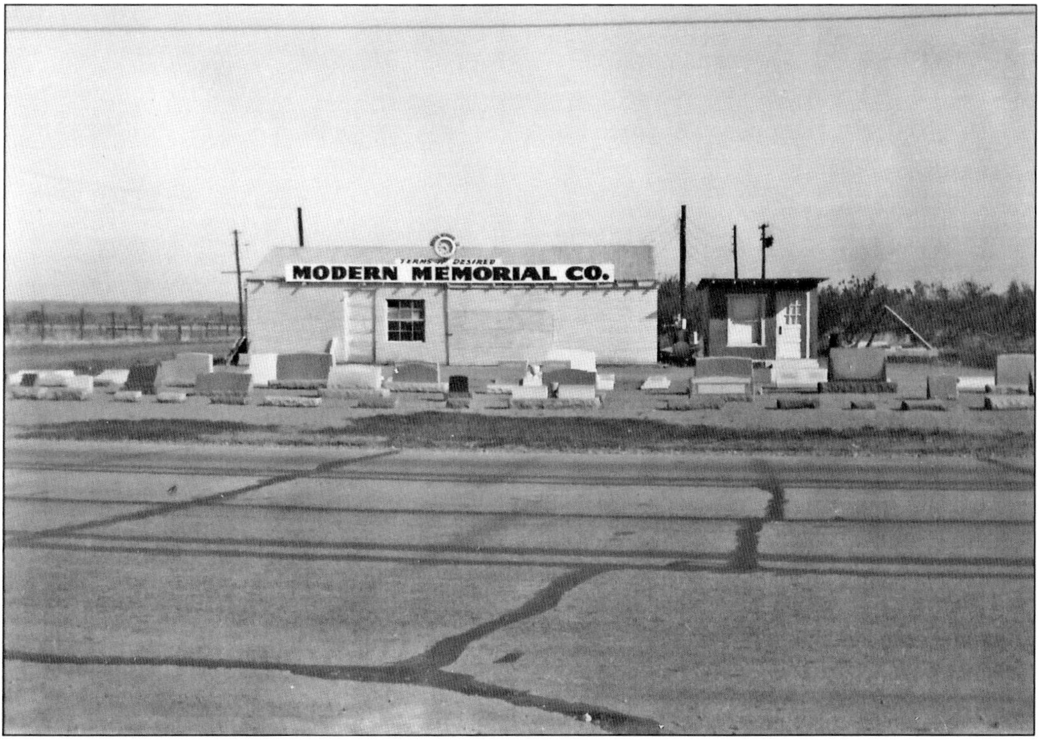

Modern Memorial, located on the Crowell Highway, was owned and operated by Fred and Clara Schmoker. The large building to the left is where they made headstones and other marble and granite monuments; it had a sandblasting room in one end. The small building to the right was the office. Earnest Schmoker was the art designer for the monuments. (Author's collection.)

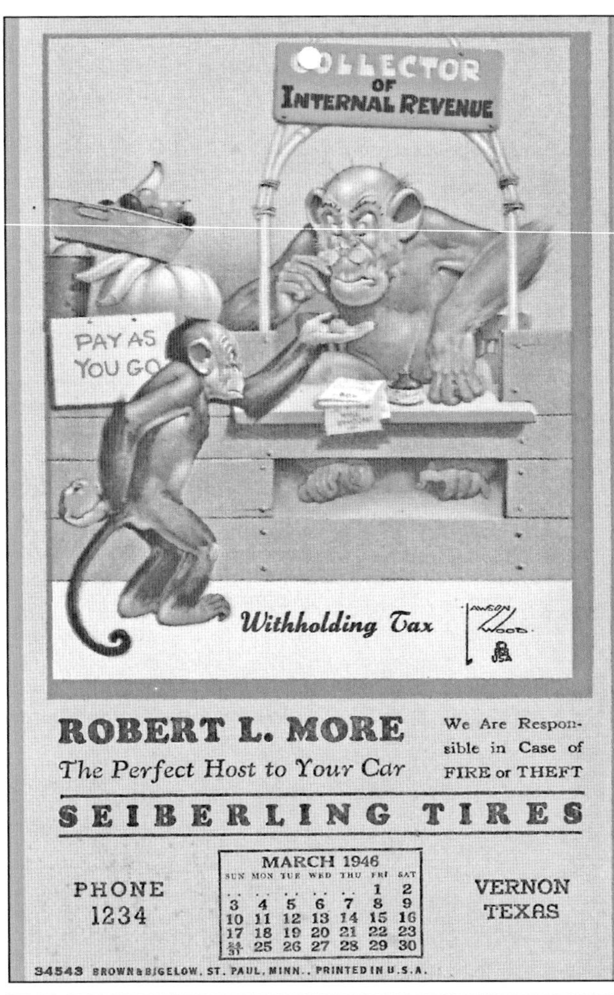

This calendar advertises the Robert L. More gas station in 1946 with the phone number 1234. This station, garage, and storage place, owned by Robert L. More Jr., sold Magnolia gasoline and oil, More's Long Life oil, Amalie oil, and Seiberling tires. Robert L. More's slogan was always "The Perfect Host to Your Car." (Author's collection.)

Alton "Al" Skelton is adding water to his radiator at Gauntt's N-D-Pendent service station, located at 1100 Main Street. Gauntt's N-D-Pendent was owned and operated by Luther L. Gauntt and offered wholesale and retail gasoline, oils, and greases, washing and lubricating, tube vulcanizing, Delco batteries, and accessories. (Author's collection.)

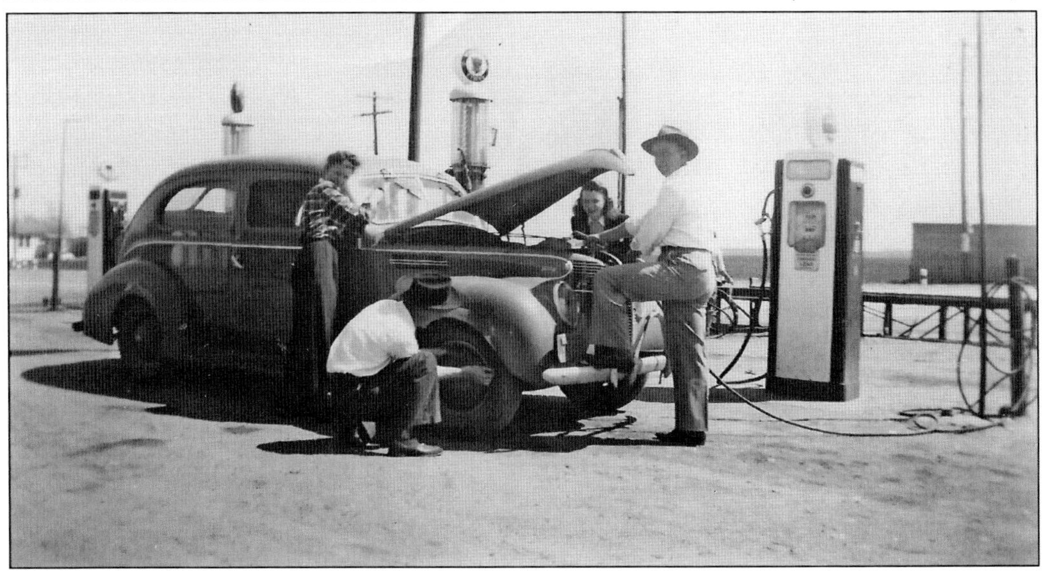

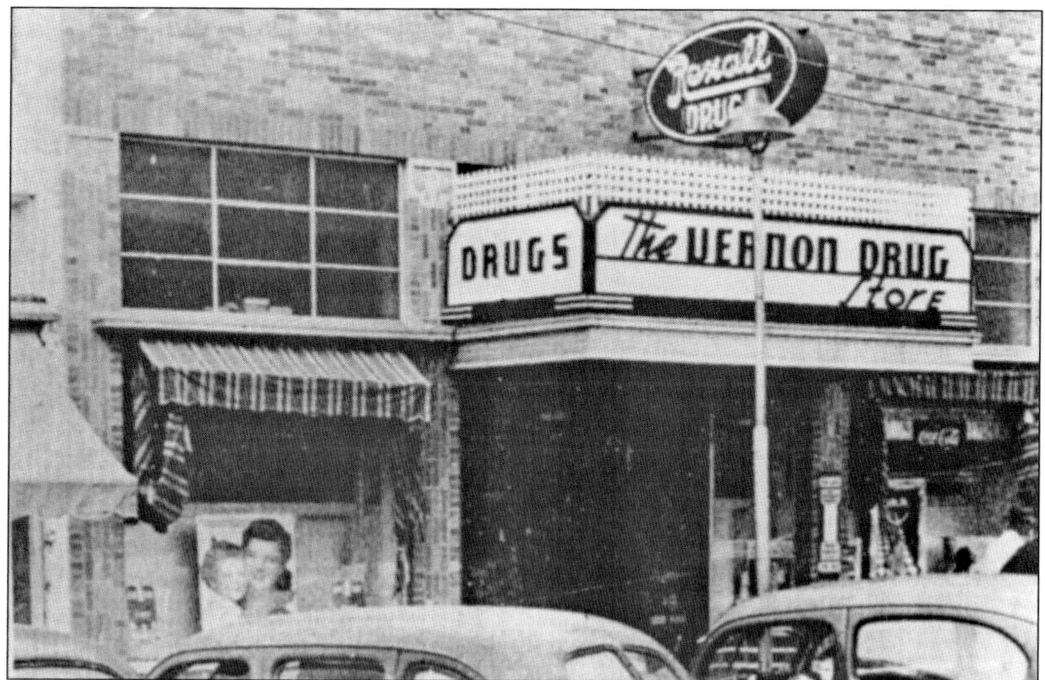

The Vernon Drugstore, located at 1704 Main Street, was established as the W.T. Dickey and Company Drugstore in 1882. By 1886, it had become the Pendleton & Fergeson, Vernon Drugstore. In 1941–1942, the drugstore was owned by George S. Hardin, R.O. Brown, and Mrs. J.J. McGaughey. Pictured in 1946, the Vernon Drugstore was owned by R.O. Brown and Ed S. Malone at the time. (Author's collection.)

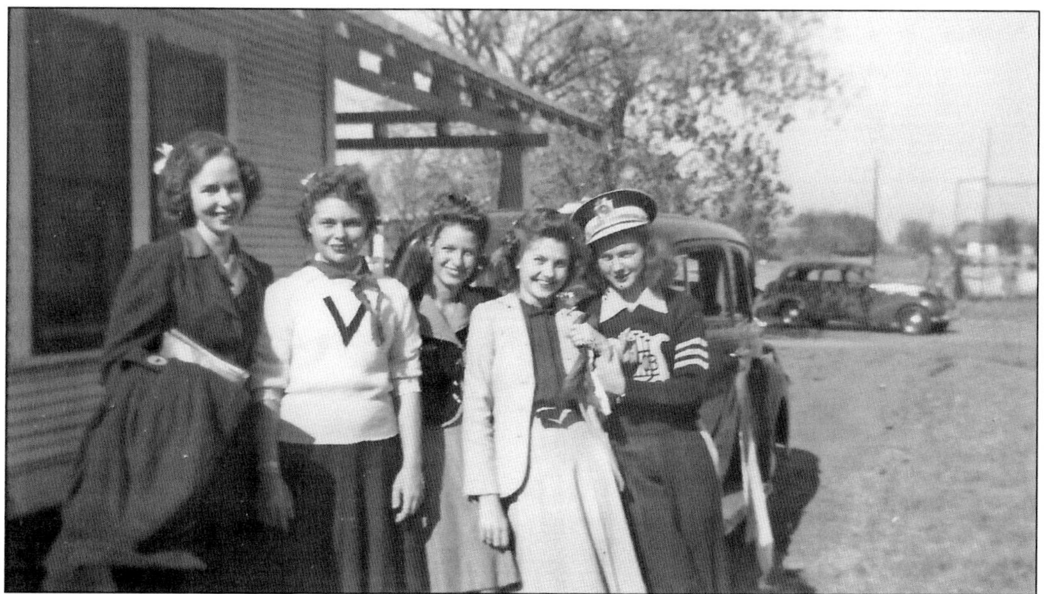

An unidentified group of girls is gathered around 1947 wearing maroon-and-white high school letter sweaters and band uniforms. Groups like this would gather after the game and head to one of the local drugstores, such as Vernon Drug, Huber's City Drug, Sewell's Corner Drug, or Owens West Vernon Drug. (Author's collection.)

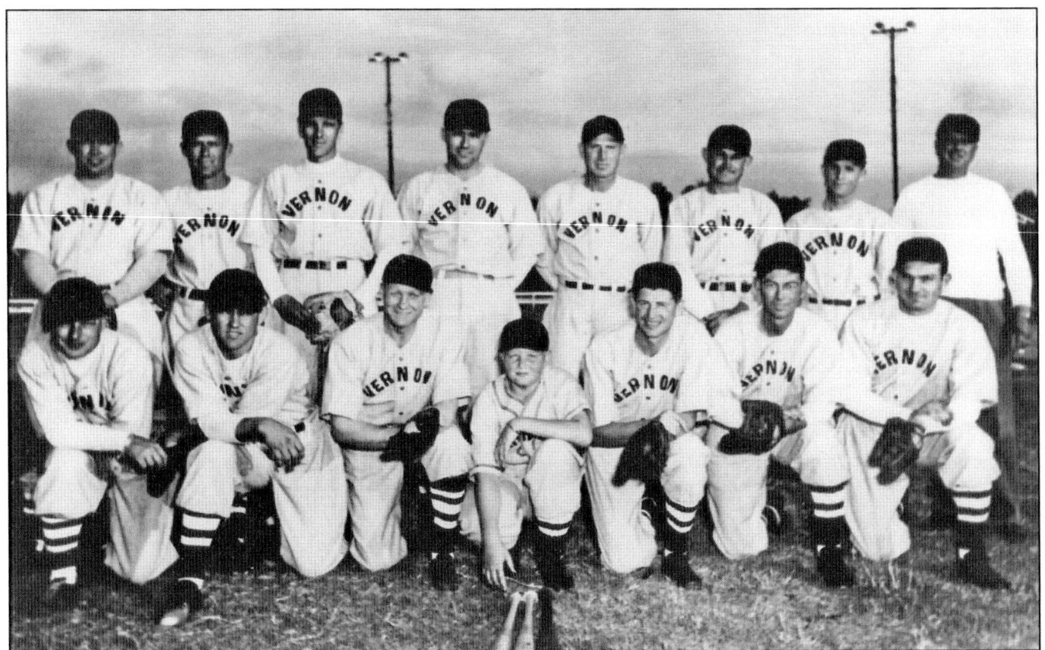

Pictured are unidentified members of the semiprofessional baseball team known as the Vernon Dusters. The Dusters played ball around the area from the late 1940s until the mid-1950s and won most all of their games. The schedule for their games included teams from Sweetwater, Big Spring, Midland, San Angelo, Odessa, Ballinger, Artesia, and Roswell. (Author's collection.)

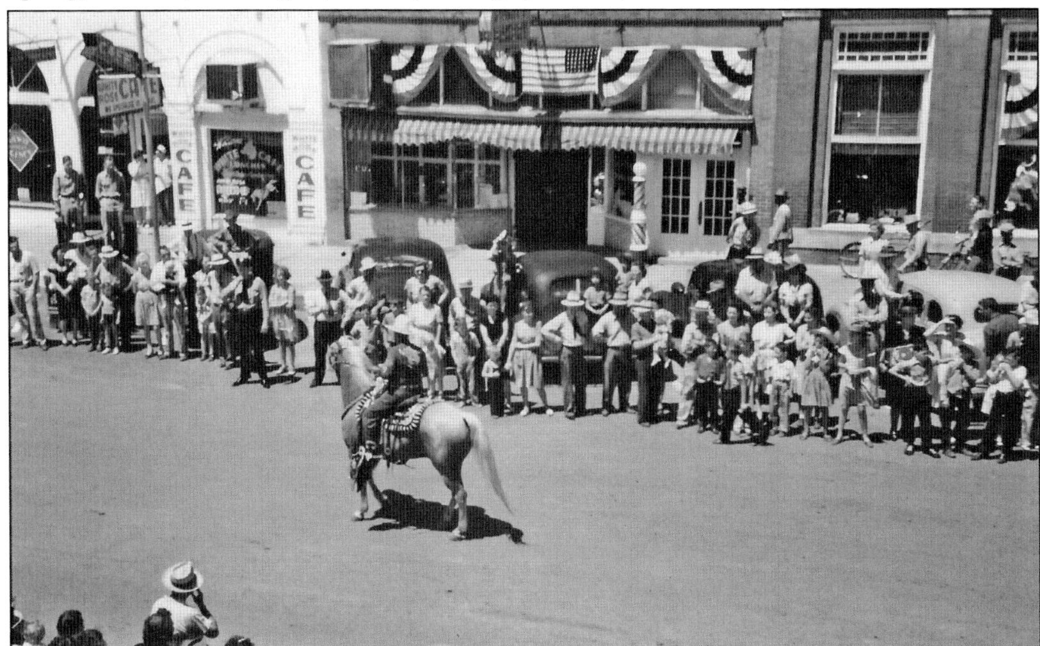

E. Paul Waggoner is seen leading the first rodeo parade in 1946 in the 1800 block of Main Street. The parade was heading south in front of Vessels and Davenport barbershop, Purity Bakery, the White Rose Café, and the Railway Express Office. E. Paul Waggoner was the owner of the rodeo and the rodeo grounds just south of Vernon. It is still in operation today. (Author's collection.)

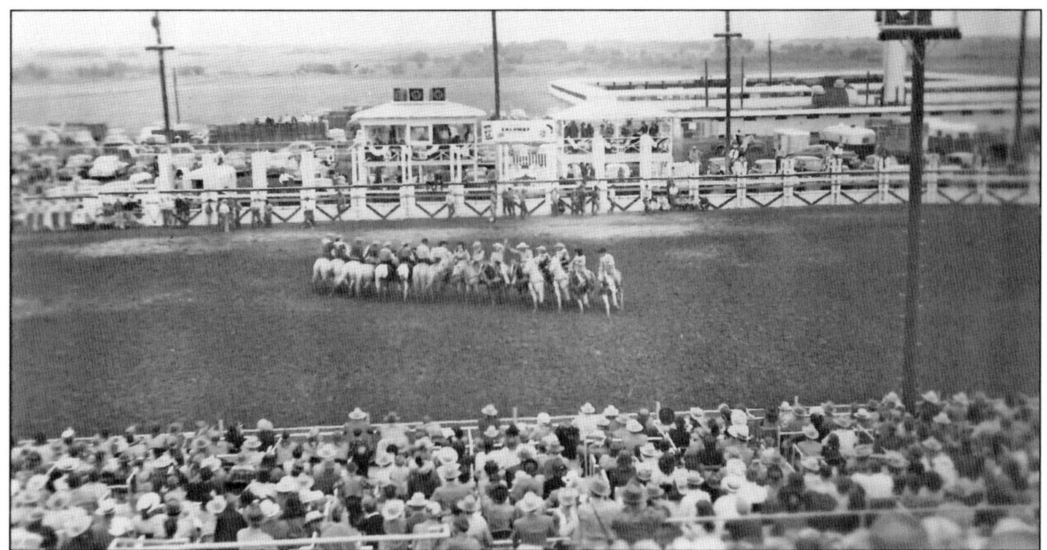

The Santa Rosa Rodeo arena is shown with the bleachers full of spectators as a group of riders performs a riding drill. The white stand, at center and overlooking the arena, is the rodeo's bandstand and announcers' booth. The horse stalls can be seen on the right-hand side at the top of the photograph. (Author's collection.)

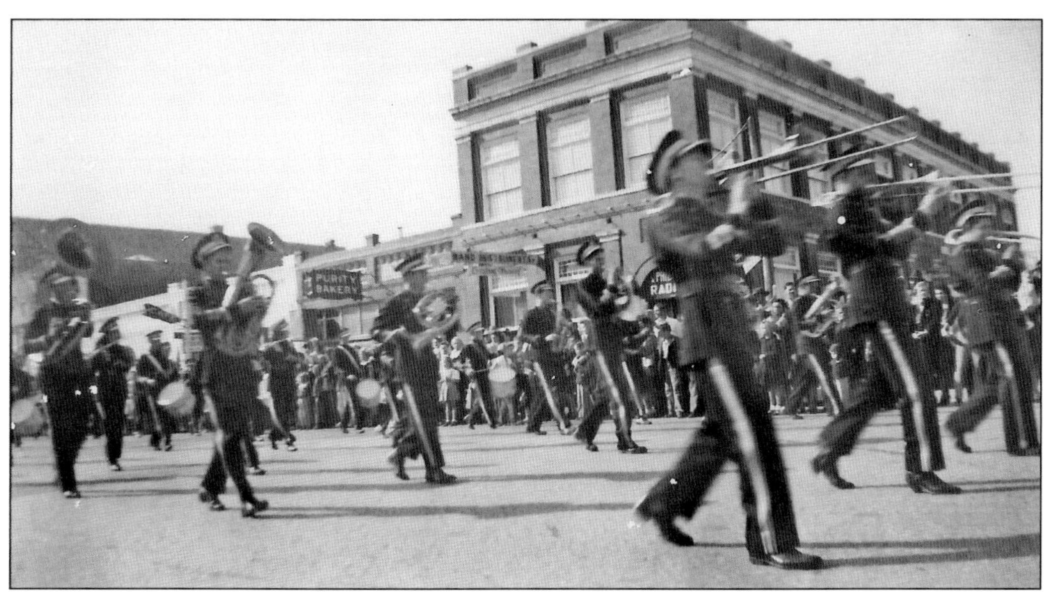

A marching band is seen in front of the Purity Bakery at 1806 Main Street, and the old Farmers State Bank Building is on the corner of Main and Wilbarger Streets. On the top floor of the Farmers State Bank Building was the KVWC radio station, and on the first floor were Barnes Appliance Store and Vernon Music & Electric, with proprietor W.W. Barnes selling Philco and General Electric appliances, radios, and records. (Author's collection.)

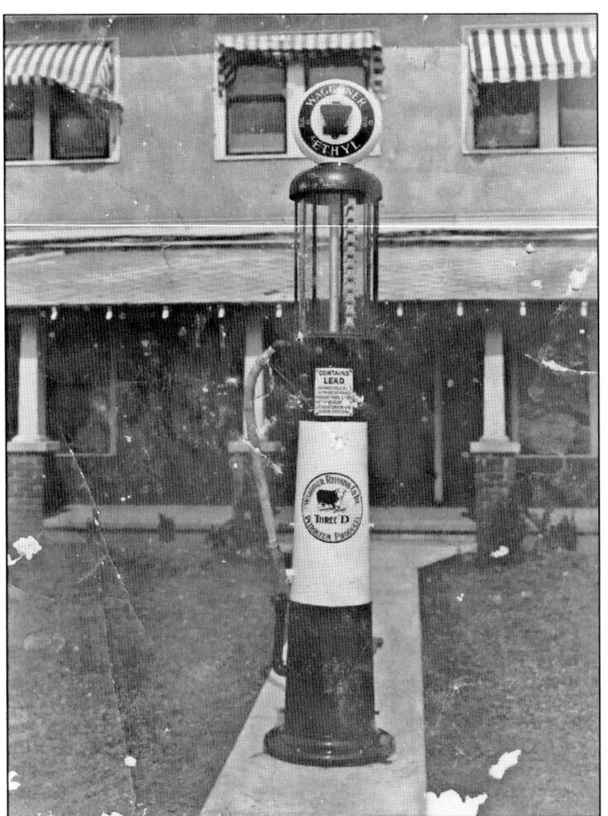

This visible gas pump on display at the Waggoner Oil Refinery in Electra, Texas, around 1947 shows a bull in a circle with Waggoner Refining Co., Inc., and Three "D" Petroleum Products lettered on the porcelain base. The gas pump globe is lettered Waggoner-Ethyl with the Waggoner Ranch Three "D" brand on each side. Two of the motor oils refined were the Three "D" brand and More's Long Life oil. (Courtesy of Mike More.)

Airmen from Victory Field can be seen standing on the corner of Wilbarger and Fannin Streets at the Wilbarger Drugstore located in the Wilbarger Hotel. Across the street from the hotel is Robert L. More's gas station and automobile storage around 1947. Probably the oldest continually operated service station in Vernon, it was built in 1914 and leased out until 1933, when Robert L. More Jr. took it over. (Author's collection.)

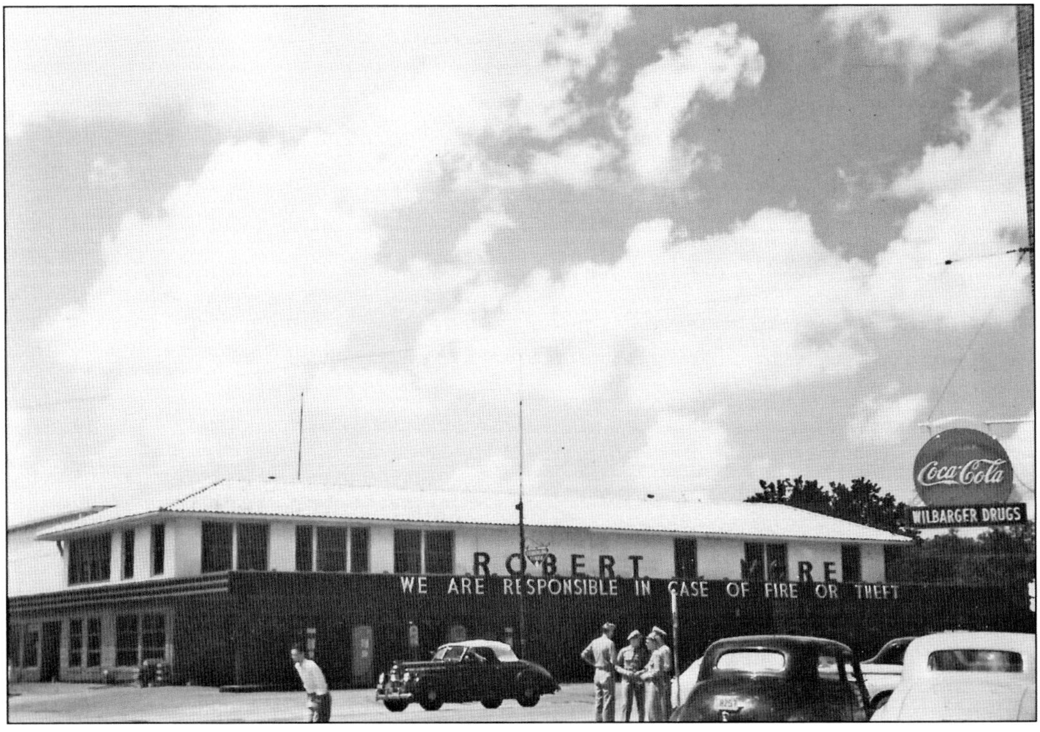

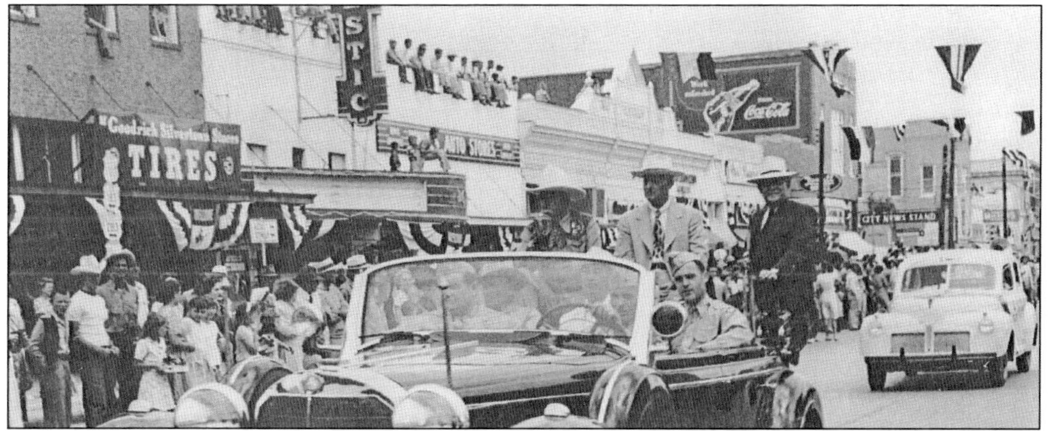

The 1946 parade, in the 1700 block of Main Street, is passing in front of White Garage, the Majestic Theater, and the B.F. Goodrich store. Herman Goerings's bulletproof car, which was captured by the 36th Division in World War II, is pictured above. Riding in the car are E. Paul Waggoner (left on top of back seat), Gov. Bradford Jester, T. Edger Johnson, and A. Garland Adair. (Author's collection.)

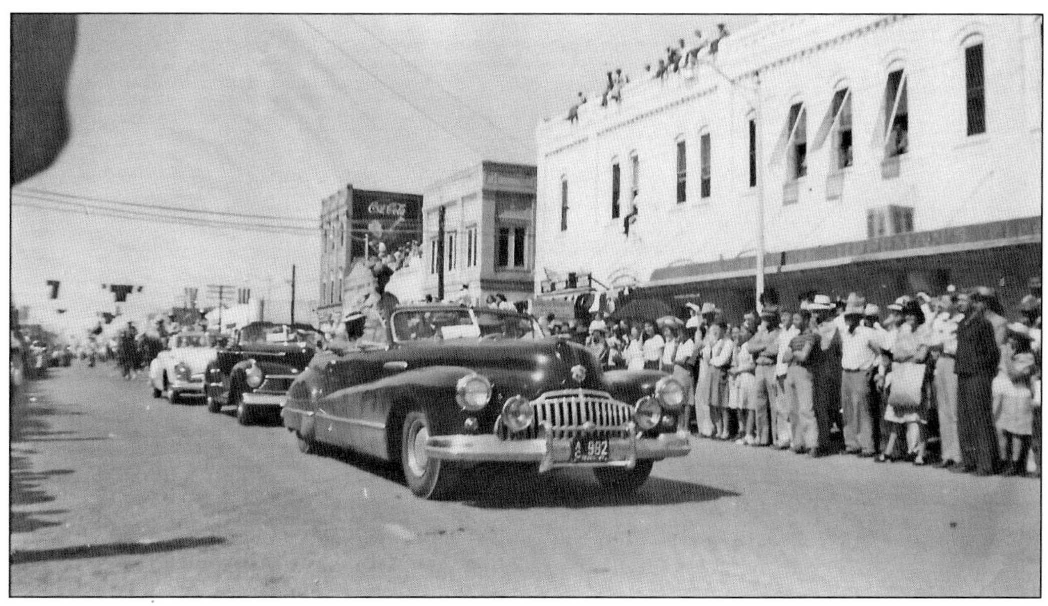

General Wainright is seen sitting on the top of the back seat of this Buick convertible, heading south on Main Street, as it passes Hoffman's Firestone, located in the old Herring National Bank Building. Looking back north is the First State Bank and Hill's Youth Center, which has a large Coke sign on the side. (Author's collection.)

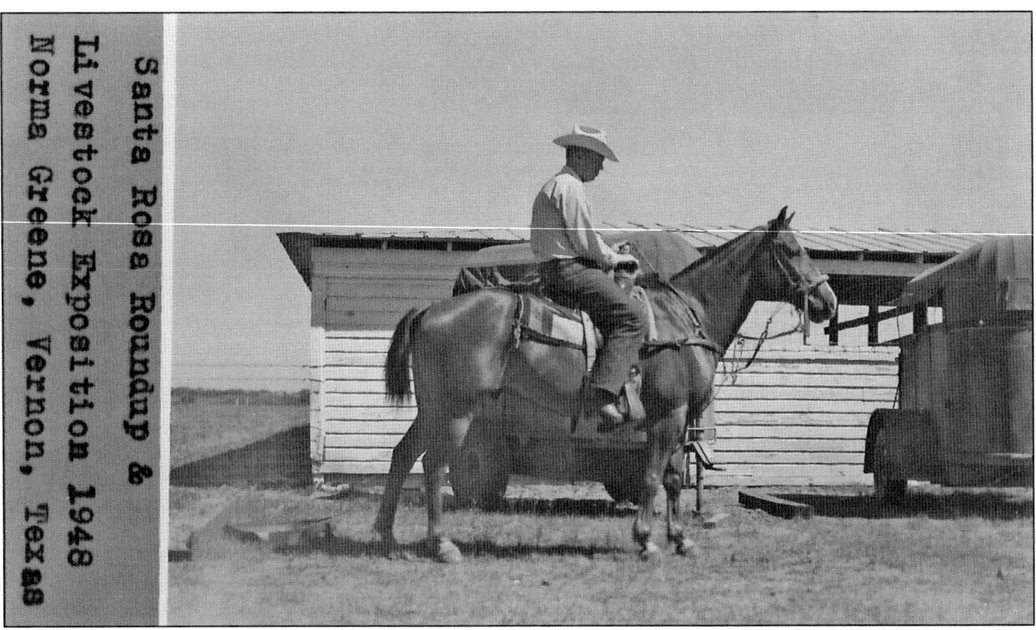

This picture taken in 1948 by Norma Greene's Studio advertises the Santa Rosa Roundup and Livestock Exposition. The exposition showed some of the top stallions kept at the Waggoner Ranch, such as Tar Baby, Pretty Bailey, Sundown, Chaparita Chief, and many more. The Waggoner Ranch foreman was Tony Hazelwood. (Author's collection.)

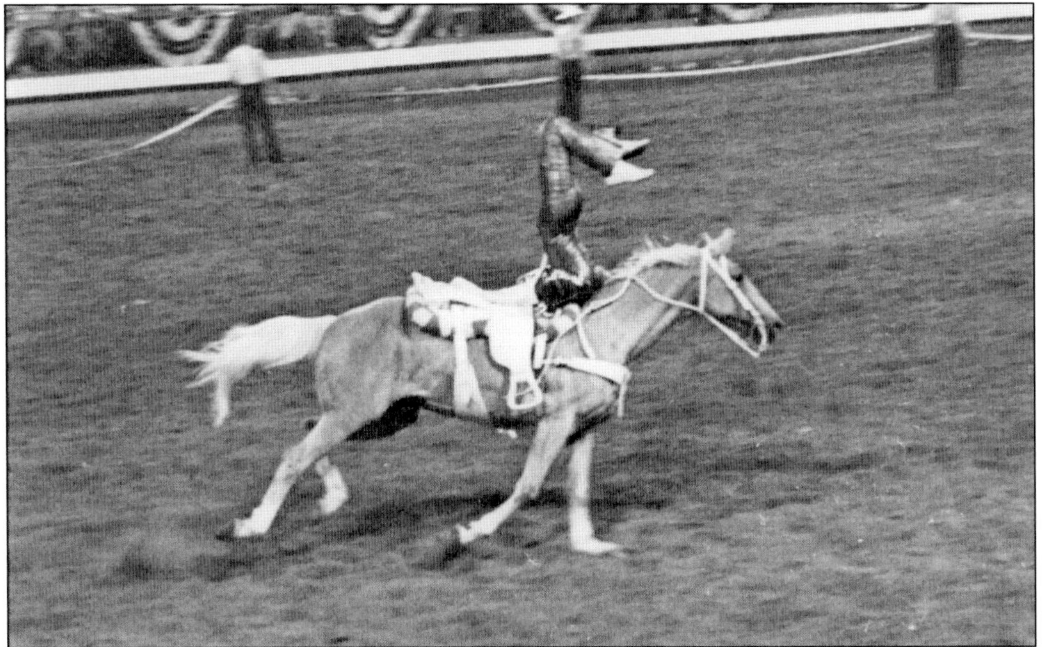

Dorothy Frizzell, a trick rider from San Angelo, Texas, is seen in the rodeo arena. While on the rodeo tour, she performed big shows all over the Southwest and was considered an expert trick rider. Incidentally, Frizzell's trick riding saddle was made in Vernon by Oliver Brothers Saddle Shop, located at 1422 Main Street. Oliver Brothers Saddle Shop owners were C.W., Claude W. Jr., and J.A. Oliver. (Author's collection.)

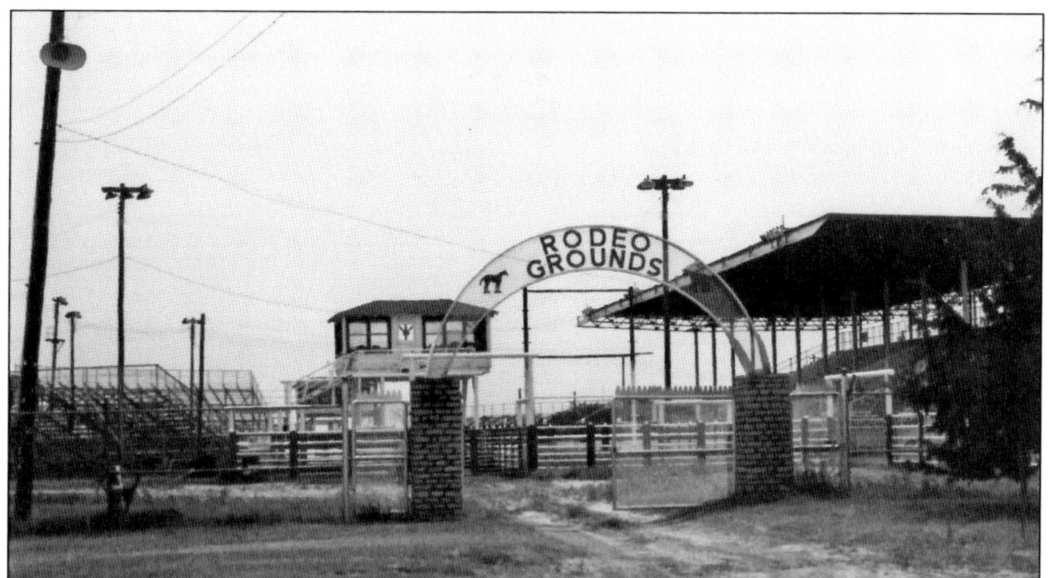

Pictured in 1947 is the entrance to the rodeo arena. E. Paul Waggoner was president of the Santa Rosa Roundup Association and the owner of the rodeo grounds. The announcer and the rodeo band were located upstairs in the center building. The covered bleachers to the right were originally at Arlington Downs. (Author's collection.)

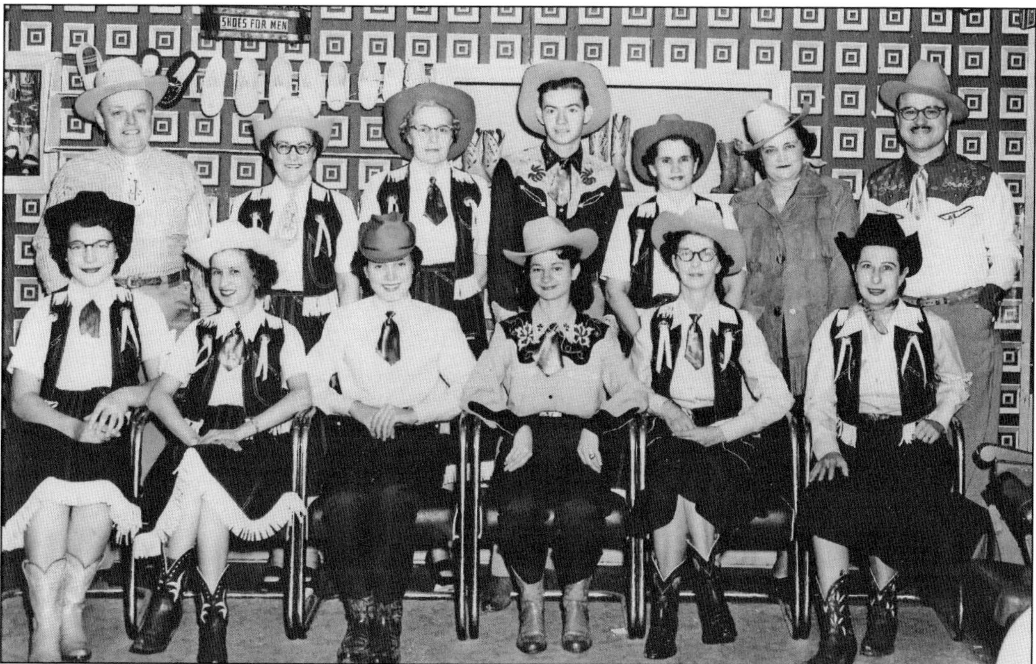

Dressed in their Western attire around 1953 are the employees of Jacobson's Department Store, located at 1526 Main Street. Originally, it was called Forman Department Store, selling dry goods and clothing through the 1940s. Those pictured are, from left to right, (first row) Alice Tull, Mary Boyd, Tommy Tull, Joyce (Perry) Schmoker, Lillian Turkett, and Polly Jacobson; (second row) Henry Jacobson, Novie May, Stella Beach, Otis Burkett, Beaulah White, Mrs. T.G. McCord, and Lou Troja. (Courtesy of Joyce Schmoker.)

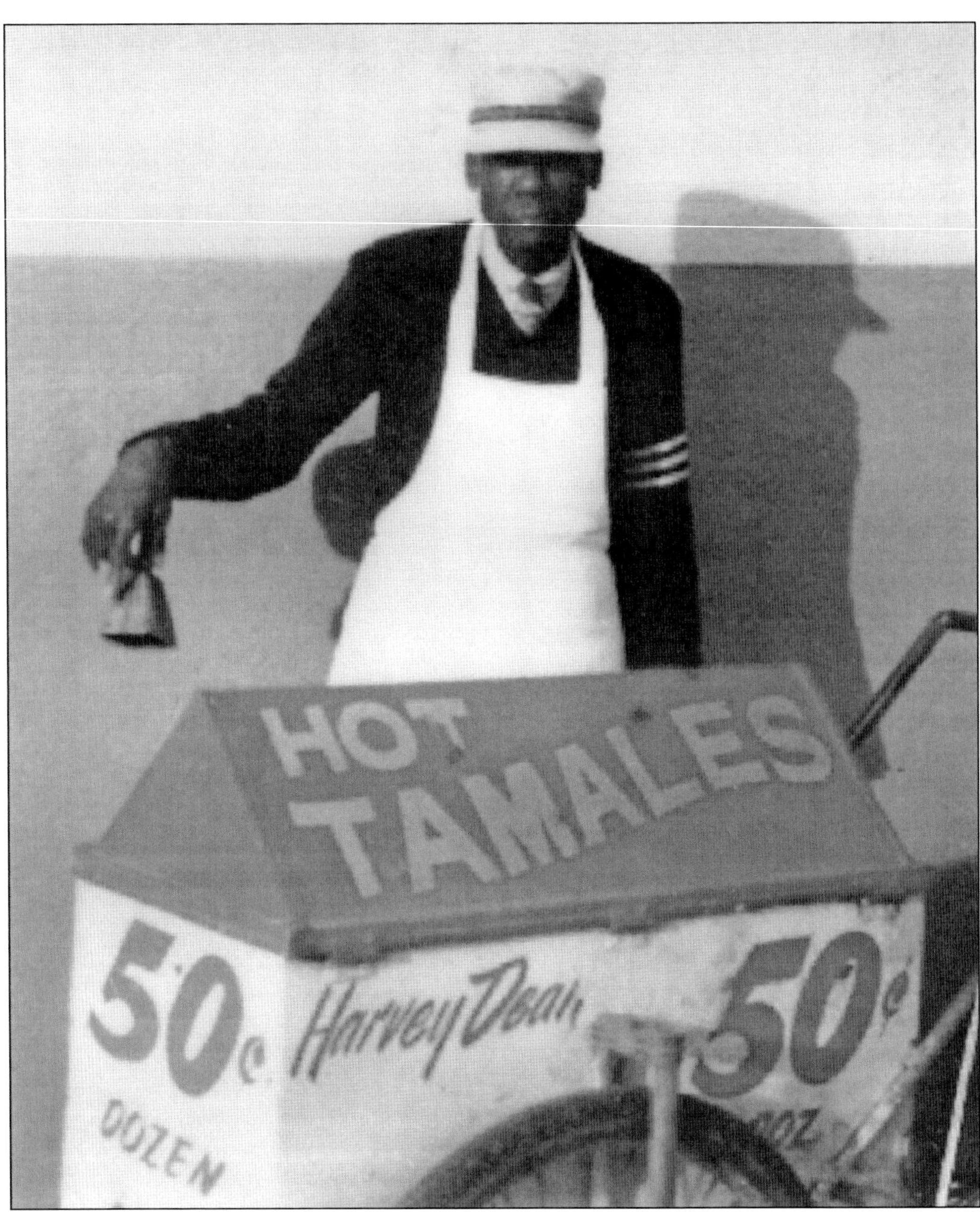

Pictured is Harvey Dean with his hot tamale cart. Everyone in town knew him as Harvey Dean, "the hot tamale king." Dean started making hot tamales in 1936 and sold them from his home at 1018 Houston Street. In 1937, he built this cart and started selling his hot tamales on the street corner; he rang his cowbell to get the attention of people as they were passing by. He would place the tamales in a metal can and then put the can on top of hot rocks in the cart in order to keep them hot. As he sold out, he would go back home and fill the can again. This business provided him with enough income to put three of his sons through college. Everyone remembers Harvey Dean being on the corner of Main and Wilbarger Streets. (Courtesy of Michael Dean.)

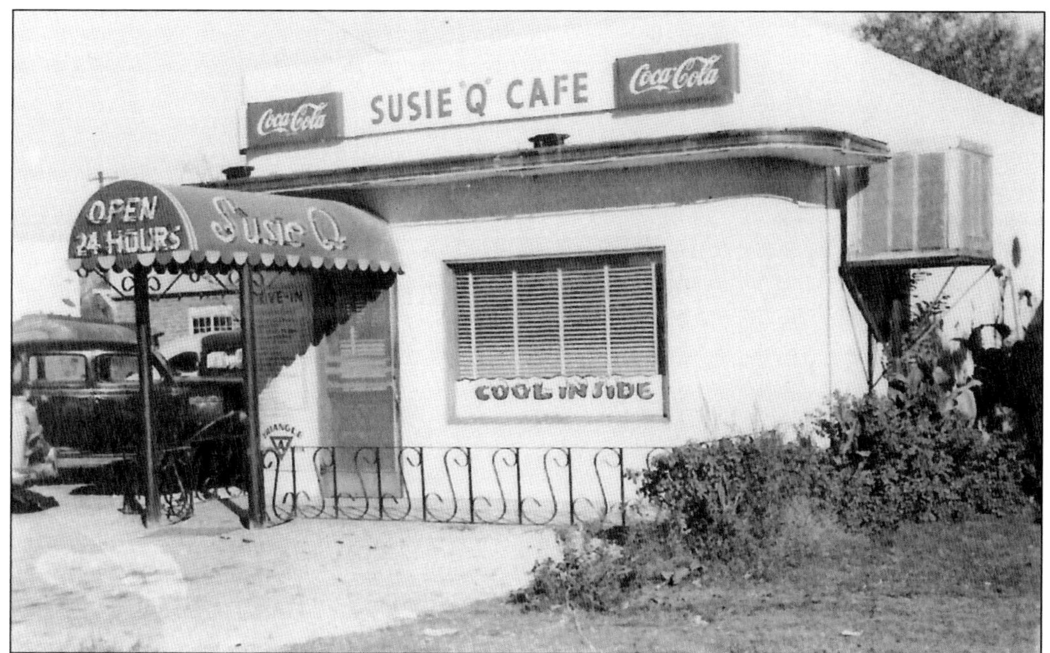

Pictured is the first Susie Q in Vernon, located at 922 Wilbarger Street and owned by Earnest L. and Lorene K. Rogers. The Susie Q opened around 1949 and was named after their daughter Sue Rogers. The advertising on the awning is all in neon. The sign in the window says, "Cool inside"; there was a water cooler in the wall. The Susie Q also had curb service. (Author's collection.)

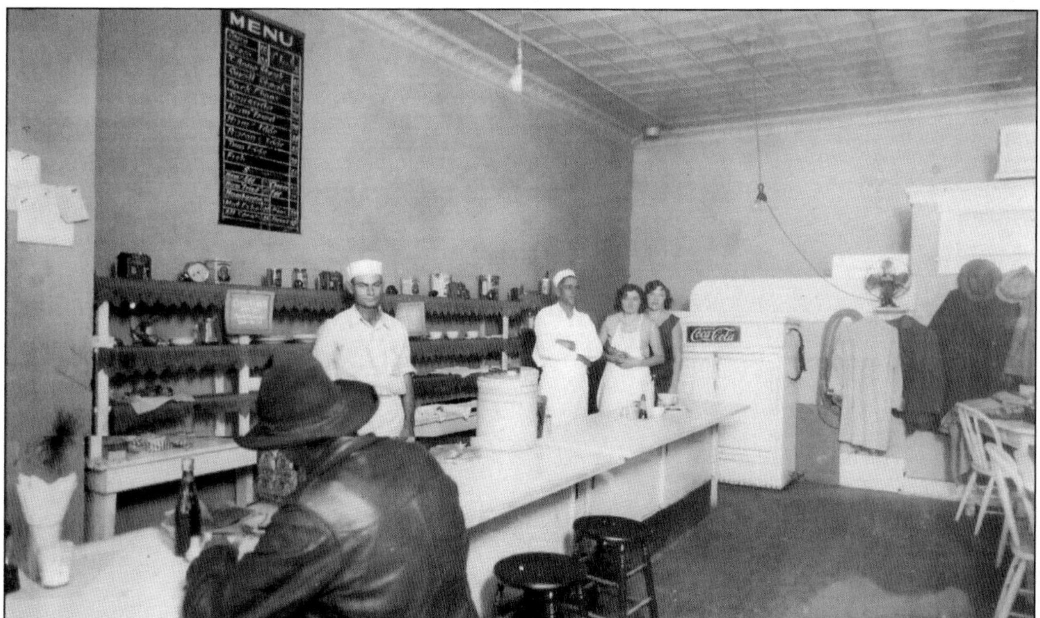

Shown is the interior of the Porter House Café in 1948, located at 1803 Bowie Street. It was owned and operated by Raymond G. Ditmore. Behind the counter is Francis (Baker) Walker, second from the right. The menu included the following: 15¢ soup, 25¢ stew, 15¢ chili, 45¢ T-bone, 35¢ small steak, 30¢ sausage, 30¢ ham fried, 40¢ ham and eggs, 40¢ bacon and eggs, 20¢ two eggs, and 45¢ fish. (Author's collection.)

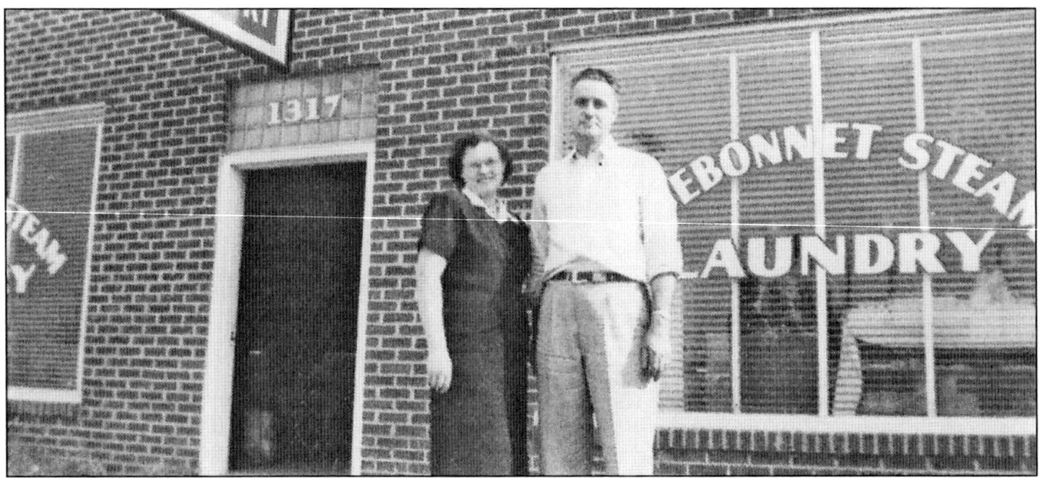

Pictured in 1948 are Rachel and Elvie Folmar standing in front of the Bluebonnet Steam Laundry at 1317 Cumberland Street. The Bluebonnet had two local pickup and delivery service routes and four out-of-town sub stations in Paducah, Chillicothe, Crowell, and Electra. Later, in the 1960s, the Bluebonnet Laundry and Dry Cleaners moved to a new location at 1220 Main Street. (Courtesy of Kevin Folmar.)

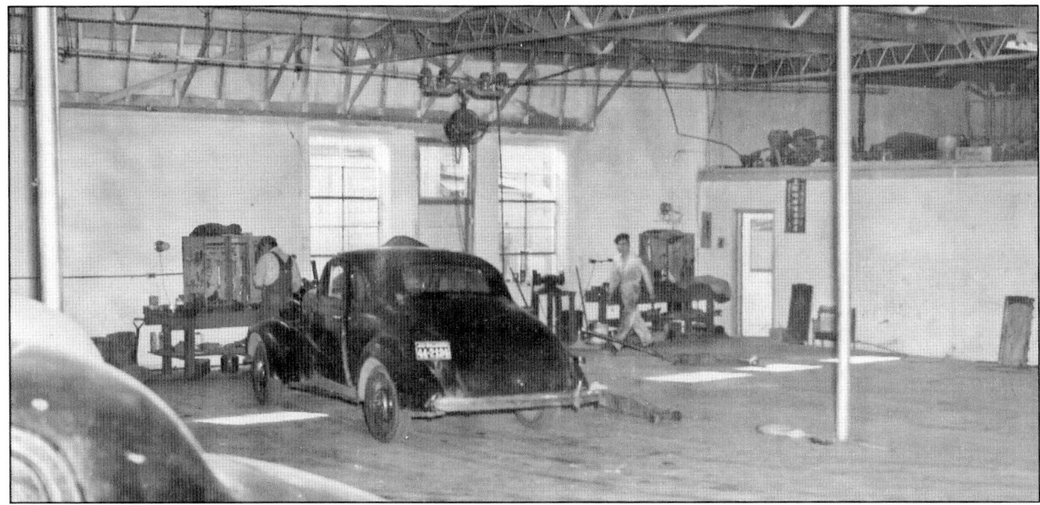

In 1949, the interior of the service department is pictured at the Johnson-Davis Motor Company. The Johnson-Davis Motor Company was owned by T. Edgar Johnson and was a Ford and Mercury dealership, selling Ford Sixes and V-8 cars and trucks. It was located at 1500–1510 Wilbarger Street. Davis was a silent partner and also T. Edgar Johnson's father-in-law. (Author's collection.)

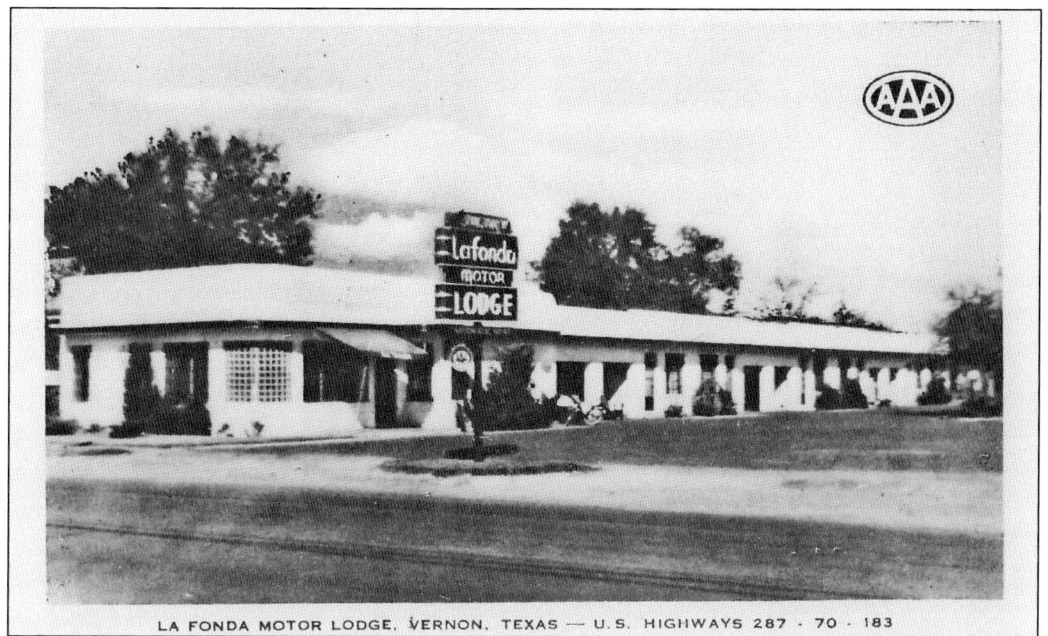

LA FONDA MOTOR LODGE, VERNON, TEXAS — U.S. HIGHWAYS 287 - 70 - 183

In 1948, the Lafonda Motor Lodge was located at 1004 Wilbarger Street, which was one of the main highways through Vernon at the time. The Lafonda Motor Lodge was owned and operated by George B. Prudom. Motels like this one were in several locations up and down Wilbarger Street on Highway 287-70-183. (Author's collection.)

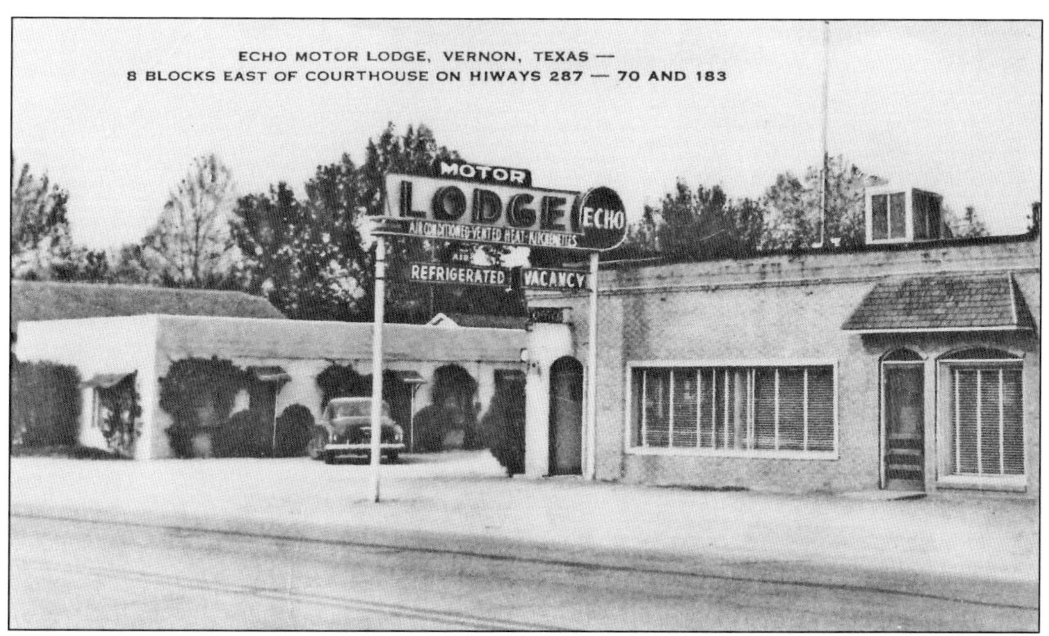
ECHO MOTOR LODGE, VERNON, TEXAS —
8 BLOCKS EAST OF COURTHOUSE ON HIWAYS 287 — 70 AND 183

This postcard was made in the early 1950s for the Echo Motor Lodge that opened in 1948, located at 816 Wilbarger Street. It was owned and operated by Henry G. Schramm. Other tourist courts on Wilbarger Street in 1948 were Cox Courts at 618, English Village Courts at 619, Greenbelt Courts at 4100, Hillcrest Courts at 3816, Mack's Camp at 4000, Restwell Cottages at 622, Spanish Courts at 3827, and the "Y" Courts at 4016. (Author's collection.)

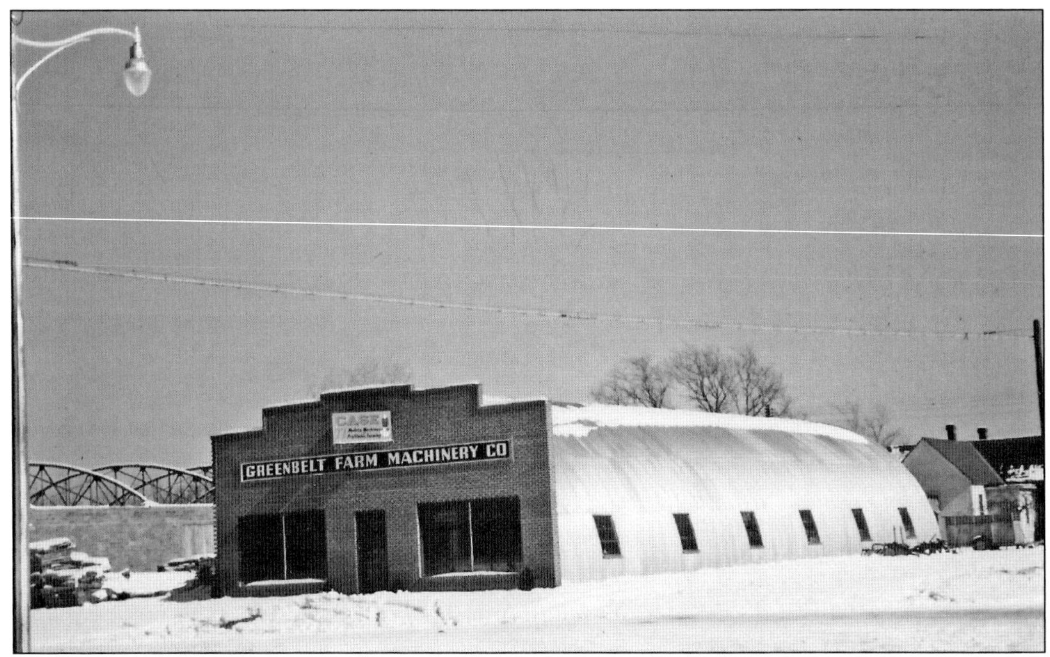

Pictured in 1948 is the Greenbelt Farm Machinery Co. Building, located at 1331 Cumberland Street. Owners of the business were Clarence A. Graf, Floyd A Graf, and Wilbert O. Graf, and they sold Case tractors and farm machinery, advertising "Modern Machinery, Profitable Farming" with the familiar logo of a bald eagle on top of the world. (Author's collection.)

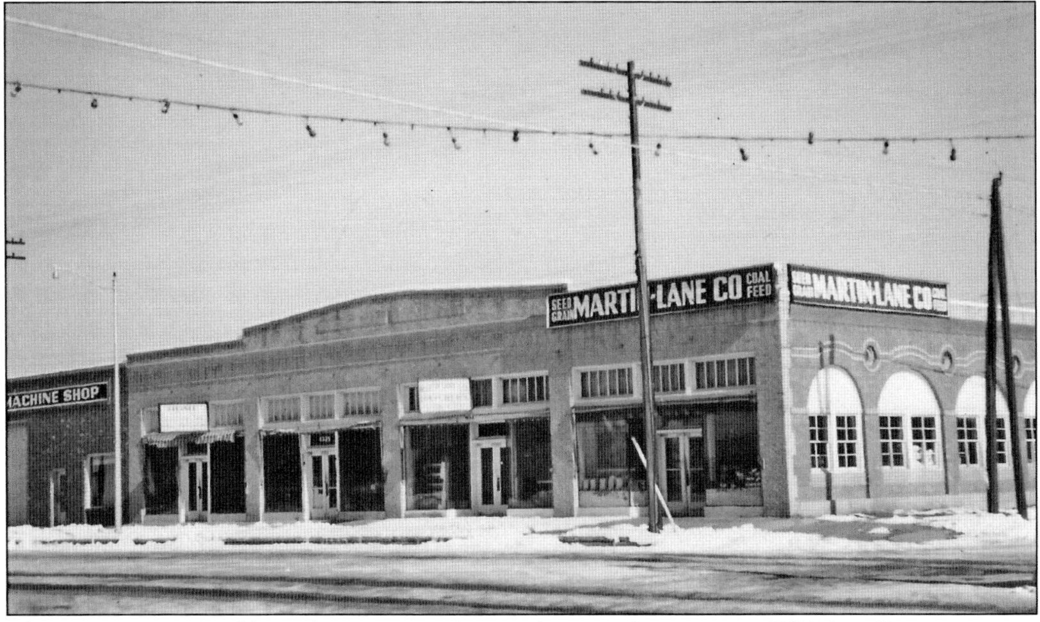

The Martin-Lane Building, shown in 1946, is in the same location at 1327 Main Street as it was when William N. Martin started it in 1921. The wholesale store was at the Fort Worth & Denver tracks between Fannin and Deaf Smith Streets. It was a wholesale and retail feed, grain, coal, garden, and field seeds store. To the left is Jones Welding & Machine Shop at 1313 Main Street. (Author's collection.)

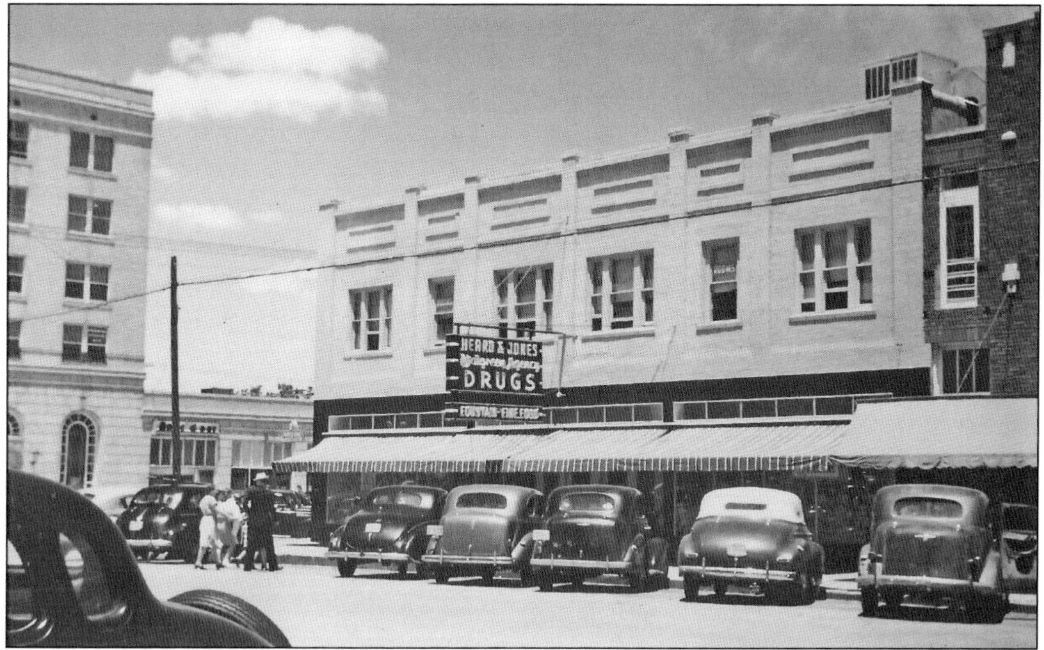

Heard & Jones, a Walgreen drugstore, is pictured in 1946 at 1830 Pease Street. The drugstore was owned and operated by Walter H. Heard and Walker B. Jones. The store offered prescription drugs, hospital supplies, cosmetics, drug sundries, pottery, gifts, school and office supplies, candies, a fountain service, and free delivery. (Author's collection.)

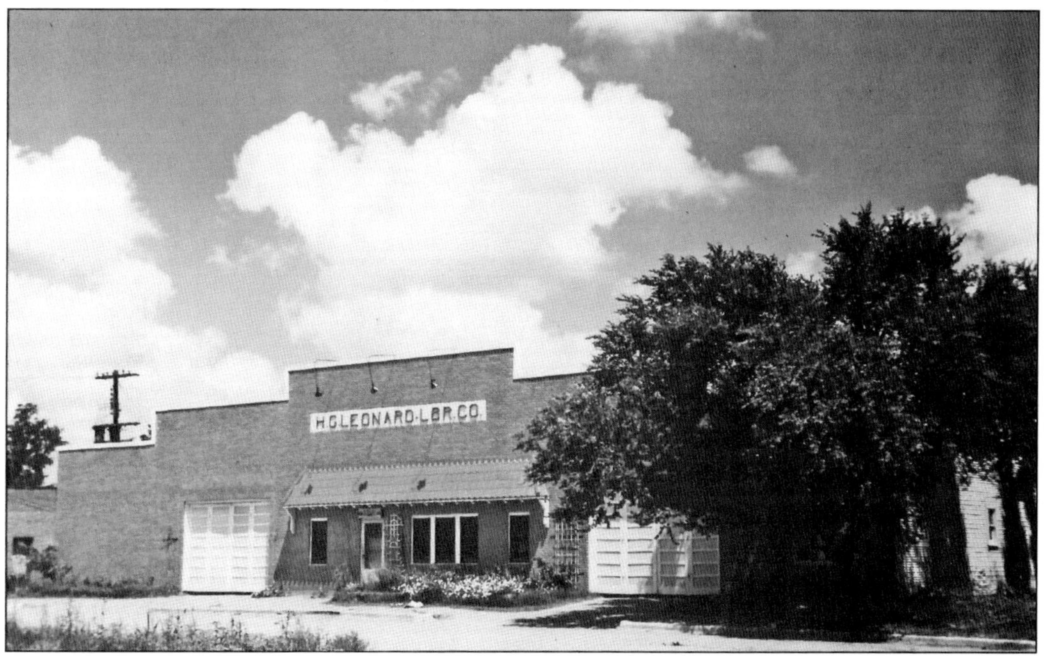

H.G. Leonard Lumber Company, pictured in 1946, went into business in 1927 on the corner of 1704 Dawson and Cumberland Streets, with Henry G. Leonard as president, H.E. Leonard as vice president, and Robert S. Leonard as secretary-treasurer-manager. H.G. Leonard Lumber Company had a complete line of builder's supplies, lumber, hardware, and paints. (Author's collection.)

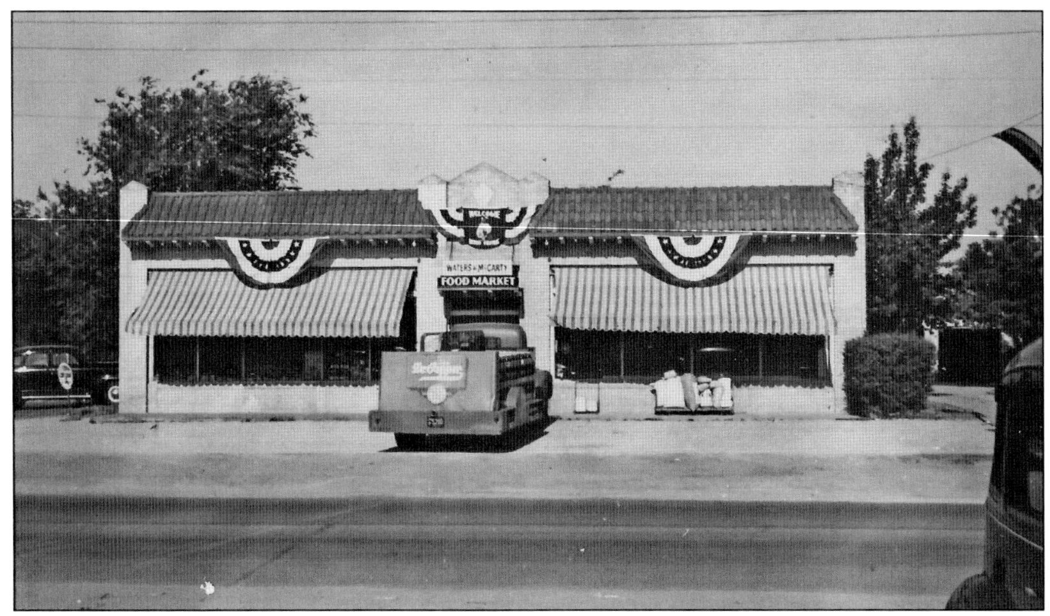

Pictured is an early Dr. Pepper delivery truck parked in front of Walter & McCarty Food Market, owned by Hershel A. McCarty, at 2428 Main Street. The store had a full line of groceries, produce, and a meat market. Around 1952, this location will become Central Market, owned by Carl A. Flores.(Author's collection.)

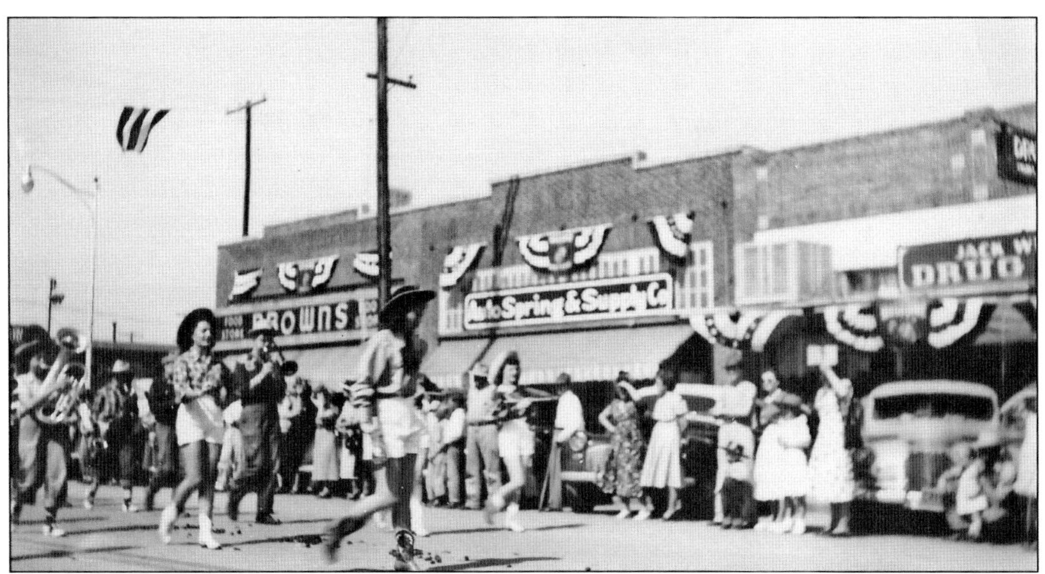

In the background of this 1949 parade, with a marching band of cowboys and cowgirls, is Browns Food Store at 1401 Main Street; Clayton Veteto owned it. The next building to the right is the Auto Spring and Supply at 1407 Main Street. The last building, pictured at right, is Williams Drugstore, owned by Jack B. Williams and located at 1409 Main Street. (Author's collection.)

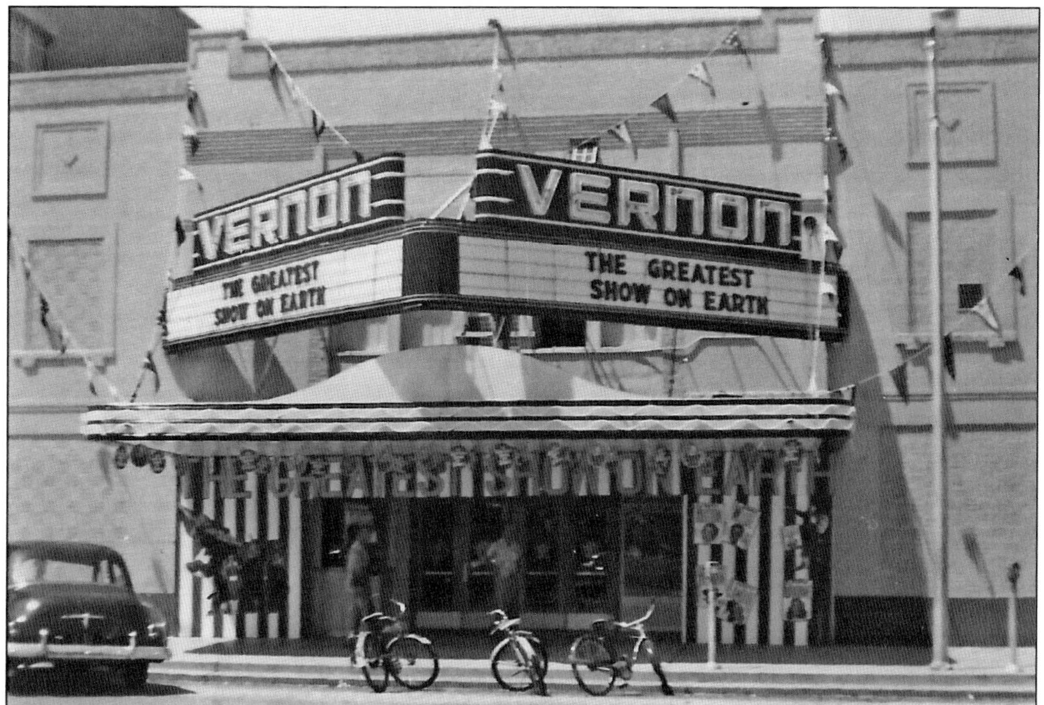

In the early 1950s, *The Greatest Show on Earth* was presented at the Vernon Theater, located at 1818 Main Street. Fred Palmer was the manager and the city manager. The Vernon Theater and the Pictorium Theater, located at 1726 Pease Street and managed by Rubin C. Jordan, were both Interstate Theaters. This was one of the last movies shown before the theater was destroyed by fire in 1952. (Author's collection.)

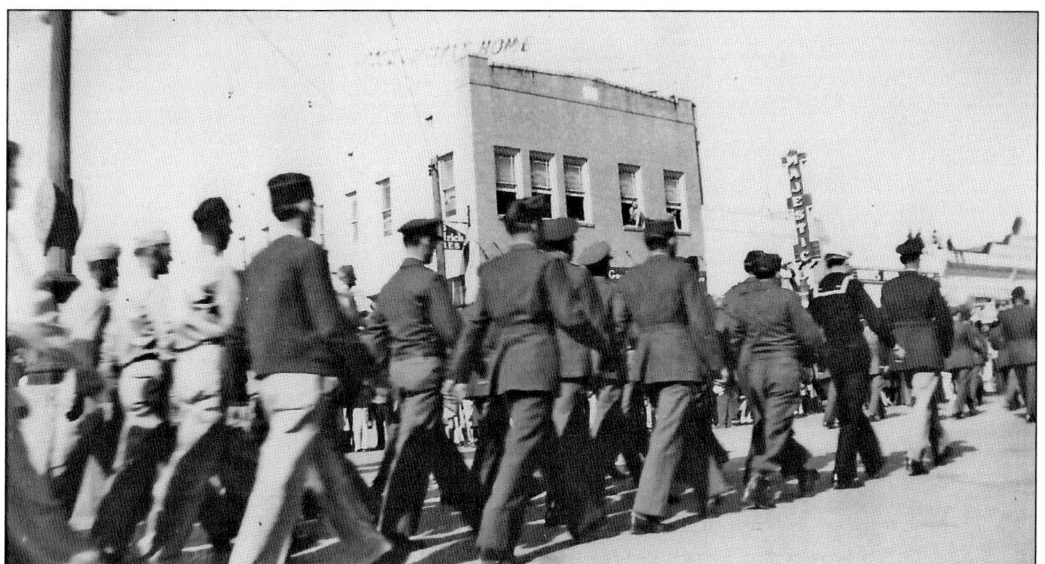

A mixed military group of Marines, Army, Air Force, and Navy servicemen are seen passing in front of the B.F. Goodrich store at 1730 Main Street. The store was managed by J. Lloyd Hill and sold tires, batteries, Motorola radios, bicycles, and appliances. The Majestic Theater, managed by Cortez C. Hamm, was located at 1724 Main Street. (Author's collection.)

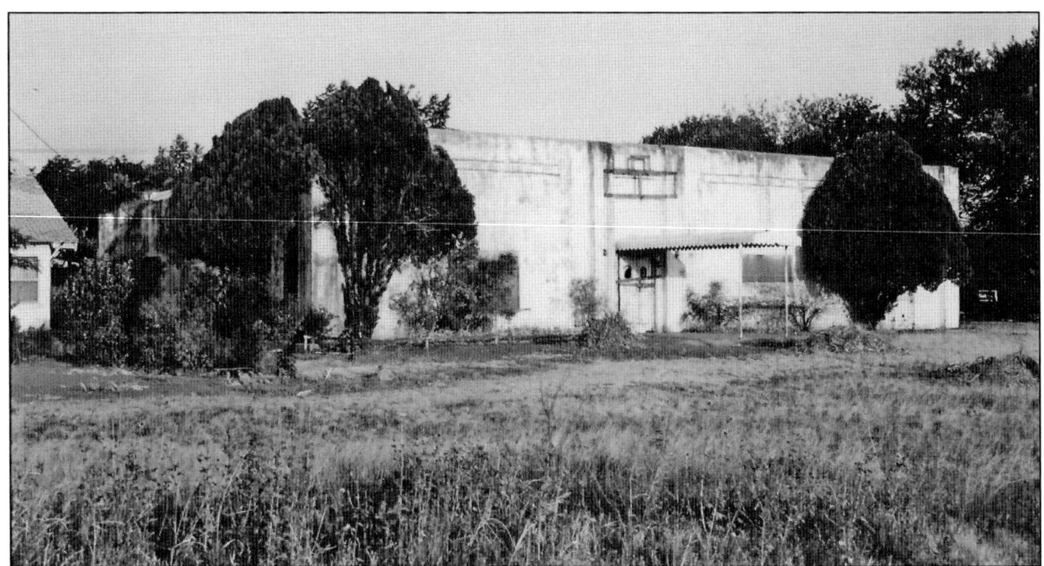

Pictured is the long-abandoned building known as "the Flame" at the entrance to the Hillcrest Country Club in the 1950s. The Flame, located at West Hillcrest and North Wilbarger Streets, was owned and operated by Orvil R. Wells as a restaurant that advertised dining and dancing. Orvil and Margaret Wells also had the Wells Shop at 1818 Wilbarger Street that sold women's clothing. (Author's collection.)

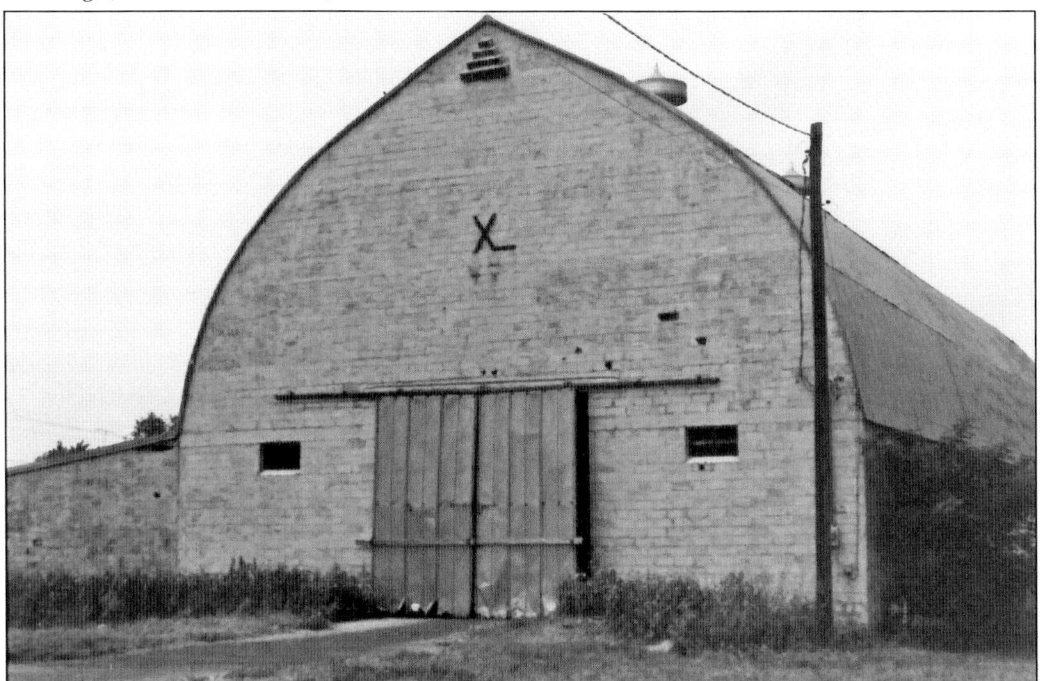

This dairy barn, located at the end of Cresent Drive and Sand Road, is owned by Grady Stowe. The dairy business played a big part in the history of Vernon. In 1891, R.A. Gilliland started a dairy on East McGee Street. Over the years, other dairies were Taylor's, J.A. Gilliland, Anderson's, Collier's, Vernon Sanitary, Massengill's, Vern-Tex, Jersey, Cook's, Triangle Creamery, Clifford Burkett, Schmoker, and the Cannon. (Author's collection.)

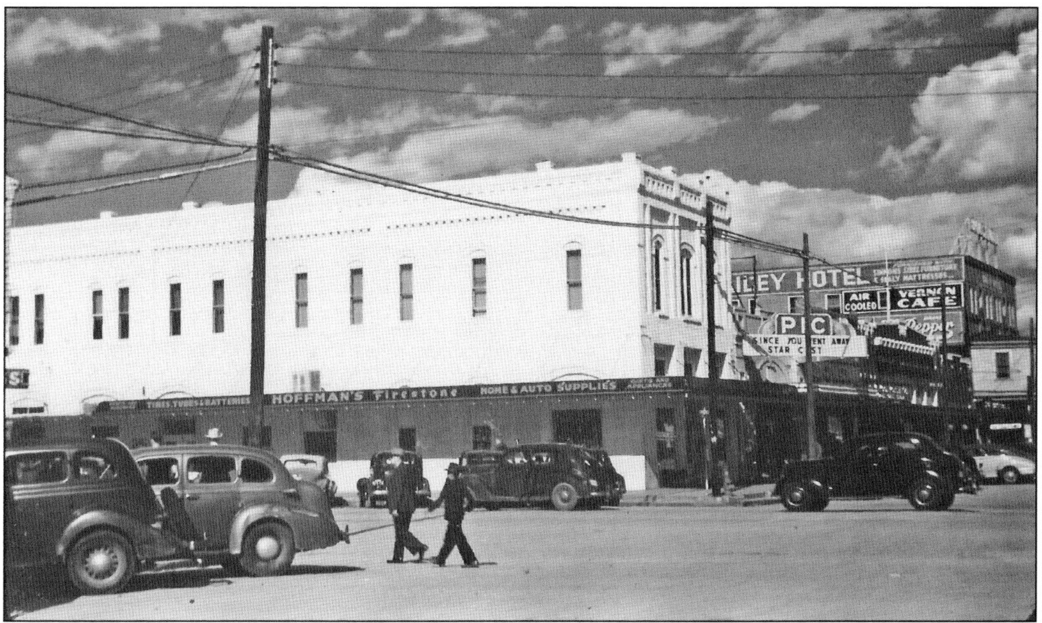

Located on the corner of Main Street at 1728 Pease Street is Hofmann's Firestone. Walter E. Hoffman was president, and Bodo Serold was vice president. The business sold tires, tubes, batteries, and household appliances. The Pic Theater, located at 1726 Pease Street and managed by Rubin C. Jordan, was an Interstate Theater. Norwood & Colman's Shoe Store was next to the Baily Hotel, owned by the Anderson Hotel System, on the corner of 1702 Pease Street at Cumberland Street. (Author's collection.)

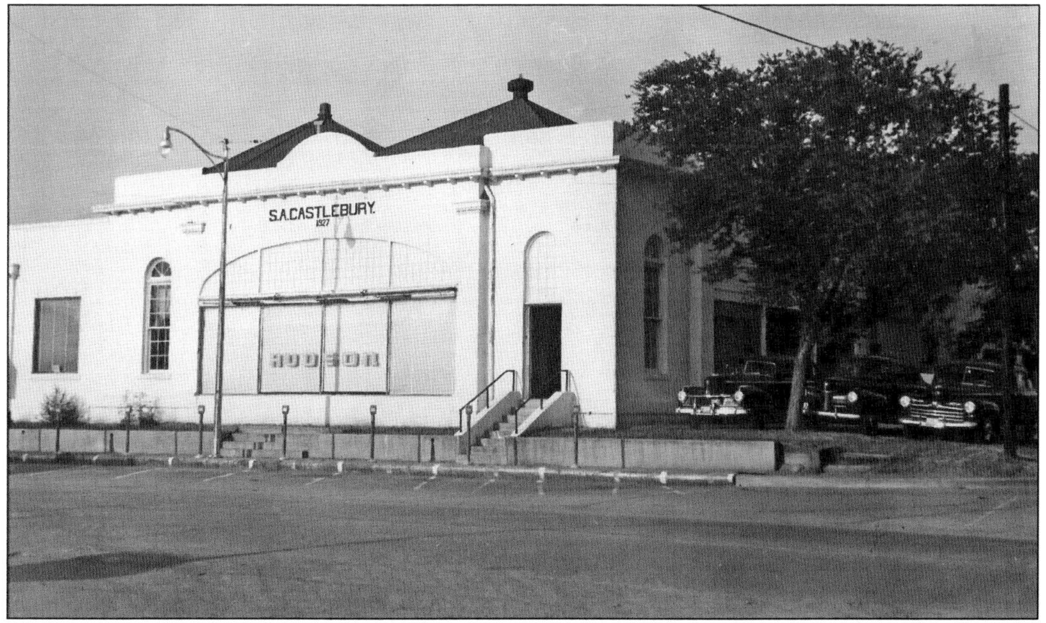

This was the Bolton-Suttle Hudson car and truck dealership, located at 1929–1931 Main Street, in 1948. Owners Charles Bolton and Lowell F. Suttle sold Hudson passenger cars and pickup trucks. Originally constructed in 1906 as the First Baptist Church, this structure was sold in 1926 to S.A. Castleberry, who had the face of the building restructured. (Author's collection.)

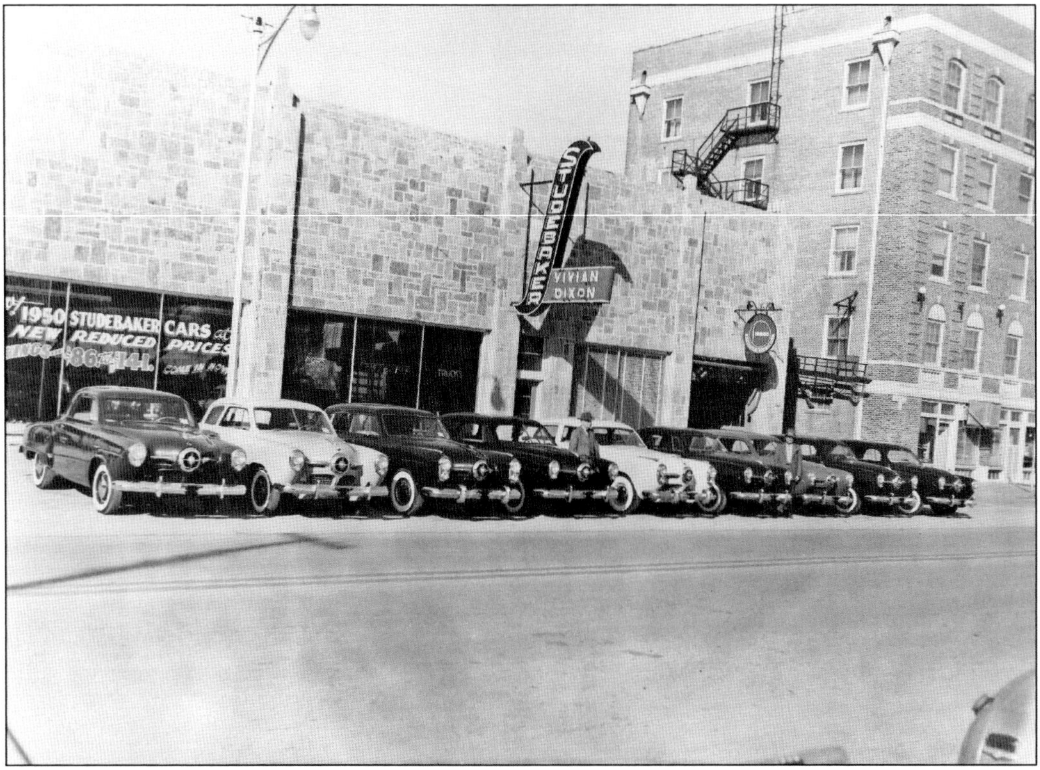

Pictured in 1950 is the Vivian-Dixon Motors, Inc., located at 1922 Wilbarger Street, with Charles Vivian as president and J.A. Dixon as secretary. Vivian-Dixon sold Studebaker cars and trucks, new and used. The last business in this building was the Firestone tire shop. This building is the future home of the Jack Tegarden Museum. (Author's collection.)

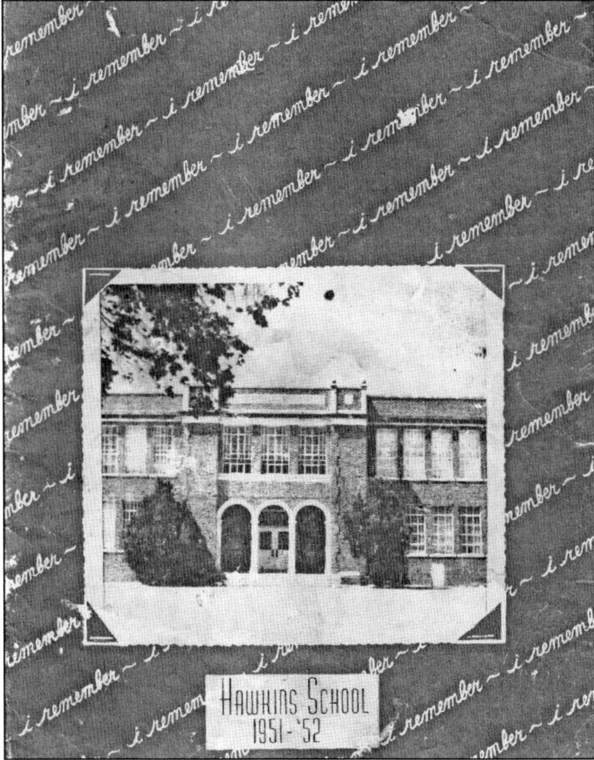

This Hawkins School annual shows a picture of the school on the front for the years 1951–1952. Hawkins School was built in 1928 and located at 2900 Yamparika Street. It was named for school trustee and banker L.G. Hawkins. It was remodeled with a wing added in 1949. US president Barack Obama's mother, Stanley Ann Dunham, is listed in the fourth grade in this annual. (Author's collection.)

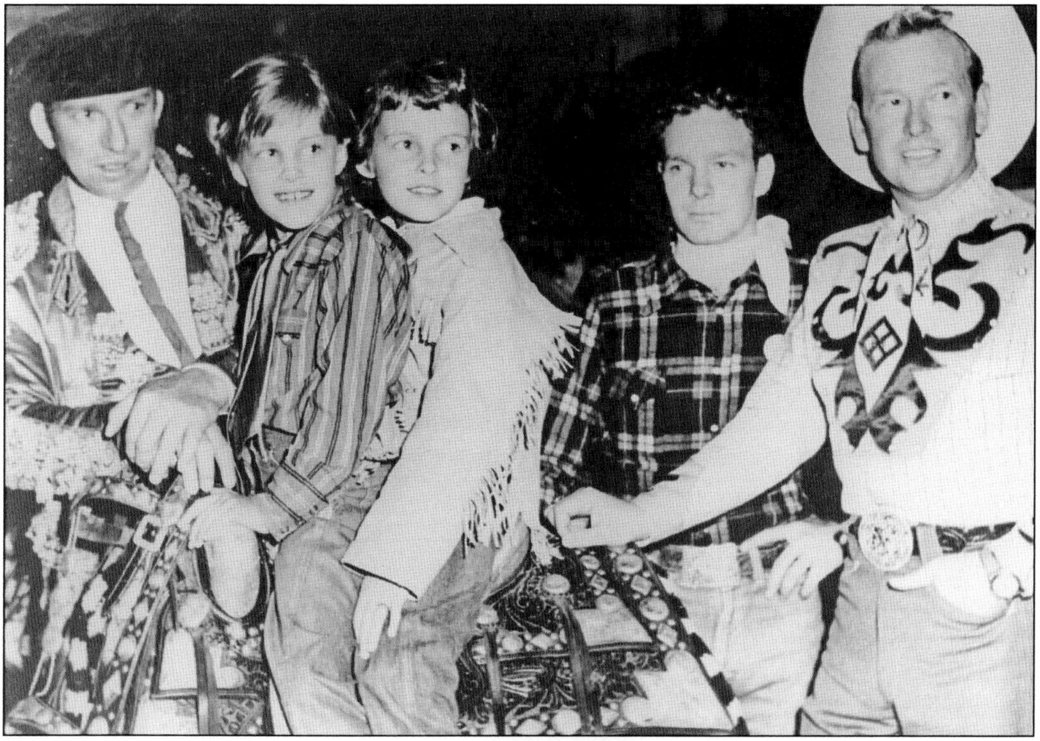

Pictured in 1952 at the opening of the Waggoner Estate Building are, from left to right, Slim Pickens, Jeri Broday, Pauline (Broday) Stow, Casey Tibbs, and Rex Allen. Jerri and Pauline are seen sitting on E. Paul Waggoner's silver-clad saddle. The Waggoner Estate Building was constructed on the same location where the First Methodist Church had been located in 1910, on the corner of Pease and Deaf Smith Streets. (Courtesy of Grady and Pauline Stowe.)

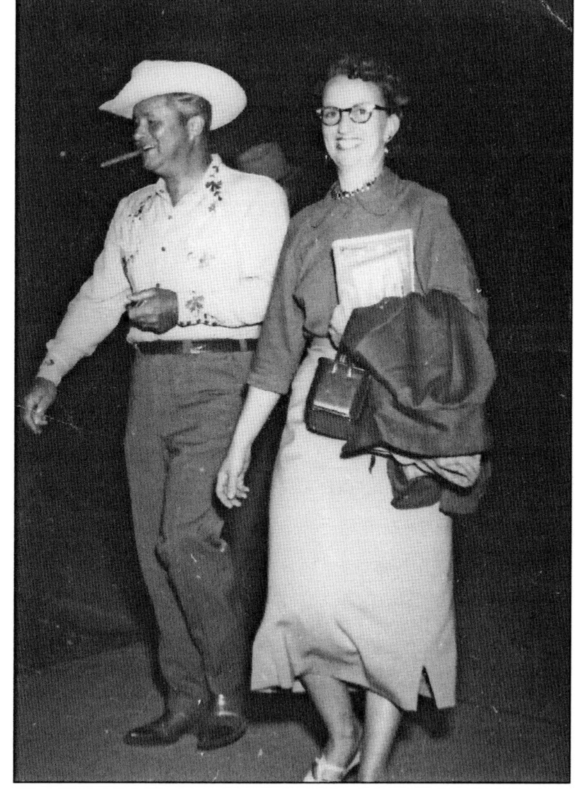

Jack and Wilma Cary are seen heading to the rodeo in 1954. Wilma is carrying the ninth-annual rodeo program in her arms. Jack Cary was the owner of Cary's Wrecking Yard at 110 North Main Street, which was across the tracks on the Altus Highway. Other wrecking yards at this time were B.R. Goodrum Salvage Company, Vernon Wrecking, and Watts Wrecking Yard. (Author's collection.)

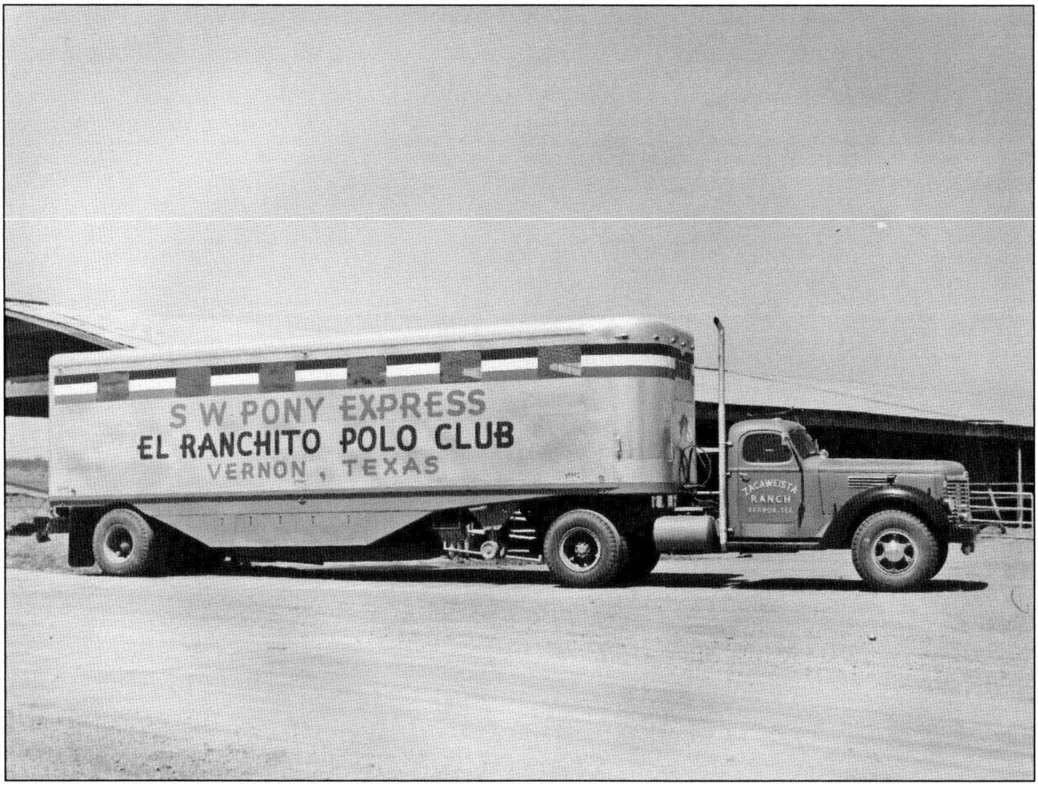

This truck was used to transport to different locations for polo tournaments. Some of the polo team members were Buster Whorton; Bill Bond; Jesse "Wild Man" Smith; one of Polo's all-time "greats," Harold Berry; and the impressible "iron man of polo," William "Billy" Skidmore. The best facilities to be found were just south of Vernon at Zacaweista Ranch, which had three large fields. (Author's collection.)

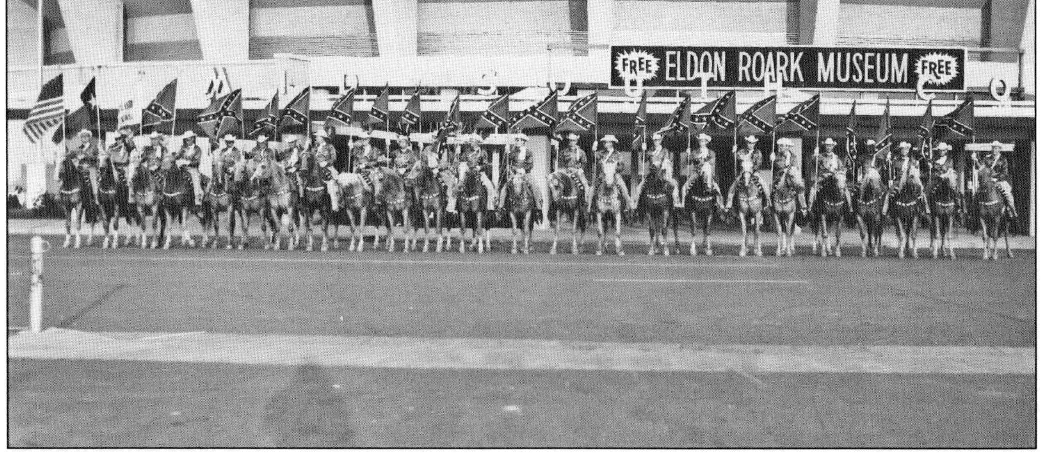

Pictured is the Palomino Riding Club at the Mid-South Fair in 1966. The Palomino Riding Club organized in 1949, was chartered in 1950, and uses precision horsemanship, matched Palomino mounts, colorful attire, and unparalleled spirit to maintain its position as one of the greatest nonprofessional riding groups. Today, the self-supporting group carries on the tradition of the Santa Rosa Roundup, started by E. Paul Waggoner. (Author's collection.)

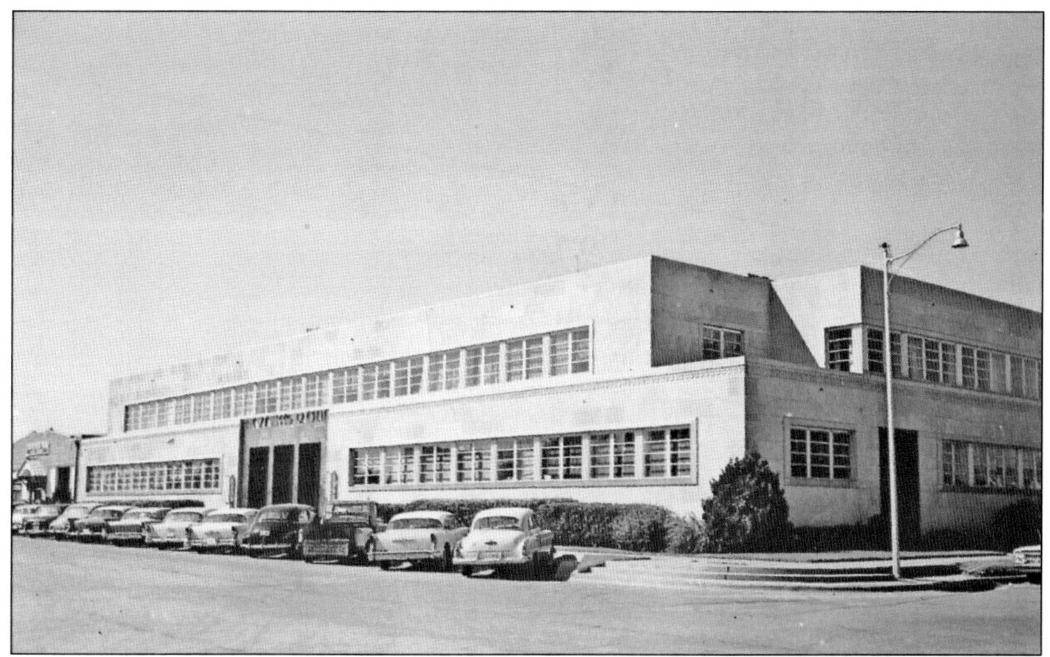

The Waggoner Estate Building, pictured in the late 1950s, was located at Pease and Deaf Smith Streets. The roots of the W.T. Waggoner Estate began with Dan Waggoner and his son W.T. Waggoner. They branded their cattle with the reversed Three "D" brand. In 1923, the present organization, the W.T. Waggoner Estate Trust, came into being. (Author's collection.)

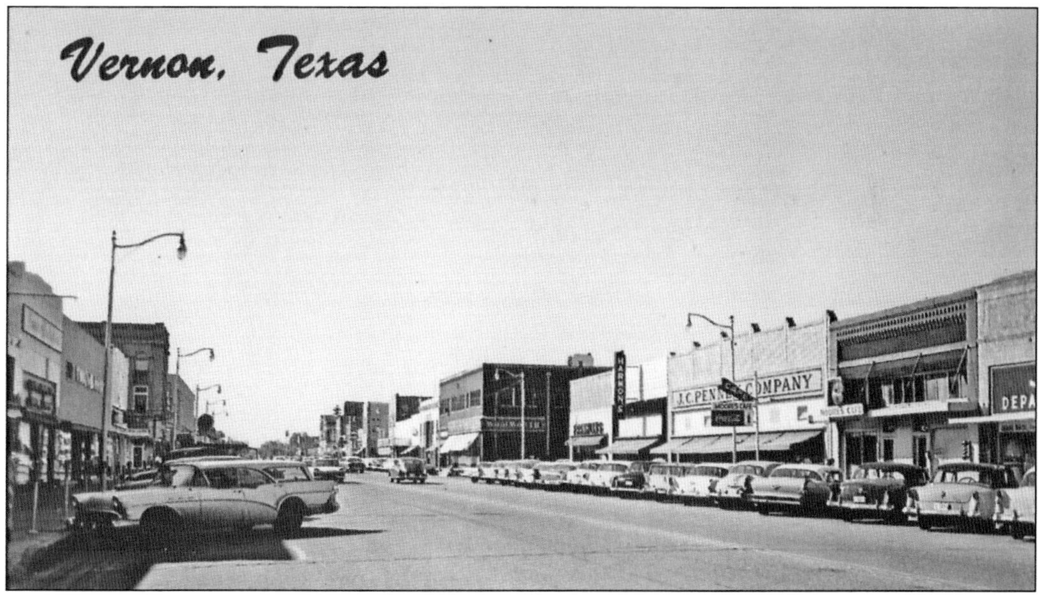

Looking south on Main Street, the first building on the left side is Whorton Furniture Company, which is now the location of Yesterdaze Antiques. Next in line are Elzy Youngblood Furniture and Sewell's Corner Drug at Texas and Main Streets. The Hill's Youth Center is to the south. On the right side of the street are Jacobson's Department Store, Moor's City Café, J.C. Penney Company, Harmons, Franklins, F.W. Woolworth, Waggoner National Bank, Moses, and Huber's City Drug. (Author's collection.)

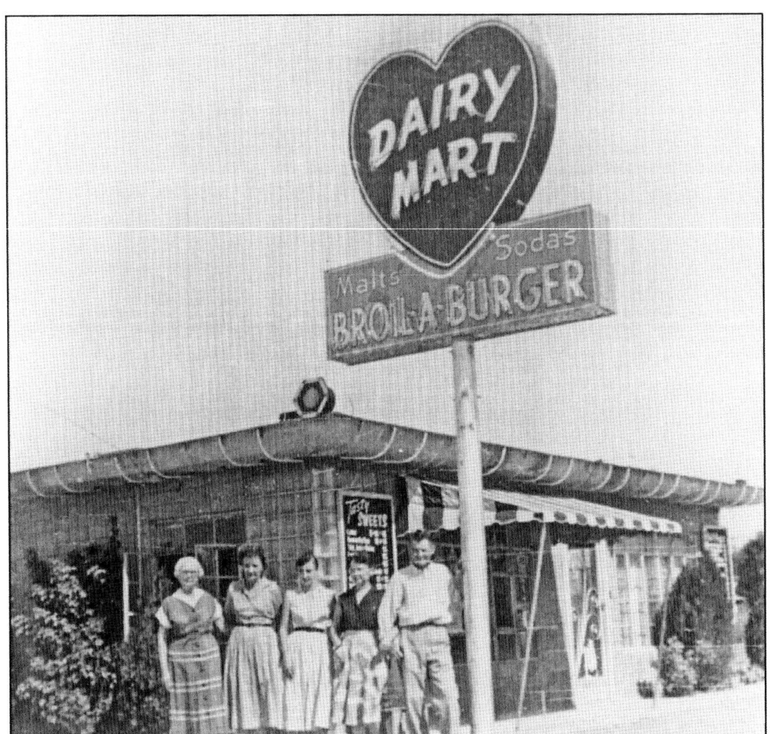

Jay T. Walker, seen standing to the right, was the owner of the Dairy Mart, located at 913 Hillcrest Street. It was also known as Jay's Burger Stop or Jay'S. Malts, sodas, and the broil-a-burger were served, but the most unforgettable item sold was the No. 4—a cheeseburger with special chili. In the mid-1960s, Jay sold the business to Clark Burkett, and it became Red's Dairy Mart, with Jerry Ming as manager. (Author's collection.)

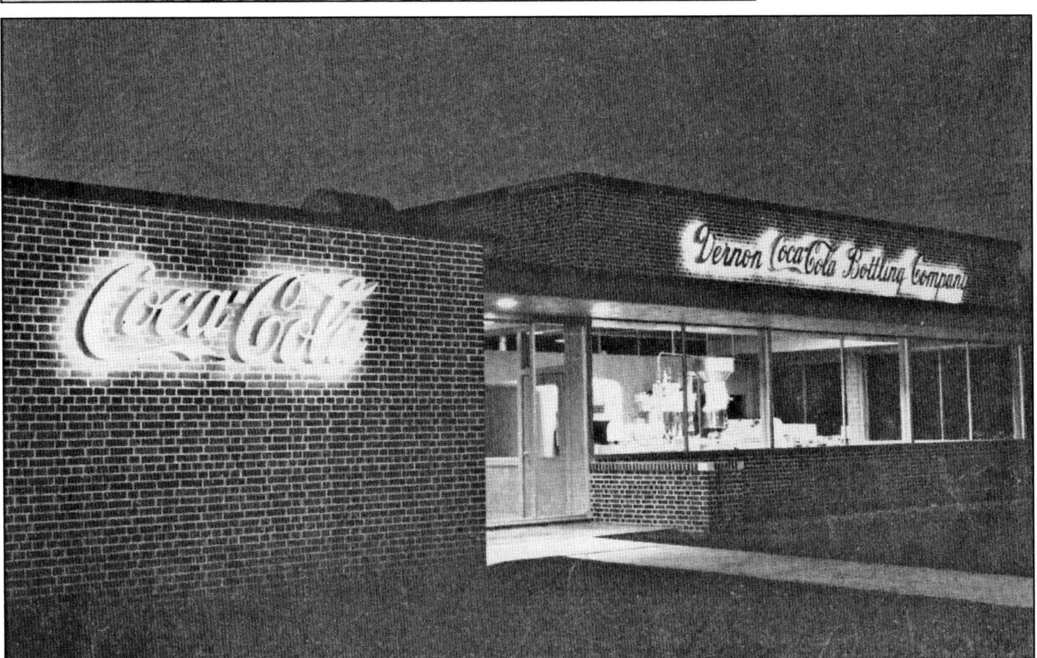

The Coca-Cola bottling company in its new location at 2900 Wilbarger Street, with Robert Lee Wilson as manager, was completed in July 1954. Eunice Wilson was the founder and owner of the Coca-Cola bottling company in Vernon and also owned the franchise covering Wilbarger, Foard, and Hardeman Counties. The Coca-Cola plant also bottled other drinks, such as strawberry, grape, and orange sodas and its own cola called Wilson's. (Author's collection.)

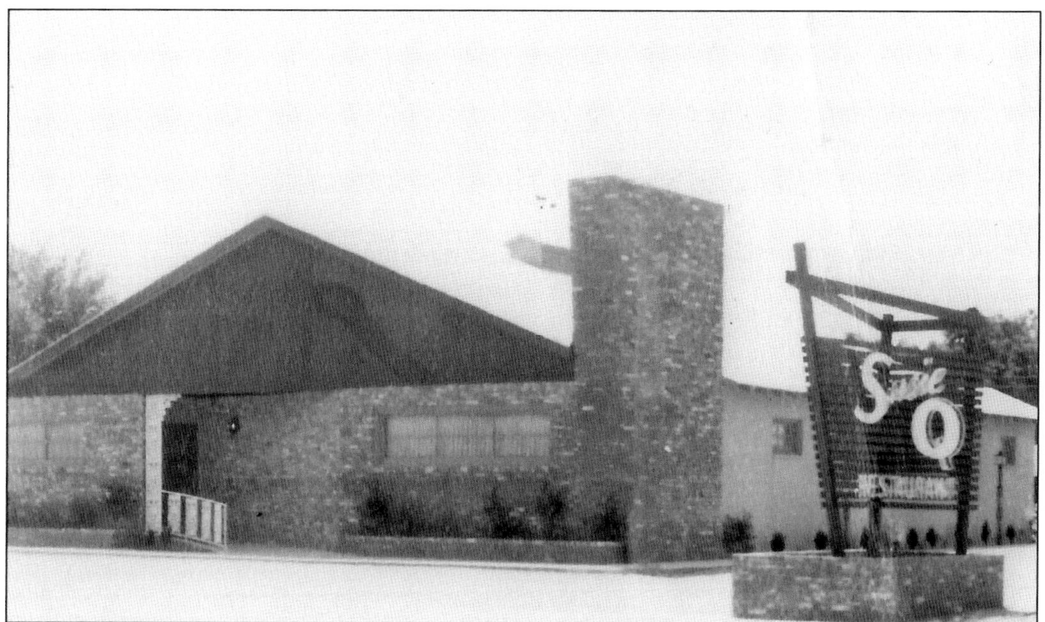

Susie Q Restaurant No. 1, as seen in the 1960s, was located at 717 Wilbarger Street. The Susie Q No. 2 was located on Highway 287 East. Earnest L. and Lorene Rogers advertised, "You are always welcome" for the two convenient locations. In 1966, the Crossroads Inn Restaurant at 1827 Expressway became the location of the Susie Q No. 2. (Author's collection.)

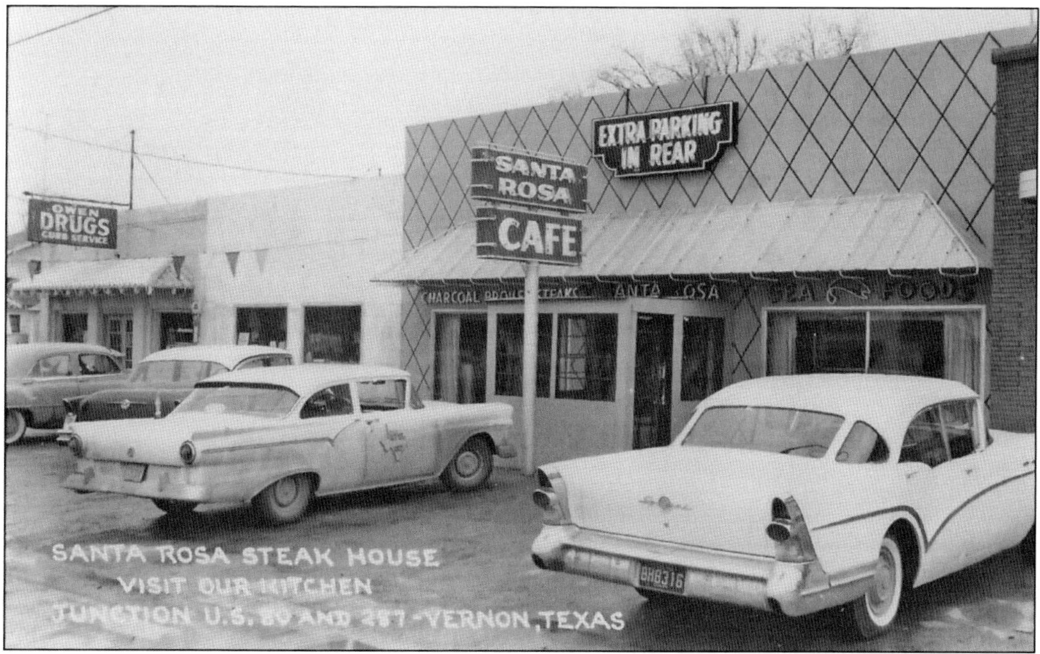

Pictured are the Santa Rosa Café and Owen's West Vernon Drug. Wayne and Paul Owen owned the Santa Rosa Café, located at 4009 Wilbarger Street at the "Y." It advertised charbroiled steaks and seafood. A 1957 Ford highway patrol car can be seen parked in front of the café. Wayne and Paul Owen also owned Owen's West Vernon Drug at 4005 Wilbarger Street, which offered fountain and curb service. (Author's collection.)

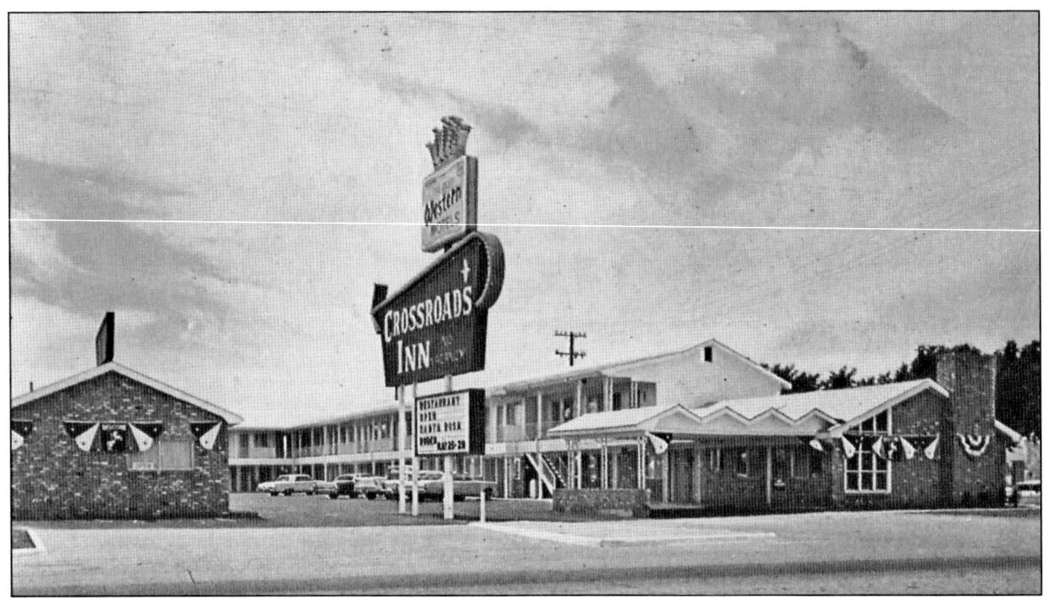

The Crossroads Inn Motel, a Best Western motel, was located at 1829 Expressway and was managed by Irene Mickle. Ruben Self managed the Crossroads Inn Restaurant. In 1966, the Crossroad Inn Restaurant became the Susie Q No. 2, owned by Earnest and Lorene Rogers. The old Susie Q No. 2 became Ramsey's Café, owned by Jake Ramsey and located next to J.L. Heard's super service station. (Author's collection.)

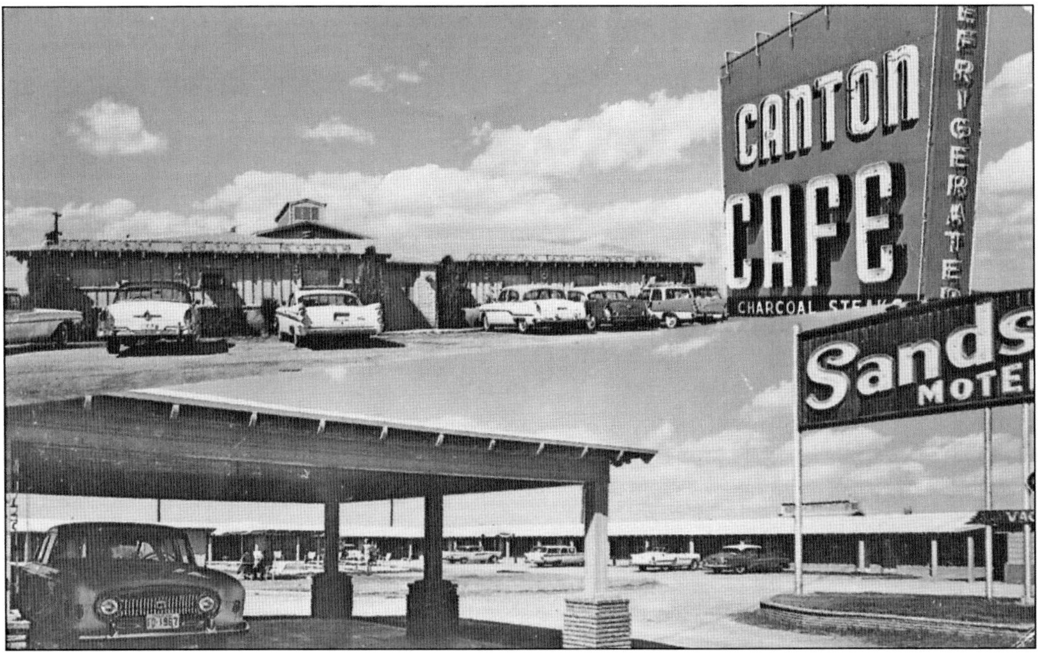

The Canton Café and the Sands Motel were built in the late 1950s. The Canton Café was located on Highway 287 East and was owned and operated by Henry Huie. Huie also owned Huie Bean Yuen Company. The Sand Motel was located at 96 East Wilbarger Street and was managed by Dallas L. Carruth. The Sands Motel and the Canton Café were both destroyed by a tornado on April 10, 1979. (Author's collection.)

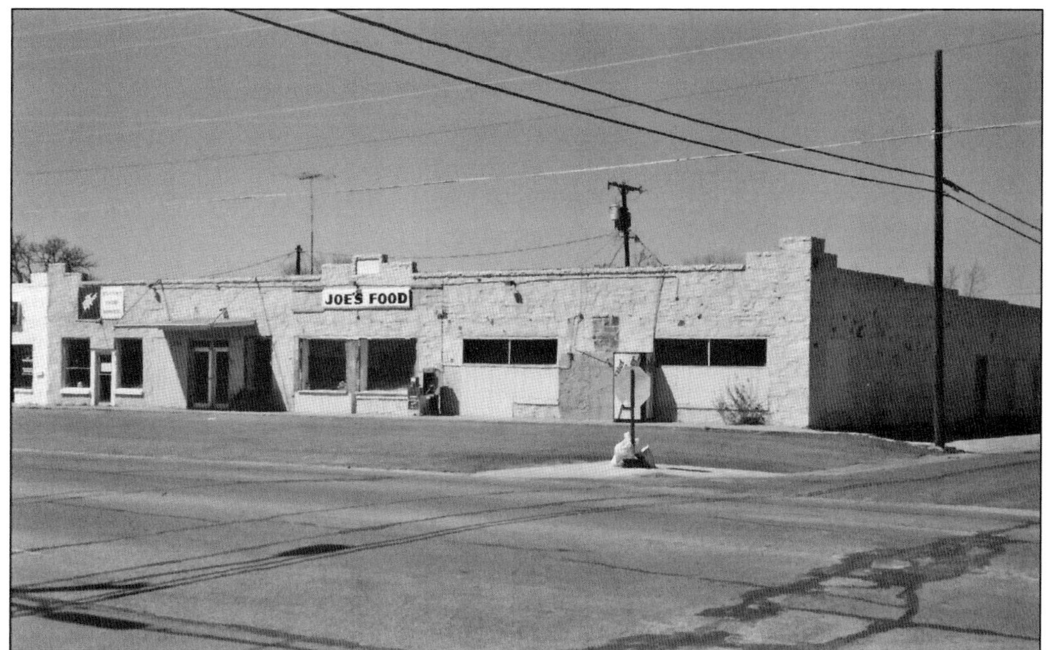

Joe and Betty Ermis owned Joe's Food Store; their daughter Cecelia Ermis Chism helped to run the daily operation. Joe started in the grocery business in the 1940s at H.A. McCartys Main Street Grocery. When McCarty lost his lease, Joe went to work in Lacy-Hamricks Food Store in this location at 3100 Wilbarger Street. The Ermis family operated the grocery business in this location from 1963 until 1996. (Courtesy of Joe and Betty Ermis.)

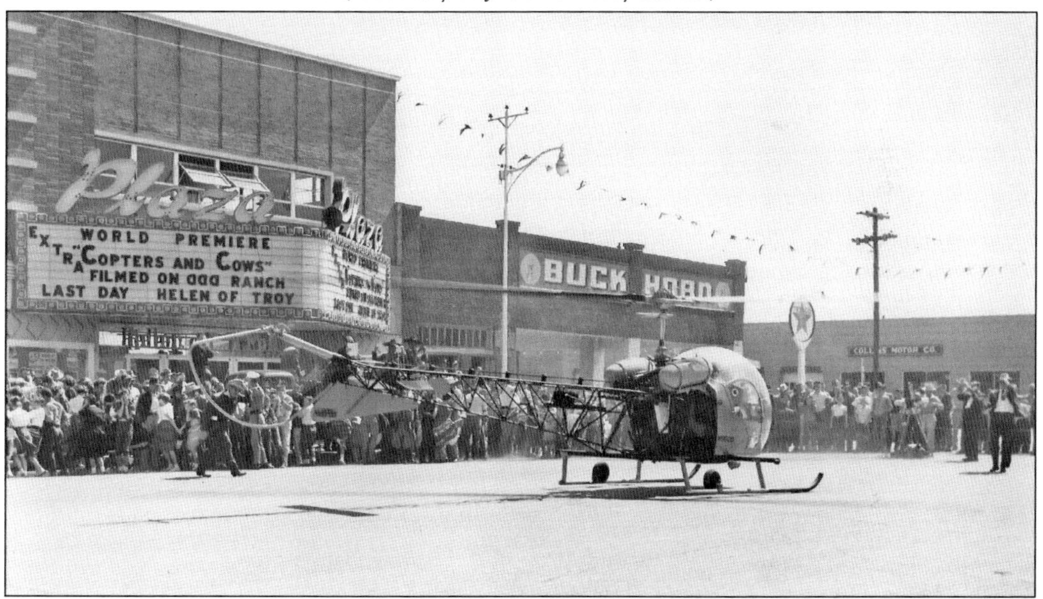

The Plaza Theater, established in 1953 and located at 1717 Cumberland Street, was managed by Thomas F. Palmer. The Plaza was the Interstate Theater's replacement for the Vernon Theater, which was destroyed by fire. Bell Aircraft and Warner Bros. short-film *Copters and Cows* was filmed on the Waggoner Ranch. On the southeast corner of Wilbarger and Cumberland Streets is Collins Lincoln-Mercury motor company at 1801 Cumberland Street. (Author's collection.)

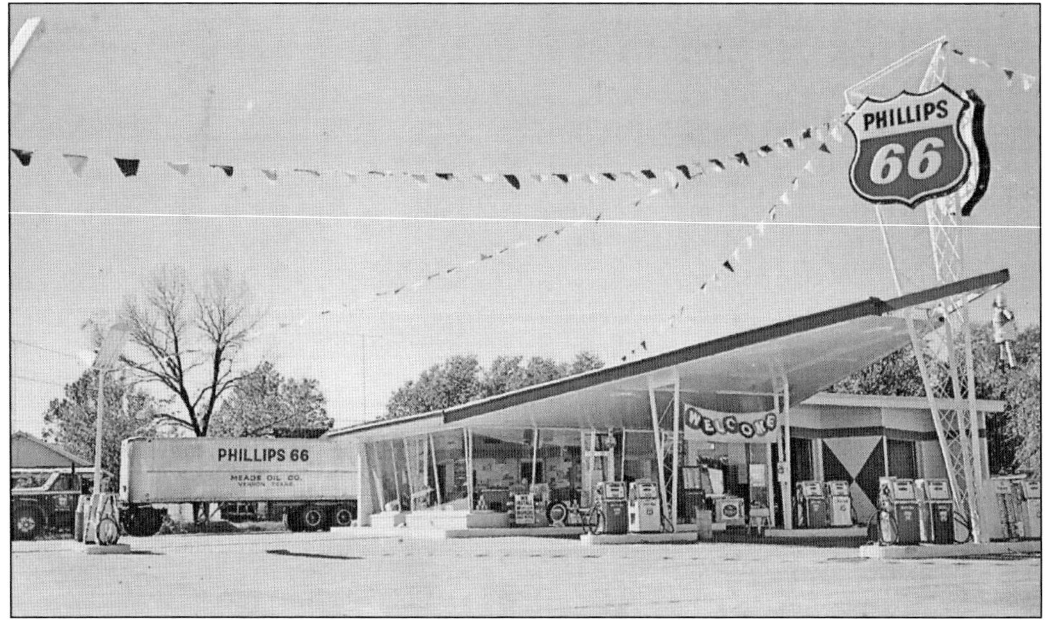

This Phillips 66 gas station, located at 3103 Wilbarger Street, was owned by Noah H. Meads and managed by Stephen H. Meads. This station was a regular stop for kids to get free air for their bikes and free popcorn. Noah Meads was the president of Meads Oil Company with Phillips 66 jobbers, located at 825 Main Street. Stephen Meads became president in the 1980s. (Courtesy of Nick Cary.)

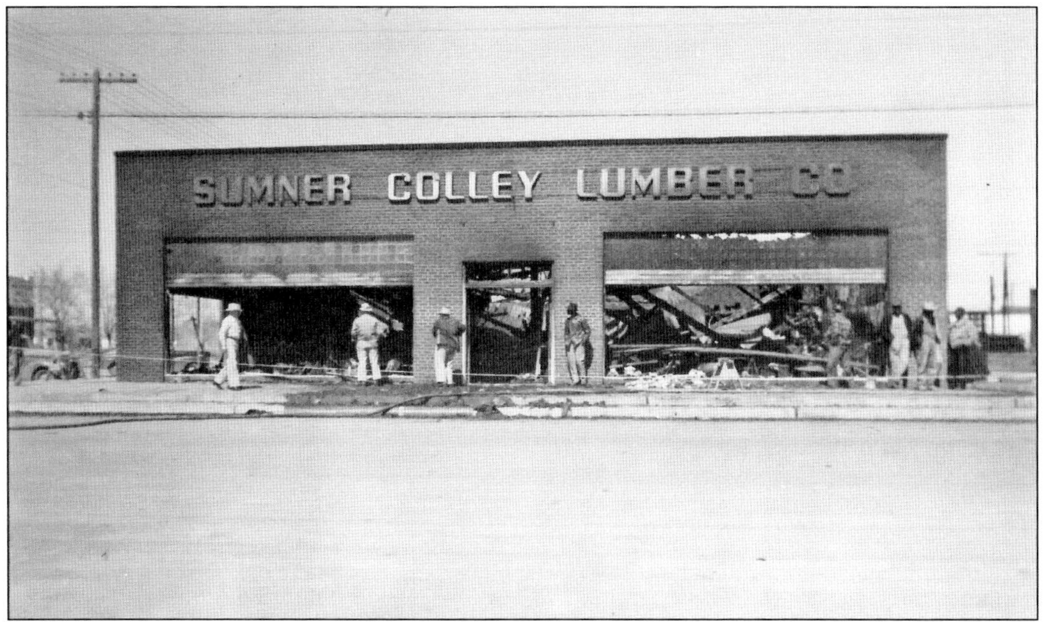

Pictured after the fire in the late 1940s is the Sumner-Colley Lumber Company. Joe C. Sumner, Hub Colley, and William F. MaGee established Sumner-Colley in 1923 at 1819 Maiden Street. It sold lumber, building materials, paints, hardware, and coal. This building was rebuilt, and Sumner-Colley is still in business today with co-owners Joe Chat Sumner and manager-owners Bob and Tim Beazley. (Courtesy of Bob Beazley.)

Pictured is the chef's head off the Pizza Point sign, located at 3205 South Frontage Road. John Hardin was the president of the business, with Reva Hardin as secretary-treasurer. Robert "Ab" Abernathy, who would become the owner by the late 1980s, managed the Pizza Point. The Pizza Point was the local hangout for school kids in the 1980s. (Courtesy of Mark Cary.)

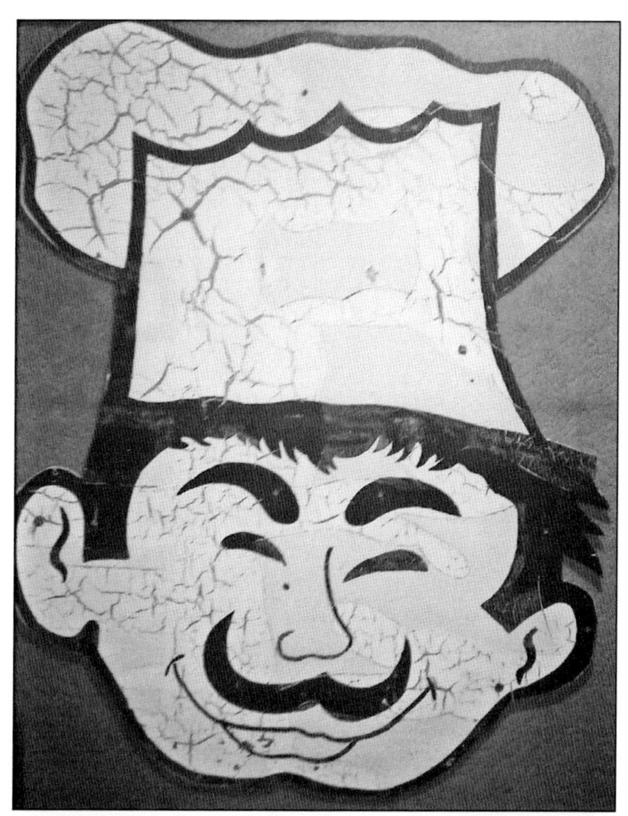

This United Supermarket is the last United built in Vernon; Allen Smith is manager. Built in the late 1990s, this is the third store constructed on this 3000 block of Wilbarger Street. The second store, shown to the right, was torn down for parking space. Henry D. Snell established the first Vernon store in the early 1930s, and the United Supermarket chain is still Snell family-owned today. (Author's collection.)

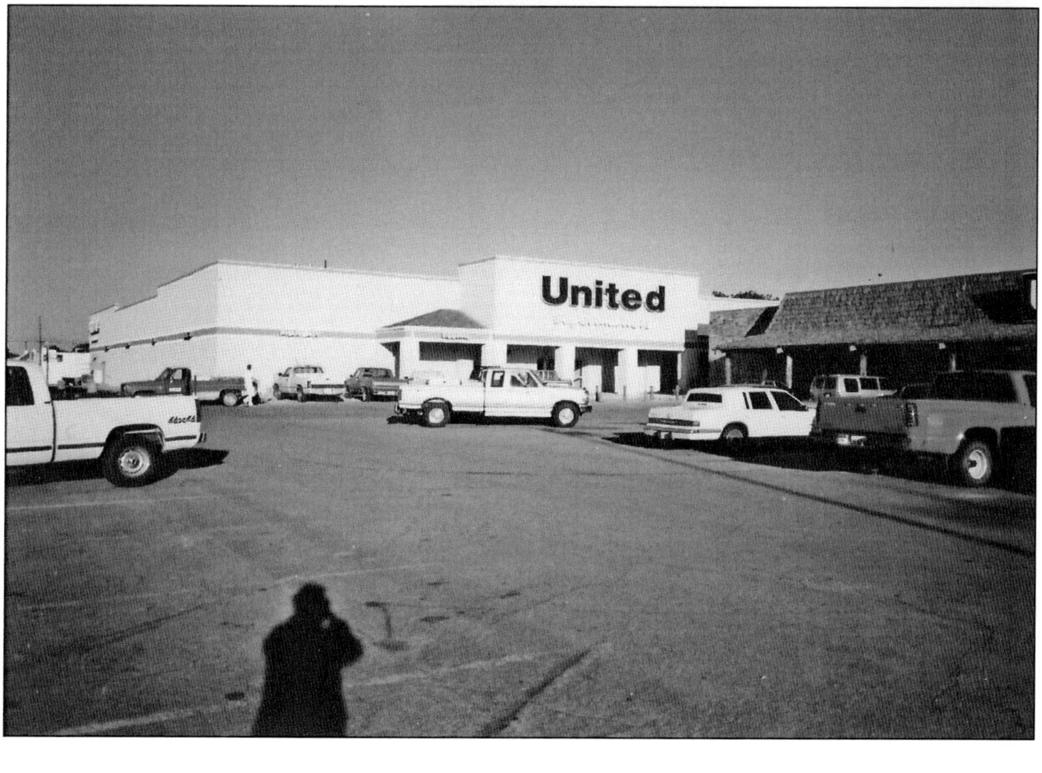

Discover Thousands of Local History Books Featuring Millions of Vintage Images

Arcadia Publishing, the leading local history publisher in the United States, is committed to making history accessible and meaningful through publishing books that celebrate and preserve the heritage of America's people and places.

Find more books like this at
www.arcadiapublishing.com

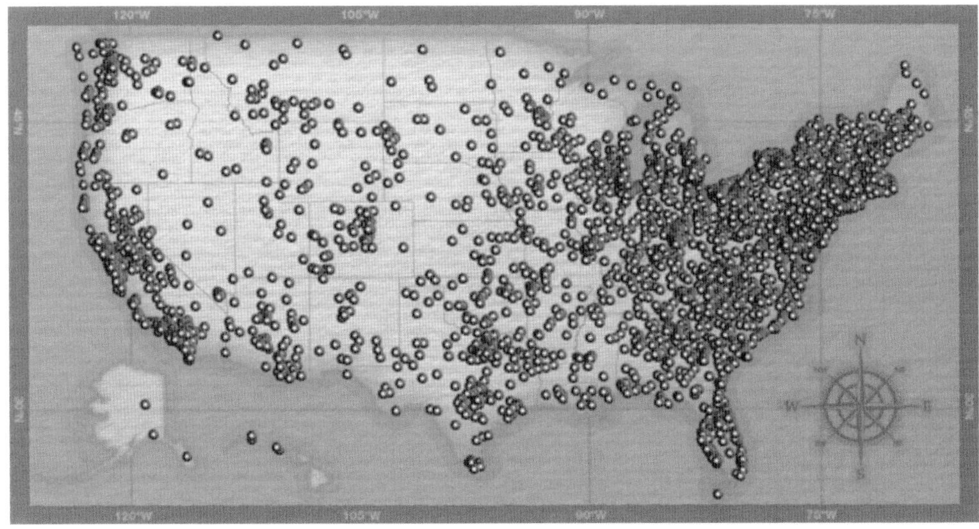

Search for your hometown history, your old stomping grounds, and even your favorite sports team.

Consistent with our mission to preserve history on a local level, this book was printed in South Carolina on American-made paper and manufactured entirely in the United States. Products carrying the accredited Forest Stewardship Council (FSC) label are printed on 100 percent FSC-certified paper.

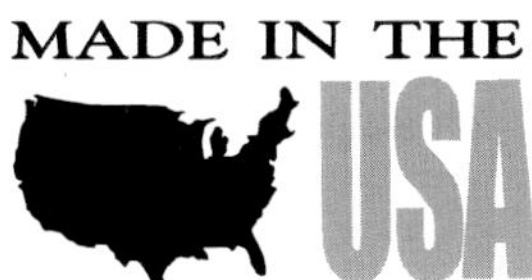